The Collapse of
the Brass Heaven

The Collapse of
the Brass Heaven

*Rebuilding Our Worldview
to Embrace the Power of God*

Zeb Bradford Long
and
Douglas McMurry

Chosen Books

A Division of Baker Book House Co
Grand Rapids, Michigan 49516

Published by Chosen Books
a division of Baker Book House
P.O. Box 6287, Grand Rapids, MI 49516-6287

Printed in the United States of America

Library of Congress Cataloging-in-Publication Data

Long, Zeb Bradford.
  Collapse of the brass heaven, The / Zeb Bradford Long and Douglas McMurry.
    p. cm.
  Includes bibliographical references.
  ISBN 0-8007-9215-7
  1. Apologetics. 2. Christianity—Forecasting. 3. Church renewal.
I. McMurry, Douglas. II. Title.
BT1102.L56   1994
239—dc20   94-15833

The purely naturalistic look at life, however enthusiastically it may begin, is sure to end in sadness.

This sadness lies at the heart of every merely positivistic, agnostic, or naturalistic scheme of philosophy. . . .

For naturalism, fed on recent cosmological speculations, mankind is in a position similar to that of a set of people living on a frozen lake, surrounded by cliffs over which there is no escape, yet knowing that little by little the ice is melting, and the inevitable day drawing near when the last film of it will disappear, and to be drowned ignominiously will be the human creature's portion. The merrier the skating, the warmer and more sparkling the sun by day, and the ruddier the bonfires at night, the more poignant the sadness with which one must take in the meaning of the total situation.

William James
The Varieties of Religious Experience

See to it that no one takes you captive through hollow and deceptive philosophy, which depends on human tradition and the basic principles of this world rather than on Christ.

Colossians 2:8

Contents

Part 1

The Brass Heaven

A Geodesic Dome of Western Design

1

Doug Discovers the Brass Heaven

Philosophy is more than a pastime for bookworms and highbrows. We all have a philosophy, whether or not we realize it. It provides the framework for our thinking and decision-making.

Westerners have chosen, by philosophy, to build "the brass heaven"—an invisible barrier of thought that separates us from God and from the spirit world. Because the Western Church (along with everyone else) has adopted brass heaven thinking, Western Christians are gagging from a lack of fresh air. The Body of Christ finds itself entombed in a metal casket of doubt, from which only God Himself can free it.

These realities dawned on Brad Long and me during the early years of our ministries.

Where Is God?

Church was an expected part of my family's weekly routine as I was growing up. But church was not the sort of place where one discovered God. God seemed little different from Superman or Peter Pan—a fictitious character people had written stories about. Did He really exist?

He never smote anyone's conscience.

He never healed anyone.

He did not heal relationships or ease heartache.

He never delivered anyone from an addiction.

He never spoke, guided, taught or counseled anyone.

He did not, so far as I could tell, convert, justify, save or sanctify.

Or, if He *did* do any of these things, no one ever spoke of it. We simply tried to be good people and go to church. Our friends did not seem to mind that God never made any appearances. They probably would have been upset if He had.

Little changed when I went off to seminary. (Like others of my generation, I saw ministers as helping professionals, like psychologists or social workers.) I heard no astonishing testimonies of the faithfulness of God in answering prayer and rewarding faith. Neither professors nor students spoke much about what God was doing in our lives, or about how we were learning to trust God each day. If someone had talked like that, we would probably have considered him a victim of a time warp from the Great Awakening, or a member of one of those sectarian churches full of simple, childlike people.

It was different from Bible times, I thought. Then, Christians believed that "God is a rewarder of those who seek Him." Biblical Christians testified about God's faithfulness because they had experienced His rewards, healing, deliverance, provision and guidance. Why didn't these things happen now?

San Francisco Theological Seminary was for me a total immersion into a contrasting view, which we will call the modern Western worldview. The summer before I entered seminary, I read the bestselling *Honest to God* by Anglican Bishop John A. T. Robinson. The book openly questioned everything in the Bible that the bishop could not rationally understand. Bishop Robinson was plowing ground that was even then being planted with God-is-dead theology, although that seed had not yet sprouted.

During my first week at seminary, the seminary president gave a speech to us freshmen: "This institution is not a preacher mill. It is a first-class intellectual institution." Most denominational seminaries, I soon discovered, want the respect of the intellects of the world, want to join their fraternities and be counted as professional, scholarly institutions. This was good news to me. I eagerly devoured the intellectual challenge of the three-week immersion in the Hebrew language that began my seminary years (although my poor room-mate was so stressed out he became sick).

Yet part of me longed for something more. I sensed the vague absence of something but could not figure out what it was. I soon developed a friendship with a Swiss student named Philippe, who had some acquaintance with the Community of Taize in France. Philippe and I started to meet for prayer—something of an oddity on campus. Our prayers were a stab in the dark, a search for—what? I had no idea why I was trying to pray, nor did the other students, who greeted our little prayer meetings with quizzical expressions and humorous comments. As to prayer, the seminary taught me what a *collect* is.

Those were days of relevant social action, not prayer. I remember long lines of students winding their way down Van Ness Avenue in San Francisco, holding candles and singing songs of protest against the Vietnam War. I remember, too, the courageous student who was tried as a conscientious objector against the military draft. His was an honest search for conscience; yet I was appalled at the rebellion, destructiveness, drug abuse and plummeting of academic standards at my Presbyterian "intellectual institution."

In my final year, Dr. James Muilenburg, my favorite professor, chose to retire from a lifetime career teaching Old Testament. He had become disillusioned and did not care to preside over the decline of academic standards invited by the growing political power of students in campus life. The student body had no time for academics and we were not interested in the Old Testament. We were searching for relevance, trying to find our way out of a sterile traditionalism that had lost its meaning. Far from having fun, we felt like moles, tunneling our way through the dirt, hitting tree roots, sewer lines and foundation stones in our groping to make a home for ourselves.

Only one thing we knew for sure. The answers to our searching would not be found in the Bible. Bible people were narrow-minded and naïve. We were advanced and experienced. How often I heard it said that "the Bible is not the Word of God; Jesus Christ is." I soon accepted this glib doctrine, though I wondered fleetingly why it needed to be an either-or proposition. Protestants had certainly changed their tune since the early years.

We did have to take a course in Bible if we wanted to be ordained. The students called this course "Baby Bible." We studied the Bible furiously to pass the exam, but closed our eyes to its relevance to anything that would improve our lives. We tried everything else in an attempt to change the world for the better—encounter groups, Marxist theory, the latest therapeutic techniques, Timothy Leary, art, dance, drama. For some, the search for meaning led to drugs, even LSD. We sampled, quaffed or drained all these and many other attempts at relevance and meaning, priding ourselves all the while in our openness.

How I Bumped My Head on the Brass Heaven

During my final year of seminary, I was offered the Fellowship for the Parish Ministry, an opportunity for an additional year of study in Europe. I chose to use the $4,000 grant to gain practical counseling experience in Edinburgh, Scotland, and became a psychiatric social worker in a hospital in the Scottish border town of Melrose. I had always wanted to help people. Now I had an opportunity to learn what the real professionals did to eradicate mental illness.

Alcoholism and depression lurk everywhere in that dark and remote country, for in winter the sun rises at 10 A.M. and sets by 3 P.M. During those long nights—well, Scotch is the national drink of the Scottish. I assumed I would learn how to eliminate alcoholism, depression and all the other blights that afflict the human mind. I was especially interested in sensitivity training, a technique in which my hospital, a "therapeutic community," specialized.

Perhaps I was expecting too much. Perhaps I had made a god of the helping professions, of encounter groups and psychology. But it seemed to me that true healing was elusive. That year in Scotland birthed in me a disillusionment that would not let go. Despite my belief in the therapeutic power of sensitivity training, what seemed to produce change was the drugs the psychiatrists administered— although I could not help but feel that drugs did not provide true healing; they merely covered over certain symptoms.

Perhaps, I thought, *true healing is not available for such as these.*

By my last week in Melrose, I felt like Robin Williams playing the part of Dr. Malcolm Sayer in the film *Awakenings*. He becomes so overwhelmed in Bainbridge Hospital in the Bronx by deranged minds, contorted bodies and fallen souls that he rushes to the window of his office to thrust it open, desperate for a breath of fresh air and a glimpse of God's beautiful world. But the window has been painted shut. Frantically he pounds it, knifes the cracks, then yanks the thing open and breathes in a draught of freshness from God's green earth.

That is how I felt that year in Melrose, except in that place of mental torment I could not even find the window, let alone open it. I was filled with the agonizing suspicion that I had nothing to give these people, even after nine years of higher education. Or no—my doubts went deeper than that. A worldview had shaped my thinking that excluded God from human affairs, that closed the window against the spiritual world and painted it shut.

As I entered my first pastoral position in Corvallis, Oregon, I felt like the man in the iron mask, his head encased by a hood of iron with scarcely an opening through which to breathe. There was in my world no freshness, no wonder. I believed only in what I could see and comprehend rationally. As to the unseen world, my skepticism was so ingrained that I doubted I could ever be free of it.

God was, I sensed, the answer somehow to my profound dryness. Yet, honest to God, I was not sure that God was not dead. I remember remarking to myself, *If God isn't really there, then we in the Church ought to admit it, stop making noises as though He were, and all become humanists. If God really is there, on the other hand, then surely the Church has the greatest ministry in the world.*

But how could I get beyond the brass heaven that had been lowered over me like a great geodesic dome from horizon to horizon?

My Window to God

A woman in my church was unique among its parishioners. Most of them looked up at me from their pews with clouded, dour faces—a leftover, I am sure, from our denominational origins in Scotland. But Wilma radiated a joy and love for me that shone like a ray of sunlight through the Presbyterian clouds. It was not that the other people were not good people. But I needed fresh air and sunshine from God, and Willie seemed to own a large share of it.

One day she came to my office and began to talk to me about the Holy Spirit. She gave me charismatic cassette tapes and books. I listened and read. Something fascinated me about this material, but something repelled me, too. I was not sure I could buy into all the teachings, but for the moment I was in no position to quibble. Spiritual dryness was making me desperate.

Later I would see the destructive power of some of those teachings to the peace of the oldline churches. But now I struggled with a more basic difficulty. Willie believed in a God who is there, who answers prayer, who rewards faith and fulfills written promises, while I doubted that God would do anything for me. *Maybe I am too intellectual for the simple, childlike faith required for an experience of God*, I thought. *Maybe I have already been turned into an incurable doubter.*

During nine years of higher education, I had learned not to rely on God. The idea of asking Him to do something for me—specifically, to pour out the Holy Spirit—injected me with deep apprehension. Both possibilities were equally frightening: that He might answer my prayer and that He might not. I was on the knife-edge separating theism from atheism, discipleship from disappointment. Which way would I fall?

The experiences of others encouraged me to believe in what I could not yet see. I was touched in part by the credible testimony of the Rev. Leonard Evans of Niles, Ohio, who described his own experience of the Holy Spirit as a "baptism of love." His early life was so much like mine that I took hope for myself. Yet I could not live on someone else's experience forever.

Is this nervous stomach what they call "the fear of God"? I wondered.

After much struggle with doubt, I took courage, along with a few members of my church in Oregon. We came together specifically to ask God to send the Holy Spirit into our lives so that we could be sure He had answered our prayers. We were tired of worshiping a theory; we wanted to know if God could be known.

I see now that I was doing just what the reformer John Calvin had written:

Therefore we see that to us nothing is promised to be expected from the Lord, which we are not also bidden to ask of him in prayers. So true is it that we dig up by prayer the treasures that were pointed out by the Lord's gospel, and which our faith has gazed upon.[1]

The Mole Hits Treasure

What happened as a result of that prayer soon affected every part of me—body, mind and spirit. As for my body, by age 29 I had been having some problems with anxiety that had produced an ulcer. Not only did the ulcer disappear after my prayer, but the anxiety that had produced it disappeared, too. People began to remark that I didn't look so nervous all the time. I was given the grace to sense that God was in my life after all.

This grace flowed in part from a decision I made at the time of my prayer to give my life to God. I had not entered the ministry out of a desire to do the work of Christ's Kingdom. But now spiritual stagnancy was forcing me to reach beyond my original ideas, to lay hold of something beyond the brass heaven of the professional clergyperson. My new faith in the personal God of the Bible soothed my anxiety and healed my ulcers.

In the spiritual area, I found a genuine love for God welling up within me. I actually wanted to sing to Him, worship Him and obey Him. This awakening was nothing I could prove or analyze, but it was the most important way God answered my prayer. Worship became for me not a dry ritual, but the freshness with which I longed to begin each day loving God.

As to my mind, I was forced to reexamine everything I had learned about God and the world, especially what I had learned in school. Slowly I realized that *my worldview had changed in a moment, in the twinkling of an eye.* By faith I had plunged my hand through the metallic fabrication of Western intellect and laid hold of something real. I could no longer accept teachings that flowed out of the brass heaven.

It is the mental part of this transformation that Brad and I want to describe in this book. During our pilgrimage of the last twenty years, the Holy Spirit has transformed our worldview, our philosophical assumptions.

I have found in the pastorate that most pastors do not speak of their personal trust in God. Western clergypersons do not usually talk this way at presbytery, classis, General Assembly or synod meetings. Normally we talk of the growth or decline of our churches, or of the latest political or denominational controversies. Rarely do we do what Paul desired to do with the Romans: "I long to see you so that . . . you and I may be mutually encouraged by each other's faith" (Romans 1:11–12).

It is not that we Westerners do not think trusting God is a good idea, but that we have drained of its meaning the idea of trusting God for any particular thing. Trusting God is a concept gone bankrupt—appropriate, maybe, for the old days of simple faith, but not for us, not for today. "I am trusting God for . . ." are words seldom spoken in most Western churches.

Why is God so absent from His Church? Why such a discrepancy between apostolic times and the present? It is not just that "miracles have ceased." Brad and I sense that a deeper, broader change has occurred in our understanding of the world and how God relates to it. These changes, we believe, reflect a profound transformation in Western thinking during the last century, a change of worldview.

The mainline historic churches have welcomed this change, by and large, and helped it along, while certain other churches, which we will call "third wave" churches (referring to the "third wave" of the Holy Spirit in the twentieth century in the mainline denominations), have not. Among the former has come a slow, relentless conviction that the worldview of the Bible is primitive—full of superstitions and unworthy of human beings in our stage of development. *We are advanced and experienced,* we have concluded, *while biblical people were narrow-minded and naïve.*

Brad and I have had to reexamine teachings we accepted throughout our university and seminary days. The building of a worldview, and of foundational pastoral teachings based on that worldview, has been one of the most exciting projects of our lives—an adventure we invite you to walk with us in the following pages.

2

Brad Discovers
the Brass Heaven

Was my home unique, or did I inhabit a world that all children do, filled with spiritual and supernatural wonder?

My mother, an artist, lived (and still lives) in a world infused with natural beauty and wonder. Hers was a life of vibrant prayer and intimacy with God. Her spiritual mentors were Glenn Clark (founder of Camps Farthest Out), E. Stanley Jones and Oswald Chambers. She communicated her spiritual sensitivity to me and my five siblings through readings and bedtime prayer. She read to us from the Bible and from C. S. Lewis, George Macdonald and John Bunyan. At home my world was inhabited by Aslan, the White Witch, the eldila, Lilith and the Shadow. Intuitively I knew these to be symbols of spiritual realities that impinge on the real world—Jesus, the Holy Spirit, angels and the devil. My world was filled with unexpected entrances into unseen realms.

Lest you think me a religious nut at the age of ten, let me add quickly that I also had a deep interest in science, loved to make gunpowder and often spent time in the principal's office for being naughty. I was dyslexic and hyperactive.

My parents were active members of a warm, loving Presbyterian church in Charlotte, North Carolina, but the world of the church was different from what I learned at home or read in the Bible and

C. S. Lewis. No one at church (although we listened to Bible stories and talked about spiritual things) expected God to do anything. At times church seemed like a dull charade, at times an elaborate, inspiring tradition. But nothing much of interest ever happened.

The Brass Heaven Descends

As I got older, I outgrew my childhood vision of the spiritual world. I learned in school that it was important to be rational and pragmatic. My faith in God slowly eroded. But this process was slowed by three intervening events.

In 1966, after ten years of school in the U.S., my family moved to Korea, where I spent my high school years. This sojourn in an Eastern land helped put my rationalism and pragmatism into perspective.

Second, after graduating from high school, I traveled in India for eight weeks, where I encountered the power of a religion alien to Christianity. On several occasions as I visited temples filled with idols, numinous powers—unseen but very real—reached out and made their evil presence felt. Something deep within me recoiled in horror. I knew in my gut that these were evil spirits opposed to Jesus, although I argued against this interpretation of my experience. I had not forgotten my childhood vision of a spiritual realm, although my rational education in the U.S. had attempted to dismember it.

A third event interrupting the erosion of my faith happened while I attended Davidson College in Charlotte, North Carolina, in the early 1970s. During my junior year, some students were into drugs. Others were involved in the occult. Several had séances in their rooms—all just for fun, of course. Most of the occult activities centered around one particular coed who was fascinated with psychic phenomena.

As a psychology major, I was interested and spent much time with her discussing these esoteric subjects. I sensed something odd about her but could not put my finger on it.

One night about midnight, this young woman burst into my room, hair and clothes disheveled, terror in her eyes. With her I sensed an evil presence that gave me the creeps—like the idolatrous presences in India.

"As I was walking across campus," she blurted out, "I started feeling invisible hands tearing at my throat and clothes. It was creepy. What's happening to me?"

I had no idea. Then into my mind came the words *In the name of Jesus, I command you to be gone*. In my confusion and fear, I had no recourse but to speak out these words, although I was not at all sure why—or what to expect.

As soon as I spoke them out, my classmate became calm, and we talked at length about what had happened.

I still did not know what to make of it. But this experience, and several others like it, tore a hole in my vision of reality. I had looked into a black abyss inhabited by entities that the Bible took for real, entities that C. S. Lewis and George Macdonald had written about but about which the Church had taught me nothing. I tried to make sense of my experience by seeking counsel from several professors whom I respected for their wisdom.

Their reactions astonished me. What I had experienced with vivid clarity, they dismissed without a thought. They did not even have categories for discussing these things. One of the professors, beloved for his erudition, laughed and told me, "Oh, yes, a lot of things seem to be going on when one is in love!"

The only one who took my experiences seriously was a psychology professor who related them to the writings of Carl Jung and William James. He assured me, however, that there was a psychological explanation for everything.

His soothing explanation left me strangely dissatisfied. I felt as though I had trespassed into a reality that my professors treated as mythic but that I knew to be real.

Light Penetrates My Brass Heaven

In 1974 I started theological studies at Union Seminary in Richmond, Virginia. There, in the very place where I thought I would find vivid experience of the things of the Spirit, I found an even deeper spiritual silence. One time, several members of the local presbytery (a court composed of ministers and representative elders) were brought before the Committee on Ministry for having received the gift of tongues and for practicing a ministry of deliverance. When this news hit the campus, it was met with howls of derision that anyone in our day could still believe in such things. Such beliefs were certainly not Presbyterian, and probably not sane.

A well-known minister who had studied the charismatic renewal came to instruct our pastoral care course on how to minister to Presbyterians infected by the charismatic disease. He described speaking in tongues as a psychological aberration providing uneducated people an emotional release from stress. The alleged casting out of demons was a tragic, misguided return to a primitive, non-scientific worldview.

"Everyone knows that these so-called demons are autonomous psychological complexes," he said. "What these people need is not some phony deliverance but the care of a good psychologist."

I felt disconcerted that this well-known minister had made no mention of Scripture in analyzing these phenomena.

Then, during my third year at Union, as part of my Doctor of Ministry program, I returned to Korea along with my wife, Laura. There we found ourselves in an environment radically different from seminary.

In Korea, God was a vital, lived reality. We found intensity of prayer and expectancy of faith. Koreans shared their spiritual struggles openly and God's power in the midst of struggle. They had a passion for the Bible, which they saw as the guide to interpreting spiritual phenomena and which they respected as the foundation for living. They also assumed that to be an effective minister, one must ask for and receive the baptism of the Holy Spirit for power in ministry.

So in Korea, Laura and I were ourselves baptized in the Holy Spirit and had many experiences of the power and presence of God. It was a glorious season of our lives.

Among the Presbyterian missionaries in Korea, I saw intelligent, well-educated people dealing maturely with spiritual issues. They were sophisticated in their understanding of reality and could discern between a demon and mental illness. They moved freely between spiritual reality and the rationally discerned empirical world, which I found refreshing. The Korean Church was moving and growing in a way that the American Church was not.

Returning to Union Seminary, immersed once again in a flat, two-dimensional world with four corners and no mystery, was a shock to my system. Again I was faced with the tension between spiritual reality and the denial of it. Western worship was controlled, safe and dull. The sermons were scholarly, the music professional, but there was no life, no expectation that God would visit us. At seminary we were well-prepared to engage in theological debate, do pastoral care with professional aplomb and preach well-thought-out sermons. But prayer, spiritual discernment and the struggles of the soul in relationship to God were passed over in silence.

As loved, nurtured and well-educated as I was at Union Seminary and at Davidson College, I recognized that these institutions were trapped in and limited by a Western worldview. While many students and professors were open to spiritual reality, they had to keep their spiritual experiences locked away in private closets.

I was profoundly puzzled by all this. How was it possible for sincere, faithful Christians to be so divorced from realities described in the Bible? Why were there such wildly different interpretations of the charismatic renewal among Christians, some seeing it as a move of the Holy Spirit and others as mere emotionalism or psychological manipulation? How was it that my church, while teaching from the Bible, lived in a world radically different from that of the Bible?

Our Need to Break Through

In 1980, Laura and I went to Taiwan as evangelistic/educational missionaries to serve at the Presbyterian Bible College. In 1982 I took a Taiwanese pastor to Korea, where he opened his life to the power of the Holy Spirit. At the same time, I received a vision for a lay training center at the Bible college to equip lay people to minister in the power of the Holy Spirit. A river of spiritual renewal was flowing among Presbyterians in Taiwan.

The lay training center came into fruition in 1984 with the construction of a $1 million facility, which has become a major retreat center for Christians. To assist in the teaching of pastors and lay people to minister in the power of the Holy Spirit, I set up seminars at the center, including one on worldview taught by Dr. Charles Kraft, Professor of Cross-Cultural Studies at Fuller School of World Mission. As he taught, I began to better understand the nature of the tension I had felt growing up.

The metallic wall I had run up against at school, at seminary and in the Church was the construct of a Western rationalistic world-view. While this worldview had provided a coherent, logical way for me to appreciate some aspects of my world, it left out other aspects altogether, which it explained away as imaginary. I have come to believe since then that many of the problems we face in the Western Church come not from our theology but from our uncon-scious philosophical presuppositions.

This conviction has compelled Doug and me to write this book. Both of us began during the '70s to rebuild our lives on philosoph-ical foundations other than those we learned as Western denomina-tional Christians with university and seminary educations. What we have learned about the nature of worldview has transformed us. The brass heaven is of our own making, and if we want to move into a fresh encounter with God, we must dismantle what we have built.

As Doug and I have broken through the brass heaven, freshness, adventure and newness have come to us—our rightful inheritance as Christians. But we see many of our fellow Christians struggling with the dryness that once hindered our own walks with God. Many of these struggles, we are convinced, come from an inadequate worldview, which blocks faith, destroys the promises of God and leaves us bankrupt at the end of the day. We think it would do us all good if Western Christians would dismantle their own brass heav-ens piece by piece. In fact, the brass heaven today is collapsing of its own weight. Let's examine this metallic, machine-like structure and the ideas from which it is made. Then we will see more clearly how to break through it and how to let the fresh breezes of God into our lives.

The Nature
of Worldviews

3

Can God be trusted? Does He heal, rescue and save? Does He put broken people together again? Can He move through the Church by His power to do His work?

Before we can settle these theological questions, we must address the more basic philosophical issue of worldview. As C. S. Lewis wrote in his book *Miracles:*

> Many people think one can decide whether a miracle occurred in the past by examining the evidence according to the ordinary rules of historical inquiry. But the ordinary rules cannot be worked until we have decided whether miracles are possible, and if so, how probable they are. For, if they are impossible, then no amount of historical evidence will convince us. . . . If, on the other hand, miracles are not intrinsically improbable, then the existing evidence will be sufficient to convince us that quite a number of miracles have occurred. The result of our historical inquiries thus depends on the philosophical views which we have been holding before we even began to look at the evidence. The philosophical question must therefore come first.[1]

Few of us examine our lives so deeply as to call into question our philosophical presuppositions. Nevertheless, our worldview is the central ingredient of our philosophy—a network of axioms about how the parts of our world operate.

25

Dr. Kraft helps us to define worldview more precisely:

> Cultures pattern perceptions of reality into conceptualizations of what reality can or should be, what is to be regarded as actual, probable, possible or impossible. These conceptualizations form what is termed the "worldview" of culture. The worldview is the central systemization of conceptions of reality to which the members of its culture assent (largely unconsciously) and from which stems their value system. The worldview lies at the very heart of the culture, touching, interacting with, and strongly influencing every aspect of the culture.[2]

Put more simply, a worldview is *the culturally determined set of filters through which we perceive and experience reality.*

Our Set of Filters

Only God apprehends reality in its absolute essence and totality. It would overwhelm our limited minds and sense organs to perceive all at once the fullness of all things. So the human mind imposes between reality and experience an elaborate set of filters. These filters limit and structure data to form manageable patterns. They limit, organize and interpret our experience of reality so that we may have meaningful thoughts and responses.

Matrices

Arthur Koestler in *The Act of Creation* uses the terms *matrices* and *codes* to define these internal organizing patterns. He explains the word *matrix*: "'Matrix' is derived from the Latin for womb and is figuratively used for any pattern or mold in which things are shaped and developed, or type is cast. Thus, the exercise of a habit or skill is 'molded' by its matrix."[3]

These filters or matrices function at various levels of perception and have different sources. The most basic ones that organize sense data come from innate neurological structures already operating during infancy:

> Seeing is a skill, part innate, part acquired in early infancy. The selective codes . . . operate on the input, not the output. The stimuli impinging on the senses provide only the raw material of an infant's con-

scious experience—the "booming, buzzing confusion" of William James; before reaching awareness, the input is filtered, processed, distorted, interpreted, and reorganized in a series of relay-stations at various levels of its nervous system; but the processing itself is not experienced by the person, and the rules of the game according to which the controls work are unknown to him.[4]

Once we leave this most basic level of processing sensory data, and move to shaping, organizing and giving meaning to experience, the origin and functioning of these filters or matrices become more complex.

It is beyond our scope to explore these processes exhaustively. Let us say briefly that they are inherited from parents, formed from the cultural air we breathe, shaped by our subconscious mind, refined by education and confirmed by experience.

In the story of Jesus and the blind man in Mark 8:22–26, we can glimpse these organizing filters at both levels—physical and cultural. By Jesus' first prayer, the man's ability to see was physically restored. But the matrices that organize perception were not, for the man said, "I see people; they look like trees walking around" (verse 24). A second prayer restored not only the innate but also the learned organizers of sense data, and the man could "see" clearly.

The following diagram from Dr. Kraft shows this process of filtering.[5]

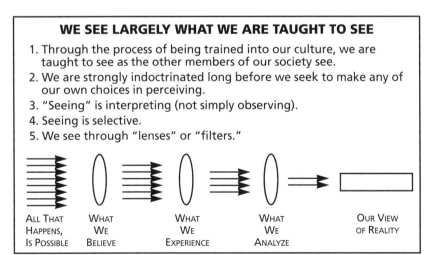

WE SEE LARGELY WHAT WE ARE TAUGHT TO SEE

1. Through the process of being trained into our culture, we are taught to see as the other members of our society see.
2. We are strongly indoctrinated long before we seek to make any of our own choices in perceiving.
3. "Seeing" is interpreting (not simply observing).
4. Seeing is selective.
5. We see through "lenses" or "filters."

| ALL THAT HAPPENS, IS POSSIBLE | WHAT WE BELIEVE | WHAT WE EXPERIENCE | WHAT WE ANALYZE | OUR VIEW OF REALITY |

Paradigms

The matrices that help us perceive and interpret our experiences are organized into what are generally called paradigms. A paradigm is a complex of filters or an extensive matrix that provides a model of how some aspect of reality works. A paradigm is a broad philosophical presupposition that helps us interpret experiences.

Let's look at some examples of paradigms:

- The world is a mysterious place that resists analysis.
- The world is a machine operating by laws easily analyzed by the rational mind.
- The species were created by God, each after their own kind.
- The species evolved from each other through natural processes.
- God is a personal deity who loves us.
- God is an impersonal force of spiritual powers and laws.
- People are basically good.
- People are basically evil.
- Time is linear.
- Time is cyclical.

Each of these paradigms has its own set of unquestioned axioms. Each has its history of development in literature and popular culture, and its champions among popular writers and teachers.

The worldview of any particular culture is full of many such paradigms. An individual's worldview is drawn from the culture but is unique to the individual's experience, temperament and education. The more liberal sector of the Church, for example, lacks a paradigm of a "personal devil" and views evil as ignorance or the result of oppressive social structures. Pentecostals, on the other hand, hold to a lively paradigm of a "personal devil." Both the liberal and the Pentecostal worldviews, being Western, have an overarching paradigm of the inalienable rights of the individual.

Often we cherish contradictory paradigms that we bring to different situations at different times. The scientist directs his or her research according to the belief that the world functions like a machine, while shifting to a paradigm of personal love when relating to his or her family.

A Worldview Is Unconscious

A worldview is both unconscious and pervasive. In fact, it is unconscious *because* it is pervasive. Like a pane of glass or the water a fish swims in, the worldview is the medium in which we see and experience. We focus our attention on what we see and experience, disregarding the medium. Most of the time, therefore, we are not aware of why we interpret our experiences as we do. Since our presuppositions are unexamined and beyond the reach of normal discussion, they are not easily modified.

Brad: When I told my professors of my encounter with the supernatural, we experienced a clash of two opposing paradigms. Their paradigm assumed the world to be entirely rational and governed by scientifically explicable laws. Mine assumed an irrational element in an otherwise ordered world and the possibility of invisible entities called demons. I believed that my college friend had been attacked by an evil spirit, while they interpreted it as a psychological event. Because it did not fit their worldview, they assumed that it did not happen. So we had a clash of worldviews, with no understanding or synthesis. To understand what actually had happened, we needed to move to another level of discourse—the examination of the paradigms of our worldviews. If we had done that, we might have had fruitful dialogue. But we did not move to that level of discourse and were unconscious of the paradigms governing our perceptions.

Apply this lesson now to the fruitless clashes of the 1960s, when the charismatic renewal first touched mainline churches. Some insisted that the "word gifts" of the Holy Spirit—gifts like speaking in tongues and prophecy—are God-given "supernatural" abilities. Others affirmed with equal passion that they are merely psychological.

Elsewhere, those who argued that evangelism is a matter of saving souls for eternity clashed with those who saw it as bringing love and justice here on earth.

Behind many of these schisms in the Church lie different paradigms and worldviews operating unconsciously.

The Shattering of My Naïve Paradigms

I will never forget the first day I spent in Calcutta, India. I arrived with a set of unconscious assumptions that the world was rational, just and good. But when I walked out of my comfortable hotel onto the Calcutta street, I was assaulted by a horde of horribly deformed beggars. Some had no legs. Others had twisted arms or open, oozing sores. Worse yet, these beggars stared blankly, empty of all hope. They cried with rasping, well-practiced voices, "*Baxces, baxces,*" which means, "Alms, alms."

If you give money to beggars, I told myself, *they'll never learn to work for a living.*

Then I passed the corpses of several people who had apparently starved during the night.

This isn't real, I told myself.

Finally a mother in rags, black desperation in her eyes, thrust into my face a baby who was nearly dead. She was pleading for help.

At this I broke. I pulled all the money out of my pocket—it might have been fifty dollars or so—and flung it at the woman. Then, turning, I raced the three blocks to the American Embassy. The embassy was not open yet, but I showed my passport to the young Marine guard and pleaded with him urgently to let me in. The doors opened and I entered the safety of the embassy.

American culture was my bulwark against the reality raging outside. For the rest of the day I felt physically sick, emotionally drained and confused. I hated Calcutta.

That evening I gathered up my courage and left the embassy. And as soon as I could, I caught a train out of that hell on earth.

What had happened to me? My trauma went deeper than an encounter with some beggars. Calcutta had challenged my unconsciously held worldview. My concept of God as present and caring about all people was badly eroded. My paradigm that the world was a good place was annihilated. The experience was so shattering that I could not deny it or shove it to one side. So I reacted in self-defense, doing the only thing I could think of to protect myself from attack. I ran.

Developing a More Mature Worldview

It took a couple of years and a personal experience with Jesus Christ before I could reconcile the kind of suffering I had seen in Calcutta with divine goodness and Christian joy. The key: the crucifixion and resurrection of Jesus Christ. The reorganization of my worldview to fit both Christian hope and the evil in Calcutta required another encounter with massive evil in another Asian country.

I lived for a few months in Vietnam during the last year before the country fell to the Communists. There I served as photographer for the Holt Adoption Agency, traveling throughout Vietnam photographing the work done with the most tragic victims of the war—children. As I saw the emaciated, listless forms of abandoned children, I was often so overwhelmed that my eyes would fill with tears and I could not see to take pictures. Vietnam, like Calcutta, seemed a futile place, devoid of God.

One day I went to photograph an impoverished Catholic orphanage. The place was falling down and the children had little to eat, but there was sparkle here; there was life. The children ran and played. Babies laughed—something I had rarely seen at the well-provisioned government orphanages where children were listless and many died for no apparent cause. I wondered at this inexplicable joy.

I stepped into a room full of cribs, each one bearing a heartbreaking bundle of skin and bones. These were the children just brought in off the street.

What hope do these children have? I asked myself.

Then I watched an old Chinese Catholic sister who, with great tenderness, lifted each of these children to her breast. She whispered to them, sang to them, loved them. I was astonished. Here was the reason for the lively, happy children I had seen in the other rooms. Here was a redeeming transformation of evil and meaninglessness.

As I watched this humble sister do what millions of dollars of American aid had failed to do, I was moved by a great mystery. Where did the love come from that enabled this woman to love these children back to life? My eyes caught sight of a crucifix on the nurs-

ery wall. It seemed as though a burst of light broke from it. I dropped
to the floor and began to weep. The source of her transforming love
was Jesus Christ.

Now I understood how the world could be so good and yet so
evil. The power of evil is everywhere, yet the power of Christ is in
the process of overcoming it. One day Jesus will put all His enemies
under His feet. In the meantime, He uses His people to make His
life-giving presence known to the world.

I cannot express exactly how my worldview was altered by my
encounter with evil in Calcutta, then by the good in the midst of
evil in Vietnam. Deep, subconscious processes were at work—
processes of which I was largely unaware. But after these encounters, I saw and experienced reality differently.

A Worldview Is Sustained by Habit

A worldview resists change because it is unconscious and unexamined. This resistance is reinforced by habit—the glue that holds
our worldview together and keeps us moving in a comfortable, well-
established matrix. Habit, while making the world predictable and
secure, also prevents us from seeing or feeling comfortable with
other matrices. Arthur Koestler helps us understand the role of habit
in filtering out contradictory data:

> Matrices vary from fully automatized skills to those with a high
> degree of plasticity; but even the latter are controlled by rules of the
> game which function below the level of awareness. These silent codes
> can be regarded as condensations of learning into habit. Habits are
> the indispensable core of stability and ordered behavior; they also
> have a tendency to become mechanized and to reduce man to the sta-
> tus of a conditioned automaton.[6]

Often in changing traditional patterns of worship in a church or
in being open to the working of the Holy Spirit, one is up against
nothing more mysterious than paradigms that have become habitual. How often has the young pastor arrived at his or her first church,
intensely aware of the potential for spiritual growth, only to be met

with that monotonous chorus, "But we've never done it that way before!"

In my first parish I had just such an experience. An 80-year-old matriarch of the church had been sick for two years and unable to attend Sunday worship. Mrs. Gardner (not her real name) was mother, grandmother or aunt to half the church—a lovable, respected lady of the Old South.

One wintry Saturday she called me and said, "Son! Do you believe the Bible?"

I said, "Yes, ma'am."

She responded, "Good! You know what it says in the book of James about elders praying for the sick?"

I said "Yes, I remember."

"Well, you get those boys"—she meant our elders, most of whom were over fifty but who were her sons or relatives—"and come down here and do what the Word of God says. Anoint me with oil so I can get healed and go to church."

"Yes, ma'am," I said. "We'll be right over."

It was Saturday afternoon and snowing. But I called each of the nine elders and explained the situation. Nine times I heard the same litany: "But preacher, we've never done that before."

My only recourse was to say, "Yes, I know, but it's in the Bible, which is the Word of God. Besides, how am I going to tell Mrs. Gardner that you won't do it?"

It was this last argument that drew the elders to her house to pray for her. I explained that the anointing oil was just a sign of the Holy Spirit and that we would trust Jesus for the healing. The nine elders were obviously uncomfortable with this procedure, but we all laid hands on her head, and I prayed and anointed her with oil.

When nothing happened, there was an audible sigh of relief. The elders' worldview had been preserved. The rationale for "never having done this before" had remained intact.

Imagine the elders' discomfort the following day when we found Mrs. Gardner sitting in church for the first time in two years, completely healed! I rejoiced at this breakthrough of spiritual power and anticipated that we would minister in this way again. But while everyone agreed that healing ministry was a good thing, the church's habitual perspective and practice prevailed. During the time I was pastor there, we never again prayed for healing with the anointing of oil and the laying on of hands.

A Worldview Both Blinds Us and Opens Our Eyes

Our worldview is a great blessing. It processes what our eyes see so that we can make sense of the world, putting billions of bits of data into a meaningful whole. It enables us to experience reality with richness and nuance of meaning because we bring with us filters constructed by the collective insight of our culture. At the same time, it excludes from our vision certain data that do not fit into its matrices.

To grasp the way a worldview both blinds and opens eyes, consider the contrast between Eastern and Western art. In most Chinese paintings you see waterfalls and mountains. A human being or two (if you can find them at all) may be off in some corner. People are blended into nature and are an insignificant feature of it.

Now consider the *Mona Lisa* by Leonardo da Vinci. The mysteriously smiling Mona takes center stage, whereas in the hazy background is swirling water and a suggestion of waterfalls.

These differences in art represent two profoundly different worldviews. The Chinese master does not usually paint from a real scene. He perfects a learned brush stroke that yields waterfalls and mountains. This style is not based on observation and experimentation but on imitation of an accepted authority—another Chinese master. The Chinese artist is also informed by Taoism, which teaches the harmony of all things. A human being's chief end is to be in balance with the rest of the world.

Mona Lisa, by contrast, reflects the paradigm that humankind is the center of the universe. It is the smile of the woman, not the swirling waters, that draws our attention. While the Western artist learned his style from other artists, he has also learned to observe reality. Leonardo, like other Renaissance artists, used live models. He even dissected human bodies to understand the mechanism by which they worked, enabling him to paint more accurately. This was the beginning of a scientific method that rests on the observation of nature—an important paradigm of the Western worldview.

The Chinese artist is blinded from seeing anatomical detail. The Western artist is blinded from seeing the harmony of all things in nature. Each sees what his or her worldview allows.

The Rabbit in the Moon

When I first arrived in Taiwan, a profound paradigm shift was ushered into my life by a triviality. While in the West we speak of "the man in the moon," children in China do not see a man but a rabbit. They have all the appropriate myths to explain how it got there, too.

Soon after arriving in Taiwan, Laura and I attended our first moon festival in mid-autumn. On a brilliant moonlit night, we sat out on the grass, ate moon cakes, shot off fireworks and admired the full moon. Everyone kept asking whether I saw the rabbit up there. Despite their attempts to show me the obvious, all my Western eyes could see was a human face largely erased by the footprints of the Apollo astronauts.

As the months sped by and I learned to speak and even dream in Chinese, my worldview started to change—and with it my perception. One night I looked up at the full moon. I saw, as if painted there by some Chinese artist, the infamous rabbit dancing on the moon, its ears flopping back in ecstasy. It was so obvious, and made such better sense than the man in the moon, that I wondered why I had never seen it before!

It may seem silly, but this new ability to see a rabbit was the harbinger of a profound change in my perception. I was beginning to see Eastern paradigms. It was to have profound consequences for me in my perception of the spiritual realm.

When the Power of God Strikes a Blind Spot

In John 9 we see a case of a worldview causing blindness. Jesus healed a man born blind. The evidence of healing was obvious, yet the Pharisees could not see it. They conducted a thorough, rational examination according to a paradigm that outlawed the signs and wonders of God. Because the healing did not fit into this paradigm, they removed the offending data by expelling the healed man from their synagogue. Later they would deal with other data that did not fit their matrix; they would nail Jesus to the cross.

And what of us? Does the Jesus of the Gospels fit our unconscious worldview? Or does the power of God strike a blind spot in our philosophical filters? When God challenges our paradigms, how do we respond?

A woman Doug and I know, Delores Winder, had an experience similar to that of the man born blind.

For nineteen and a half years her spine and hips had been deteriorating. The doctors gave no hope for a cure, but her pain was so excruciating that they performed a surgical procedure called a percutaneous cordotomy. This procedure, performed only on terminal patients, burns out the pain centers in the brain.

After this operation, Delores had no feeling on the right side of her body from the waist down. On the left side she had no feeling from the breast down. Because she had no feeling, she would often unwittingly cut or burn herself. She could walk only with assistance. Her body was encased in a body cast, her neck in a brace.

In 1975, at the request of her son, Delores went to a Kathryn Kuhlman meeting, during which she began to experience a burning sensation in her legs—a medical impossibility. By the end of the meeting she enjoyed full feeling (not pain) throughout her body. Her healing was verified by Dr. Richard O'Wellen of Johns Hopkins Medical School, who was present. She took off her body cast and walked out of the auditorium fully restored. Today, as we see this spirited, energetic woman moving nimbly from person to person in prayer (Delores has a wonderful prayer ministry), we are filled with wonder and thanksgiving at the power of God.

Yet this healing created difficulties. For years Delores and her family had been members of a loving, caring church. But when God answered prayers for healing differently than everyone expected, she was ostracized by the very people who had been praying for her. Her church studiously ignored the healing; there was no announcement from the pulpit nor any public thanksgiving. Though they had suffered with her through her ordeal, they were deeply embarrassed and frightened by the healing, for it challenged their worldview.

Even Delores had difficulty accepting her healing. It did not fit into her worldview, either. She soon wished that God had healed her in a more ordinary, less miraculous way.

"I can say these things about my church," she says, "because they are facts, and because the person most threatened was myself. My worldview had no place for this kind of miraculous intervention by God. If the church people had a hard time dealing with the miracle, I had an even harder time. I only believed in Jesus the Savior. I had no place in my world for Jesus the Healer. The miracle blew away everything that I had believed about Jesus and the way He works. I was angry at God and wanted to move away to a place where no one knew me, and start over again.

"That first year was extremely difficult. I had to adjust to a new view of Christianity and discover from the Bible that Jesus is more than the Savior of our souls. For months I wrestled with Scripture and started to rebuild my worldview to include the possibility of Jesus working miraculously."[7]

Our constructions of reality are always, to some measure, incomplete and limiting. Like Delores, we are challenged to see more as God sees and to experience the immensity of the world as God created and moves within it. The paradigms that God invites us to try, which give us a hint of His perspective, are provided in the Bible. In Scripture as nowhere else, we find the paradigms through which we may view reality as our Creator views it.

But the first step to seeing as God sees is to make conscious the unconscious presuppositions that presently determine our Western way of seeing.

4

Where Is
the Power?

Brad: Our worldviews have not grown up in universities and think tanks. They have been cultivated by societies to address human need. At the core of every worldview stands this question: Where is the power to control our lives so that we may survive and even prosper in this hostile world?

Human need is the *Go* space on the Monopoly board of life. A worldview provides clues as to how we may tap into power sources as we move around the board.

According to Dr. Charles Kraft, worldviews look for power in any of three realms—natural, human-social and spiritual. Sources of power in these areas may include the following:[1]

The Sphere	The Means to Control It
Natural-material sphere (Light, water, the sun, minerals, etc.)	Folk medicine Crafts Science Technology Magic Medicine, etc.

Human-social sphere (Parents, eldership, government, the family, chieftainship, etc.)	Social organization Confucianism Ethics Government Psychology, etc.
Spiritual sphere (God, the Holy Spirit, angels, demons, spirits of the dead, etc.)	Shamanism Witchcraft Religion Yoga, etc.

Let's look at these different spheres and sources of power in turn as each is embraced by a particular worldview.

The Natural-Material Sphere

Western cultures have moved toward the first of these three power options—the material. We can manipulate nature through science and technology to produce everything from stereos to steroids, from computer chips to potato chips.

Having walked many a filthy street with open sewers in the developing world, I fully appreciate how the Western worldview has materially improved the quality of life. Once during a family reunion, I overheard some women talking about their childbirth experiences. With a shock I realized that, of the five of them, four would, but for the benefits of medicine and technology, probably have died giving birth because of complications they experienced.

Our lives are packed full of the benefits and achievements that are a byproduct of this worldview. According to Genesis 1:27–31, God gave us the mandate to take dominion over the earth, and we have used this mandate to advantage (although we have used it irresponsibly at times, too).

The Human-Social Sphere

The Chinese have built their worldview not on the material realm but on social relationships. To the Easterner, such relationships are vested with power.

Confucianism, for example, gives great weight to the human-social sphere. This elaborate system carefully delineates the positions of all individuals within family and society. At the top of this system is *Shangdi*, the Emperor of Heaven, to whom belongs one's ultimate allegiance. Beneath God is the emperor of the nation, who receives his authority from *Shangdi*. The family reflects a similar order, with the father at the head of every household. Children are duty-bound to love, respect and provide for parents through filial devotion.

A central doctrine of Confucianism is the "rectification of names"—the idea that order and harmony result when each person fulfills the requirement of his or her office. The father exercises love and oversight over the family. When children fulfill their obligations of filial piety, the family enjoys peace and harmony. This system has contributed for centuries to the preservation of Chinese civilization.

In its elaborate family system, welfare programs and rest homes for the aged are practically unheard of. Indeed, they are an offense, for each family takes care of its own. Once Laura and I found a sick old man lying in front of our home in Taichung, Taiwan. We called the police for help. When the police arrived, the first question they asked the man was, "Where is your family? Why aren't they looking after you?" What Western policeman would ask such a question?

It is in these family and social relationships that cultures shaped by Confucian teaching find power for living. Chinese culture is a culture of relationships, wherein lies its source of power. Those who can get things done are those who have *gwansyi,* the "pull" of relationships.

I experienced this firsthand in a dramatic way. At the Lay Training Center, where I helped start an annual conference for Christian businessmen, we invited as speaker for our first conference the vice president of the Republic of China, Lee Dung Wei. (Dr. Lee, a Presbyterian, became president of the Republic of China.) To our amazement he accepted our invitation. While he was at the Center, we established with him *gwansyi,* a relationship.

Two years later my sister Ruth came to stay with us in Taiwan for several months. She was having so much fun that she forgot to extend her visa.

On Christmas Eve, when I took her to the airport to catch her flight back to the States, we were shocked to be told, "There is no way she can leave. Her visa has expired by over a month. She must go to the police in Taipei City and get this straightened out."

The police were adamant. Never, we were told, had anyone been allowed to leave Taiwan with a visa expired by that much.

By this time my sister was in tears. I finally prevailed on a police officer to give Taipei headquarters a call and check with the authorities. He agreed but assured me it was futile.

Twenty minutes later he returned, a look of amazement on his face.

"Who are you?" he asked. "You must really have *gwansyi*. After checking your records, the chief of police approved your sister's departure."

This is just a small instance of how relationships serve in Asia as the source of power.

The Spiritual Sphere

Doug: To illustrate the third power alternative, we turn to aboriginal Native American cultures, which looked to spiritual power—the faith of animism.

The Salish tribes in the northwest U.S. and British Columbia, like most other aboriginals, treasured their *sumesh* pouches. Each Salish man assembled a bag of charms given him by the guardian spirit on whom he relied for protection and blessing. To find out which animal spirit was to be his personal guardian, he went to a lonely place during his teen years to pray and fast. During that time he would make contact with some animal that would impart its spirit. This spirit was believed to bequeath certain powers that would remain with a warrior for the rest of his life. These spirits were trusted for prowess in battle, for success in food-gathering and for virtually everything important for survival.

The spiritual world, organized under the watchcare of a distant and little-known Master of Life, was full of powers, all interacting according to laws revealed by the true power-brokers of Native American culture, the shamans.

When Chief Joseph of the Nez Perce nation decided to wage war against the whites, it was because his shaman advised him to do so. When the Salish Flatheads refused to form an alliance with him, it was because their shamans prophesied that war with the whites was futile and that Chief Joseph's plans would come to nothing.

Power Sources in Western Culture

Thus do societies build their worldviews around sources of power. Every culture remains firmly convinced that its worldview is correct and that abandoning its source of power would bring widespread catastrophe. Western culture is no exception.

Building on Dr. Kraft's observations, I want to identify three principles related to power sources in Western culture.

Investment

First, *what we designate as the main source of power will determine where we invest our time, money and energy.* We Westerners invest ourselves in the advancement of science and technology and reward those who develop these areas. Electric toothbrushes, children's computer games, sixty-inch televisions—all are evidence of Western mastery of the material world and are greeted as successes of Western expertise.

Yet our psychiatric hospitals and prisons are filled to overflowing, and we are seeing more and more of the traumatizing behavior that puts people into those places. I have more than a dozen people in my congregation who have made a career in the helping professions. They are supposed to fix the traumatized and addicted people in our midst. But they have an impossible job because our society is weighted against them—a society that values not spiritual and social power but material power.

One out of eight American women today will be raped during her lifetime. Rape is the most rapidly growing crime in America. It is fed and encouraged by the pornography industry, by Madonna and the music industry, and by Hollywood. These industries help to perpetuate the myth that women secretly want to be raped. Lust is running unrestrained in our society, and we have put our confidence in material methods to combat it. We turn up our noses at social and spiritual influences, which we no longer consider relevant sources of power to help us.

There was a time when most Westerners might have listened to these words of Jesus: "Anyone who looks at a woman lustfully has already committed adultery with her in his heart" (Matthew 5:28). This wisdom might have empowered us to avoid the difficulties in which we now find ourselves. But Jesus' spiritual insights are ignored by Westerners in our post-Christian era. His authority, which flows from the spiritual realm, goes unrecognized. Besides, in the so-called "quest for the historical Jesus," Western scholars question openly whether the words of Jesus really came from Jesus at all. Science has purportedly, through higher criticism, found a way of scientifically evaluating the historicity of everything biblical.

We invest our energies in science. These attempts at scientific Bible study have created the illusion that Jesus' words are unreliable. We have science now. It is better.

As a nation, we exalt not only sexual energy but the technological wizardry to stimulate sexual energy in our homes. Videocassette recorders are available to almost everyone who wants one, and we pride ourselves in our freedom to view whatever we want. Video is a material industry that no longer pretends to serve an ennobling or moral purpose. We invest in what we believe—and Westerners believe in the material world and the technological power to regulate it.

In the context of such a culture, therapists and pastors must try to bring healing to sex addicts and their victims. They fight Western philosophy every step of the way.

Causality

Brad: Second, *what we designate as the main source of power will determine our understanding of cause-and-effect relationships.* We Westerners tend to see our problems as caused by a lack of material things or material knowledge.

Most sickness, we believe, is caused by natural laws that have been broken, and we need more scientific knowledge to discover drugs to solve the problem. We do not believe that the spiritual world influences the material world, or that God rewards those who seek Him (except perhaps in heaven after we die). We have lost the conviction that events are caused by the spiritual world impinging on our here-and-now.

Accordingly, what in another age might have been perceived as spiritual or moral problems are reduced to "sicknesses" and medical problems today. Do we have problem pregnancies? Rampant sexual addiction? AIDS? Even excessive violence? Science and medicine will find the answers to these curses. Let us spend more money on government research. Because we do not see the social and spiritual causes, we do not believe in social and spiritual solutions. Teens cannot possibly control their sexual urges, despite the evidence that in our own past, Christian teaching, appealing to the commandments of the One from above, enabled most young people to remain chaste.

I remember vividly my first class in ostensibly values-free education. Our high school guidance counselor, an atheist, assured us that there was no reason to feel guilty over venereal disease or accidental pregnancy. "These medical problems can be taken care of by penicillin and abortion," she explained. Problems are caused physically and are to be solved physically.

In the East, causation is viewed differently. If a business fails in Taiwan, the Chinese might attribute the failure to the fact that the *fēngshwěi* was wrong—that the location determined by geomancy (a kind of geographical divination) was not aligned properly to bring in money.

Our Presbyterian mission in Taiwan had a valuable piece of land that we wanted to hand over to the Taiwan Presbyterian Church for development. In a final committee meeting, we were trying to decide whether to go ahead with the project. It seemed like a good decision, but I could tell that several of the Taiwanese businessmen were undecided.

I asked the contractor, a Presbyterian elder, about it. He affirmed that it was an excellent investment.

Still I sensed the unease among the Taiwanese.

Finally I asked the question that apparently no one else dared ask in the presence of American missionaries. In recongition of the Chinese worldview, I knew I had to ask. "Look, I know you're a good Presbyterian, but we do live in Taiwan. How is the *fēngshwĕi* of the building location?"

He grinned sheepishly. He knew better. "I hired a geomancer to come and check out the mission property. He assured me that the *fēngshwĕi* is excellent and that the spiritual forces are aligned perfectly for us to make a lot of money."

The decision to go forward was unanimous.

Power Brokers

Third, *how these spheres of power are weighted will determine whom we invest with control over our lives and our institutions.* Those who mediate power are given rights to control our social system. Westerners now give these rights to those skilled in the use of material power.

For two hundred years the U.S. has accepted the conviction "that all men are created equal; that they are endowed by their Creator with certain unalienable rights." This spiritual concept grew out of the biblical paradigm that all people are created in God's image. Our nation stood not only for its own interests but for principles.

When some Americans wanted to deny those rights to slaves, guarding the plantation economy at the expense of those principles, others (like revivalist Charles Finney and author Harriet Beecher Stowe) held spiritual principles higher than economics. Among those who opposed abolition, some argued that black slaves were not human beings, for they possessed no eternal soul and should not be granted the unalienable rights accorded to whites.

The Civil War was a victory of spiritual principle over material prosperity. Many believed that America's strength came from her principles, which were based on spiritual realities rooted in the Word of God. Alexis de Tocqueville, an objective French observer, confirmed this impression during his visit to our country in the 1840s. The strength of America, he said, came from "pulpits aflame with righteousness." Abraham Lincoln, pointing to the Bible, wrote that "all the good from the Savior of the world is communicated through this Book; but for the Book we could not know right from wrong. All the things desirable to man are contained in it."[2]

Here, then, lay the source of power behind much of the abolition movement. Those with proven expertise in that power were entrusted to control our lives and our institutions.

Today, by contrast, we look to medical science and technology. Doctors (however mistrusted) have become the new high priests of American culture, replacing the spiritual leaders of the past.

When the Supreme Court considered *Roe v. Wade* in 1973, its decision turned almost exclusively on the testimony of certain doctors to tell the court whether babies in the womb were to be regarded as human beings. If they were, the fetus must be accorded the unalienable rights we grant to every human being.

On this key point the doctors vacillated. The possession of a soul could not be proven since there is no physical evidence to show that a fetus has a soul or is created in God's image. (Nor can it be proven, of course, for an adult human being.) Richard Neuhaus wrote:

> For the first time . . . it was explicitly stated that it is possible to address these issues of ultimate importance without reference to Judeo-Christian tradition. . . . For the first time in American jurisprudence, the Supreme Court explicitly excluded philosophy, ethics and religion as factors in its deliberation.[3]

Among Supreme Court justices imbued with the new worldview, the question revolved around physical fetal development. Pregnancy was divided into trimesters, with the idea that a fetus is more human-like and more "viable" with each passing month. Because the Court approached the issue from a physical rather than spiritual direction, it decided that a fetus could legally be "terminated" up to the moment of birth (though termination was discouraged under some circumstances in the last trimester). Which circumstances would indicate abortion was to be determined by the physicians.

Only at birth, then (in the eyes of society), does the fetus become a human being deserving our protection. Medical doctors have become power brokers holding the power of life and death over millions of unborn Americans—a power doctors were fighting for when they testified during *Roe v. Wade*. To quote David C. Reardon,

> What the Court upheld was not the woman's choice per se, but the physician's freedom to treat his patient in whatever way he saw fit. Only the woman's own doctor, the Court insisted, is qualified to determine her "health needs." . . . The Court placed little or no emphasis on the woman's choice, but instead insisted that the final decision "is inherently, and primarily, a medical decision, and basic responsibility for it must rest with the physician."[4]

A Biblical Illustration

For another illustration about power sources and power mediators, we may look to the biblical story of the healing at the Gate Beautiful (Acts 3:1–10). The miracle caused conflict because it challenged the prevailing power paradigms. To begin with, Peter and John lacked both the social class and the academic credentials to exercise power. They were not Judeans but Galileans—simple, unlettered men who had no money, could not debate with the rabbis, knew no one in the temple with whom they could curry favor. Yet they demonstrated that they were in touch with a source of power. They had been with Jesus and attributed their power to Him.

This claim fell completely outside the Sanhedrin's power paradigms, which placed the power of God exclusively in the Law and the Temple system that they managed. God was apparently working outside their system. Feeling threatened, they tried to gag the disciples. Then Gamaliel, who seems to have possessed some remnant of respect for the power of God, dissuaded them from doing to the apostles what they had done to Jesus.

The fundamental question raised at the Gate Beautiful was this: "What is your source of power?" When Peter was met by the astonished crowd, he said, "Why do you stare at us as if by our own power or godliness we had made this man walk?" (verse 12). Likewise, the first question put to Peter by the Sanhedrin was, "By what power or what name did you do this?" (Acts 4:7).

The basic issue in every culture and age is power.

The Power of the Cross

Jesus Christ confronts the worldview of every culture with the power of God. John the Baptist prophesied, "After me will come one who is more powerful than I . . ." (Matthew 3:11). Paul characterized the power of Christ as the power of the cross. "When we were still powerless, Christ died for the ungodly" (Romans 5:6). Above all things, Paul did not want "the cross of Christ [to] be emptied of its power" (1 Corinthians 1:17).

The Scriptures convey that the power of God is without parallel in the natural, social or spiritual spheres. It takes precedence over all other powers. But in portraying this power as "the power of the cross," Paul conveys how different this power is from all others. It cannot, like other powers, be manipulated or controlled.[5] We can only surrender our lives to it and let it flow through us. We must approach this power as Paul described:

> Your attitude should be the same as that of Christ Jesus: Who, being in very nature God, did not consider equality with God something to be grasped, but made himself nothing, taking the very nature of a servant, being made in human likeness. And being found in appearance as a man, he humbled himself and became obedient to death—even death on a cross!
>
> Philippians 2:5–8

Jesus sets up His cross at the center of every worldview of every culture. The cross speaks a message into that worldview: that every source of power—spiritual, social and material—is tainted and corrupted. Only the power of God escapes these curses, and His power is available only to those who empty themselves and give their lives over to God the Father, as Jesus did. "If anyone would come after me," He said, "he must deny himself and take up his cross and follow me. For whoever wants to save his life will lose it, but whoever loses his life for me will find it" (Matthew 16:24–25).

The Gospel injects divine and foreign paradigms into every worldview. The One who died on the cross ascended to the right hand of the Father—the executive hand, the power hand. Jesus shows us that death to self can lead to the power of God, and that the power of God extends to all three realms—spiritual, social and material.

In the spirit realm, Jesus confronts and triumphs over spirits that invite us into manipulation and control—the spirits of shamanistic, animistic and pagan cultures. God invites us into a covenantal relationship by which we are free to love Him and in which He preserves our freedom from the influence of controlling spirits. Paul made it clear that we are not to go back to "the elemental spirits of the universe" (Colossians 2:8, RSV) to do their bidding or gain their friendship.

In the social realm, Jesus confronts the power of legalistic social control, the binding power of the Law. The Law is an external device enforced upon the depraved by controlling people. That this control is necessary we do not question. It keeps us from destroying one another. But its influence is a restraining one, not a creative or freeing one. The power of the cross brings us to our knees, invites repentance in the midst of our manipulative ways and writes God's laws on our hearts. In Galatians Paul made it clear that we are not to let well-meaning people take away our Christian freedom given by the Holy Spirit. The power of the Holy Spirit is distinct from the power of the Law, which relies on social and political pressure.

In the material realm, the cross of Christ confronts us when we manipulate people as though they were rats or monkeys in an experiment. The cross of Christ shows us the emptiness of Western material attainments when those attainments stand by themselves. Jesus placed little value on material possessions in comparison with the words that proceed from the mouth of God; and Paul counted them all garbage compared with the surpassing worth of knowing Jesus.

Before we look at how Western philosophy has affected this Gospel of the cross, let's try to understand Western paradigms more fully.

The Western Worldview

Brad: What, then, are the paradigms with which Westerners build their worldview?

Charles Kraft has given the broad outlines of the Western worldview in his book *Christianity with Power*. I will never forget the first time Dr. Kraft showed me two charts comparing cultures from the Bible with cultures from the West and from the developing world. They were a burst of light into what I had suspected for many years but had never fully articulated. Following is the first of these charts:[1]

BIBLICAL CULTURES	WESTERN CULTURES	2/3 WORLD CULTURES
Spirit Sphere (God is greatest concern)	Spirit (God)	Spirit Sphere (often little concern for God)
Human Sphere	Human Sphere	Human Sphere
Material Sphere	Material Sphere	Material Sphere

This chart shows that the Western worldview diverges from the worldviews of the biblical and developing worlds in its rejection of spiritual reality. In the West, the spirit world occupies an insignificant part of the picture. The West, confident in its material successes, has become loutish and ignorant in the spiritual arena. We analyze ourselves as though human beings had more in common with rats and monkeys than with God. Many of us doubt that the spiritual world exists. Those who believe in it are not sure it bears much relevance to everyday life.

The result of our willful ignorance of the spiritual realm is just what you might expect. Beneath the glossy facade of material prosperity, we are a culture in decline. Recently William J. Bennett, U.S. Secretary of Education from 1985–88, quantified this decline by releasing the following statistics, which offer evidence of the cultural decline of the United States and, by inference, of the West:[2]

Eight Cultural Indicators

Average Daily TV Viewing		Average SAT Scores		Percentage of Illegitimate Births		Children with Single Mothers	
1960	5:06 hours	1960	975	1960	5.3%	1960	8%
1965	5:29 hours	1965	969	1970	10.7%	1970	11%
1970	5:56 hours	1970	948	1980	18.4%	1980	18%
1975	6:07 hours	1975	910	1990	26.2%	1990	22%
1980	6:36 hours	1980	890				
1985	7:07 hours	1985	906			(Source: Bureau of the Census; Donald Hernandez, The American Child: Resources from Family, Government and the Economy)	
1990	6:55 hours	1990	900				
1992	7:04 hours	1992	899				
(Source: Nielson Media Research)		(Source: The College Board)		(Source: National Center for Health Statistics)			

Children on Welfare		Teen Suicide Rate		Violent Crime Rate (per 100,000)		Median Prison Sentence*	
1960	3.5%	1960	3.6%	1960	16.1	1954	22.5 days
1965	4.5%	1965	4.0%	1965	20.0	1964	12.1 days
1970	8.5%	1970	5.9%	1970	36.4	1974	5.5 days
1975	11.8%	1975	7.6%	1975	48.8	1984	7.7 days
1980	11.5%	1980	8.5%	1980	59.7	1988	8.5 days
1985	11.2%	1985	10.0%	1985	53.3	1990	8.0 days
1990	11.9%	1990	11.3%	1990	73.2	* "Serious crime": murder, rape, robbery, aggravated assault, burglary, larceny/theft and motor vehicle theft.	
				1991	75.8		
(Source: Bureau of the Census; U.S. House of Representatives)		(Source: National Center for Health Statistics)		(Source: FBI)		(Source: National Center for Policy Analysis)	

These statistics suggest that the problems of Western nations go beyond a simple failure to structure public education or provide good professional law enforcement training or stop drug traffic at the borders. They suggest that there may be something wrong with the culture itself—something deep, basic and pervasive; that we have placed our trust too narrowly in material power.

Biblical Paradigms Show the Way

Biblical paradigms present the proper balance and understanding of how the spheres of power fit together. The book of Genesis reveals that men and women were given dominion over nature (although a biblical worldview does not justify the arrogant, all-consuming pursuit of material power that preoccupies Westerners today). The Bible also teaches that God values the material world He made—so much so that He sent His only Son to enter into it, sanctify it and purchase it.

In the Bible it is the spiritual world that provides the wellsprings for the meaning of life and the power for living. "Man does not live on bread alone," Jesus said, "but on every word that comes from the mouth of God" (Matthew 4:4).

> "So do not worry, saying, 'What shall we eat?' or 'What shall we drink?' or 'What shall we wear?' For the pagans run after all these things, and your heavenly Father knows that you need them. But seek first his kingdom and his righteousness, and all these things will be given to you as well."
>
> Matthew 6:31–33

And what could be more non-Western than the words of Paul: "We fix our eyes not on what is seen, but on what is unseen. For what is seen is temporary, but what is unseen is eternal" (2 Corinthians 4:18)?

I sensed the tension between biblical and Western paradigms whenever I moved between Eastern and Western cultures. In India or Taiwan I could believe in God and trust Him daily for guidance and provision more easily than I could in the United States. The worldview in these other cultures is "porous"; there is interchange between us and the spiritual world. In the West, by contrast, the material realm is oppressively "brassy" and nonporous.

This difference was brought sharply into focus for me right after returning from Taiwan in 1989. While we were still unpacking, our six-year-old daughter Rebecca accidentally tripped, fell and hit her head on the rocking chair. She came to me screaming, with a bleeding gash in her forehead.

Having been involved in a healing ministry in Taiwan, my first impulse there was always to pray first, looking to God to heal. I know that if this accident had happened in Taiwan, I would have sought God first (although I would not have neglected medicine), for God is above the practice of medicine. But here it did not cross my mind to rely on God or to pray.

I bundled Rebecca into the car and took her to the emergency room.

At the hospital, since there were no nurses on duty at the time, I helped the doctor sew stitches to patch up the wound. At about the fourth stitch, it suddenly dawned on me that I had not prayed or included God in my picture of how to solve the problem. Instead, I had turned instinctively to the power source of Western society—medicine.

I stopped the doctor and asked if we could pause for prayer. She shrugged as if to say, "If you want to, go ahead." Though I felt foolish, I prayed. Then we continued to sew her up.

Later I regretted the way I had behaved toward God. I realized how pervasive and powerful is the Western worldview that places trust in the material sphere and relegates God to the fringes of life.

One reason for our failure to turn to spiritual power in times of need is that the Western worldview is nonporous. The brass heaven admits no communication between the spiritual and material worlds.

The Bible can help us correct this false and asphyxiating situation. Because God wants to involve Himself in our lives, a biblical orientation is radically God-centered and God-dependent. Jesus said that He could do nothing on His own authority but only what He saw His Father doing (John 5:19). He depended on the Father for everything. But this concept is difficult for us Westerners to comprehend. It runs against our most basic orientation, which is toward personal control, personal rights and mastery over the material world.

An Absent God?

Though the Easterner is more open than the Westerner to the spiritual realm, there is an important difference between the biblical worldview and the worldview of the Eastern and developing worlds. The following chart from Dr. Charles Kraft—the second one that was so eye-opening for me—shows this difference:[3]

BIBLICAL	WESTERN	2/3 WORLD
God Sphere ------- Spirit Sphere	God Sphere ------- Undefined	God Sphere ------- Spirit Sphere

In the developing world, God occupies only a remote corner of the picture; while the biblical worldview presents us with not only a strong picture of the spiritual world, but with God as an active part of it. Biblical people experienced the holiness and power of God.

One evening during seminary, I, too, was given a glimpse of the awesome majesty of God, high and lifted up. I had just finished my doctoral exams and was out late for a walk with David, my friend and next-door neighbor. We were praying, praising God and doing silly, joyful things like jumping over the rose bushes in the median strip of the boulevard. It was about one in the morning when we came to the soccer field that separated our houses.

In the middle of the field we were offering up a prayer of thanksgiving when it happened. Without warning, we were overwhelmed by the glory of God. Instantly we both fell to the ground, prostrated by God's presence, where we lay for a long time. I was filled with visions of the glory and majesty of God. It was as if a current of stars and all created matter was rushing upward toward a vortex, and *YHWH*, in piercing, brilliant light, was at the center of it.

David experienced the same thing. That is how I know this was not just a private, subjective experience impossible to verify.

After a long time, the presence lifted and David and I were able to get up. We did not dare say a word to each other, but basked in the glory of the high God.

While the God of the Bible is indeed exalted and holy, He appears frequently among people and is intimately involved in the lives of those who place their trust in Him.

He also involves Himself in the rising and falling of nations. The interfacing between God and us happens in part through the Holy Spirit. The apostle Paul took for granted that the Holy Spirit interfaced with the human and material spheres. Recall: "I know a man in Christ who fourteen years ago was caught up to the third heaven . . ." (2 Corinthians 12:2).

The Holy Spirit changes hearts, gives spiritual gifts to the Church and works signs and wonders. The Church, said Jesus, would do the works that He did because He gave the Holy Spirit from on high (John 14:12).

Other Spiritual Beings

The Bible speaks of other spiritual entities besides God: angels, seraphim, cherubim, the devil, evil spirits, spirits of the dead. For many of the believers in Bible times, angels were real beings who had entered into their experience. Fully one-third of Jesus' recorded ministry consisted of freeing people from evil spirits. He also said that the Church would have to contend with this hierarchy of evil beings.

The developing world takes these spiritual beings very seriously (as we saw in the chart on the last page). Even Western-educated Taiwanese believe in the spirits of the dead, and worship their ancestors. Unlike the biblical worldview, however, so much attention in Taiwan is given to these ancestral spirits that the one high God is driven into the background. This is typical throughout the developing world. Although most Taiwanese are hugely aware of the spiritual realm, they see God as beyond reach.

Go to any active Buddhist temple. In the first courtyard you find images of many different gods. Often you see the Red General, the god of business. The goddess of mercy is there, too, garbed in flowing robes. Several images of Buddha occupy niches about the place. This is a center of great commotion. People are coming and going. Incense is being burned. Prayers are being offered. Many people are bowing and making offerings. Paper money is being burned for use by ancestors. Look over there in a corner. A spirit medium is in a trance, in the grip of some spirit that can check out the circumstances of the dead or help solve domestic or business problems. The first courtyard is a busy place in which I have often strongly experienced the presence of evil spirits.

If you keep walking past the ornate, dragon-inlaid rooms into the outer courtyard, you come to a part of the temple with an entirely different atmosphere. Here, all is serene. You can see at the very back, amid calm dignity, a solitary plaque that says *The Emperor of Heaven*. Nothing happens here. In fact, it feels like many a Western church I have visited! Everything is decent and in order and no one expects anything to happen. Those who enter this courtyard give careful respect to a distant God whose existence is recognized but who does nothing to help them with their broken hearts and desperate needs. This emperor is so distant, he is all but obscured by the brass plaque that bears his name.

All the attention in this Buddhist temple is directed toward other spirits who influence the daily lives of people.

Thus, while the spiritual realm occupies a large part of the worldview of the developing world, God the Creator and Ruler of all things plays a minor role. As in the Western worldview, He is out of reach.

Our Blindness to the "Excluded Middle"

Dr. Paul Hiebert of Trinity Evangelical Divinity School spent many years as a missionary in India. He discovered that Indian people, like the Taiwanese, take seriously these lesser spiritual beings. He discerned that their worldview was three-tiered:

The top tier is high religion based on cosmic personalities or forces. It is very distant. The bottom tier is everyday life: marriages, raising children, planting crops, rain and drought, sickness and health, and what have you. The middle zone includes the normal way these everyday phenomena are influenced by superhuman and supernatural forces. There is no question in their minds that every day they are influenced by spirits, demons, ancestors, goblins, ghosts, magic fetishes, witches, mediums, sorcerers, and any number of other powers.[4]

As a Christian missionary in India, Dr. Hiebert was expected to deal with spiritual beings, just as Hindu holy men did. But he, like most Western missionaries, was blind to this "middle ground" of the spirit world. He described how his submersion in Indian culture affected him:

> The reasons for my uneasiness with the Biblical and Indian world-views should now be clear. I had excluded the middle level of super-natural but this-worldly beings and forces from my own worldview. As a scientist, I had been trained to deal with the empirical world in naturalistic terms. As a theologian, I was taught to answer ultimate questions in theistic terms. For me, the middle zone did not really exist. Unlike Indian villagers, I had given little thought to spirits of this world, to local ancestors and ghosts, or to the souls of animals. For me, these belonged to the realm of fairies, trolls and other myth-ical beings. Consequently, I had no answers to the questions raised.[5]

His Western education had not equipped him to deal with spiri-tual powers—divine or demonic. He wanted to treat spiritual power as mythical or imaginary, as German theologians like Rudolph Bult-mann had advised.

Paul Hiebert's paper "The Flaw of the Excluded Middle" has become a seminal work for Western missionaries who plan to carry on Christian missions in non-Western countries. The paper implies that Western missionaries are ill-equipped to minister in the devel-oping world from the paradigms and biases of Western culture. We would be more effective if we returned to the paradigms of the Bible.

The Double Life of Western Christians

In the West, some Christians believe in the existence of demons, angels and the Holy Spirit purely because the Bible says that they exist, but in practice they exclude these realities from daily life. They have crowded out spiritual realities that biblical people took for granted.

This trend has set us free from superstition and erroneous explanations of natural phenomena. We can treat mental illness with drugs and psychotherapy instead of with futile exorcisms. But in the process we have dismissed from our minds spiritual beings that do influence our lives. When people are truly dealing with demonization, drugs and psychotherapy are ineffective. Needed today is a proper discernment of the psychological, physical and spiritual influences that trouble or bless us.

But to the Westerner, God is in His heaven, we are here on earth and there is nothing in between. This is a comfortable arrangement. We do not have to worry about spiritual powers that take us beyond the reach of the rational. We gain security from this worldview—a security that we can maintain as long as we stay in Western countries, Western hotels and Western embassies, and ignore the impact of spiritual power all around us.

Our ability to ignore spiritual power has, more than anything else, contributed to the construction of the brass heaven that covers Western culture. In one sense it is a protective shield, in another sense a casket. We have constructed an agreeable philosophy that says, "We don't need to worry about spiritual things. We can take control of our destiny simply by ruling out all spiritual power. Let's agree on it. Spiritual power does not exist—or if it does, it is irrelevant to everyday life. In either case, we don't need either the power of demons or the power of God."

Here, too, is the reason for the terrible dryness of many Western churches. We have our theologies in order. Our rituals flow smoothly. Many of us are sincerely trying to do what pleases God. The reality, presence and power of God are unheard of, and we are grateful for that. We have the form of religion, but lack the power thereof. This is just as we prefer it.

Most Western Christians, then, live a strange double life. We say that we believe in Jesus Christ, Immanuel, the God who is with us. Yet we are governed by a worldview that excludes the Christian experience that has always been central to the faith of Christians.

Before turning our attention to how the Western worldview has hindered Christian experience, let's try to understand how we got like this. In part 2 of this book, Doug and I will trace the construction of the brass heaven through the thinking of a few key leaders of the West.

Part 2

How Did We Get Like This?

6

Before the Brass Heaven: Augustine

Doug: If we Westerners are to understand where we are, we must examine how we got here. The present Western worldview is largely a twentieth-century creation, though it was birthed in the eighteenth century and reached adolescence in the nineteenth. Before recent times, however, another worldview prevailed throughout the West, a worldview full of paradigms of the power of God and perceptions of the spiritual.

No one was more influential in bricklaying the earlier worldview than the fifth-century theologian Augustine. He played a key role in the West by replacing pagan paradigms with Christian ones. As a young man he sorted through the worldview options available to him and troweled together one that would serve the West well for fourteen centuries. Martin Luther, an Augustinian monk, drew often from Augustine's writings. John Calvin quoted him more frequently than anyone but Jesus Christ. Only in the Enlightenment were Augustine's foundations abandoned.

In his *City of God*, Augustine described the growing sense in leaders like Seneca and Cicero that paganism lacked integrity. The Roman world was hungry for a new worldview to replace that of dying paganism. Plato had prepared the way for that new worldview; Jesus and His apostles had supplied the main paradigms; and now Augustine articulated them so that they turned European culture to Christ.

Let's look at the course of Augustine's early life and see why he settled on biblical paradigms. These we discover in his *Confessions*.

Search for a Worldview

Augustine began his search for a worldview where many young Westerners begin theirs today—at New Age spirituality. The New Age religion of the Roman Empire was Manichaeism, a spiritual brew into which was thrown bits of Babylonian paganism, scraps of Buddhist ethics, chunks of Zoroastrian mysticism, a broth of Greek Gnosticism and a smattering of Christian names and external analogies. The followers of Manes claimed to present ancient knowledge revealed by spirit powers to those who were initiated into its disciplines. Manichaeism held that the material world was evil, the spirit world good. But its "revelations" of the spiritual realm were very different from those of the Bible. Its source of information was what New Agers today would call "spirit guides"; in those days they were called *archons*.

Manichaeism was *occult*, offering deeper knowledge hidden from the masses and revealed only to initiates. It was *Gnostic*: Those who came into this faith were looking for a secret knowledge from which they could gain power for living. It was *ascetic*, recommending fasting and strict morality—severity to the body leading to the spiritual power of the archons. It was *neo-pagan*, an attempt to present the old paganism in a new form that would appeal to intellectuals.

This is why Augustine as a young man was attracted to it. He was an intellectual to whom Christianity, as contrasted with Manichaeism, seemed moronic. The Bible was dull, devoid of intellectual challenge—"for my swelling pride turned away from its humble style, and my sharp gaze did not penetrate into its inner meaning" (III.9). Yet as he passed through his twenties, Augustine was less and less at home with Manichaeism. The more he explored it, the more preposterous and disappointing it became. It lost its power over him.

By the time Augustine moved from Carthage to Rome, he was ready to explore other alternatives. Here he met the Academic philosophers and read their writings. The Academics, like modern scientists, were skeptics who refused to believe anything that could not be proven. Augustine himself, tiring of his own naïveté, was reluctant to believe someone just because that someone had good credentials. By age thirty, Augustine had read so many philosophical and mystical writings that he was reluctant to trust any of them. Rebounding from Manichaeism, "there half arose a thought in me, that those philosophers whom they call 'Academics' were wiser than the rest, for they held, men ought to doubt everything." Augustine began to take a cynically superior attitude toward anyone who believed anything by mere personal testimony.

Academic philosophers helped him to think skeptically. To their mentor Aristotle, the spiritual realm seemed preposterous. Yet Augustine was reluctant to reject spiritual reality entirely because of certain experiences of his youth, especially the near-death experience of his closest boyhood friend.

This friend, while unconscious on his deathbed, had been baptized by the local priest, after which the boy had miraculously recovered consciousness and regained his health. Later Augustine joked with him about the stupidity of baptizing an unconscious person. But his friend turned on him, changed by his near-death experience, healing and baptism.

"He was horrified at me," Augustine wrote later, "as if I were an enemy, and he warned me with a swift and admirable freedom that if I wished to remain his friend, I must stop saying such things to him" (IV.8).

His friend's baptism, sudden recovery and inward change impressed Augustine deeply. This and other experiences of spiritual power stuck in his memory.

The Question of Epistemology

The Academics were as different from the Manichaeans as the tortoise is from the hare. Manichaeans raced with every spiritual concept that came down the pike, while the Academics belabored every idea under the sun, trying to prove it true before carrying it on their shoulders. Augustine tried to be a tortoise—"for I wished to be made just as certain of things that I could not see, as I was certain that seven and three make ten" (VI.6). This desire would become the foundational passion of the Enlightenment.

Augustine sought for certainty (as we also must) by examining how people can know truth—the question of epistemology. Epistemology is at the heart of any body of philosophy. It asks, *How can we discern what is true from what is false?* As far as Augustine was concerned, neither the Manichaeans nor the Academics had developed an adequate epistemology. He complained that the Manichaeans made "rash promises of sure knowledge" on the one hand and then commanded "that so many most fabulous and absurd things be accepted on trust because they could not be demonstrated" (VI.7).

The Academics, on the other hand, refused to accept the word of credible witnesses. Skepticism seemed an impossible creed to live by. Augustine came to believe that we cannot do without credible witnesses. In his *Confessions* he provides a dozen examples of the futility of trying to live without credible witnesses. For instance: "I thought of how I held with fixed and unassailable faith that I was born of certain parents, and this I could never know unless I believed it by hearing about them" (VI.7). In the normal affairs of life, it is necessary to accept a hundred times a day the word of credible witnesses. Epistemology cannot outlaw this brute fact—which, of course, bears upon the Bible, which is claimed to be divine revelation given to us by credible witnesses.

The Scriptures had power, as Augustine soon found out, to reveal the spiritual realm to him and to base our lives on a bedrock of truth: "Not those who believe in your books . . . but those who do not believe in them are the ones to be blamed" for our lack of certain knowledge in life. The Bible shows us the proper relationship between the spirit realm and the material, for at its heart is the testimony of the One from above.

So, though Manichaeism had seemed absurd, not a credible witness, Augustine was not ready to give up all spiritual reality as mythical, nor to disbelieve everyone who testified to it. The Bible became more and more credible to him—not because it appealed to reason, but because it revealed what reason could not attain.

> Since we were too weak to find the truth by pure reason, and for that cause we needed the authority of Holy Writ, I now began to believe that in no wise would you have given such surpassing authority throughout the whole world to that Scripture, unless you wished that both through it you be believed in, and through it you be sought.
>
> VI.8[1]

If we are forced to accept the testimony of credible witnesses, the Bible presented itself as more credible to Augustine than Manichaeism because of its "holy lowliness." The Bible was unpretentious, full of humility, written by simple people and not by those trying to gain a reputation for themselves. It was also permeated with the integrity of holy character—the character of God. Its prophecies, moreover, had come true; history vouched for it.

But these reasons do not entirely explain Augustine's decision to place his whole confidence in the Bible, rather than in science or in Gnosticism, to convey true and accurate paradigms. *He was looking for power that made a difference in life.* It was his experience of the power of God's Word that decided his epistemology. He called the Manichaean message, in contrast to that power, "senseless and seducing continency," a "shadowy and counterfeit virtue." Manichaeism had not changed his life, though he had given it a dozen years to do so.

The Problem of Savagery

Augustine was deeply troubled by the savagery of human nature and of Roman culture. In the book *I, Claudius,* the emperor Claudius the details this savagery at the highest levels of Roman government. There seemed to be no way out of this steady retreat from civility into barbarism, either in Manichaeism or in Academic skepticism. But Augustine saw hope for power in Jesus Christ and in the Bible.

While in Rome, for example, he was enjoying the friendship of Alypius, one of his students. Alypius was invited by several friends to attend the Amphitheater, where gladiatorial combat was the main attraction. He was shocked at the idea of patronizing such a gross, low-minded display, but he consented to go anyway.

> When they had entered and taken whatever places they could, the whole scene was ablaze with savage passions. He closed his eyes and forbade his mind to have any part in such evil sights. Would that he had been able to close his ears as well! For when one man fell in the combat, a mighty roar went up from the entire crowd and struck him with such force that he was overcome by curiosity. . . . He opened his eyes and was wounded more deeply in his soul than the man whom he desired to look at was in his body. . . .
>
>   As he saw that blood, he drank in savageness at the same time. He did not turn away, but fixed his sight on it, and drank in madness without knowing it. He took delight in that evil struggle, and he became drunk on blood and pleasure.
>
> VI.13[2]

Augustine was appalled to see this student become addicted to the Amphitheater. Alypius became consumed with barbarity, violence, blood and gore. Neither the philosophy of the Academics nor the myths of the Manichaeans could save him. But "from all that you [God] rescued him with a hand that was most strong and yet most merciful, and you taught him to put his trust not in himself but in you. But that was long afterwards" (VI.13).

The power of God in Christ decided the matter for Augustine— power to redeem us from savagery. The power of Christ was, for Augustine, the one and only power that could transform people and write God's laws on their hearts.

But it was some time before Augustine tasted that power for himself. While in Rome he discovered the writings of Platonic philosophers.

The Schoolmaster of Platonism

Plato had discerned the nature of God—the supreme reason, the efficient cause of all things, eternal, unchangeable, all-knowing, all-powerful, just, holy, wise and good. Clement of Alexandria said of

Platonic philosophy that "it was to the Greeks what the law was to the Jews—a schoolmaster to bring them to Christ."

Plato's ideas, when compared with other ideas coming out of pagan Greco-Roman culture, are remarkable. They prepared the Greek world for the Gospel. Platonic thought was a fertile garden in which Christianity took seed and flowered, as Augustine intimated:

> You procured for me certain books of the Platonists. . . . In them I read, not indeed in these words, but much the same thought . . . that "In the beginning was the Word, and the Word was with God, and the Word was God. . . ."
>
> VII.13

As Augustine began to apprehend God through the writings of Plato, his worldview began to admit biblical paradigms. Yet he soon realized that Platonic philosophy was incomplete. By itself, though it had some truth, it had no power.

> It is one thing to behold from a wooded mountain peak the land of peace, but to find no way to it, and to strive in vain towards it by unpassable ways, ambushed and beset by fugitives and deserters, under their leader, the lion and the dragon. It is a different thing to keep to the way that leads to that land, guarded by the protection of the heavenly commander, where no deserters from the heavenly army lie in wait like bandits.
>
> VII.27[3]

Platonic philosophy without Christ at its center worked no better than scientific skepticism or New Age religion. It did not rescue people from savagery. It led to analysis paralysis. It produced no change. It provided only the background for something God had accomplished in Christ, yet it did not tell what God had done.

Augustine was led to see first the spiritual realm as Plato described it, then Christ, "the heavenly General," at its center—at which point Augustine had attained the age of 33.

The Power of Lust

What finally drove Augustine to give his life to Christ was his besetting sin of lust—the consuming passion of the West to this day. He had struggled with lust for many years: "But I, a most wretched youth . . . had even sought chastity from you, and had said, 'Give me chastity and continence, but not yet'" (VIII.17). It galled him that, despite all his learning, he had no power to overcome the lust of his heart for women, which kept him perpetually ashamed. He saw in himself an inner conflict, conscience leading him in one direction, lust another. In torment he felt as though he had not one mind but two—one civil, the other barbarous.

One day there came from Africa a friend, Pontitianus, who reported quite simply that he had turned to Christ and Christ had freed him from lust. Augustine complained bitterly of this: "The unlearned start up and 'take' heaven by force, and we with our learning, and without heart, lo . . . we wallow in flesh and blood!" (VIII.19).

Power Over Savagery and Lust

God was forcing Augustine to confront the real issue: Where are we to find power for living, power to overcome savagery, violence and lust? Not in the material world and its skeptical sciences. Not in the mysticism of the Gnostic cults, nor yet in the Greek philosophers. Pontitianus was presenting Augustine with a fourth option: Power over savagery comes from Jesus Christ.

As Augustine complained of his inability to live a clean life— "How long? Tomorrow and tomorrow? Why not now? Why not is there this hour an end to my uncleanness?"—he heard the voice of a child singing in the street: "Take up and read; take up and read."

> Instantly, with altered countenance, I began to think most intently whether children made use of any such chant in some kind of game, but I could not recall hearing it anywhere. I checked the flow of my tears and got up, for I interpreted this solely as a command given to me by God to open the book and read the first chapter I should come upon. . . .
>
> So I hurried back to the spot where Alypius was sitting, for I had put there the volume of the apostle when I got up and left him. I

snatched it up, opened it, and read in silence the chapter on which my eyes first fell: "Not in rioting and drunkenness, not in chambering and impurities, not in strife and envying; but put you on the Lord Jesus Christ, and make not provision for the flesh in its concupiscences." No further wished I to read; nor was there need to do so. Instantly, in truth, at the end of this sentence, as if before a peaceful light streaming into my heart, all the dark shadows of doubt fled away.

VIII.29[4]

Augustine finally related the fact that confirmed his worldview and set it in place for countless Westerners: "Now was my mind free from the gnawing cares of favor-seeking, of striving for gain, of wallowing in the mire, and of scratching lust's itchy sore. I spoke like a child to you, my light, my wealth, my salvation, my Lord God" (IX.1).

Augustine had discovered that there is a power to free human beings from savagery and lust: the power of Christ as described in the Bible. Augustine was to rebuild his worldview around that power.

Central to his worldview, too, would be the awareness that his own conversion was the result of his mother's faithful prayers. She died a few months later. It was as though God had kept her for that one ultimate purpose—to pray for her son until he had tasted God's power to redeem him.

Three Foundational Principles

Augustine established a number of foundational principles that guided Western culture for more than a thousand years:

1. *Knowledge is power.*
2. *There are three possible sources of knowledge:*
   a. The rational knowledge attained by skepticism (later, the foundation for modern science).
   b. The occult, Gnostic knowledge of neo-pagan religion (the foundation of today's New Age beliefs).
   c. The Word of God, openly proclaimed in Jesus and the Bible.
3. *The power most likely to tame our self-destructive, savage nature comes from the third source.*

If the central issue in our search for a worldview is the question of where we find power for living, then Augustine's discoveries are still relevant today, when lust for sex and violence seems insatiable and leads to the acting out of our savage nature.

But the foundations built by this spiritual and intellectual giant were undercut by others who believed they had a better worldview and a more fascinating power to offer humankind.

7

The Brass Heaven:
Descartes and His Builders

Doug: It was René Descartes who first proposed that we all return to the skeptical philosophy of the Academic philosophers, whom Augustine had rejected early in life. So we give to this seventeenth-century French mathematician and philosopher the title "Father of the Enlightenment." His contribution to Western culture is like the recent Biosphere experiment in which a colony of eight people in Arizona moved into a gigantic glass house and purported to seal it off from the rest of the world to see if they could survive as a self-contained unit.

Descartes proposed that Westerners build such a philosophical house. He wanted to escape a gnat that troubled him—"that it is much easier to have some vague notion about any subject, no matter what, than to arrive at the real truth about a single question, however simple that may be."

> Since scarce anything has been asserted by any one man the contrary of which has not been alleged by another, we should be eternally uncertain which of the two to believe. It would be no use to total up the testimonies in favor of each, meaning to follow that opinion which was supported by the greater number of authors.[1]

Since truth cannot be arrived at democratically, Descartes set out to establish a new way to dig down to bedrock, to lay foundations for a new worldview. Unlike earlier philosophers, he quoted neither philosophy nor Scripture. He wanted to use but two digging tools, experience and deduction, and thus seal off his mind from the rest of the world.

> By a method I mean certain and simple rules, such that if a man observe them accurately he shall never assume what is false as true, and will never spend his mental efforts to no purpose, but will always gradually increase his knowledge and so arrive at a true understanding of all that does not surpass his powers.[2]

So Descartes rejected "the reliable witness" as a valid source of truth. Remember that Augustine had found skepticism untenable as a way of life. Descartes, a Catholic, relied on human authority and Scripture in his personal life, although he saw this dependence as a temporary nuisance:

> As it is not sufficient, before commencing to rebuild the house which we inhabit, to pull it down and provide materials and an architect . . . unless we have also provided ourselves with some other house where we can be comfortably lodged during the time of rebuilding, so . . . I formed for myself a code of morals for the time being which did not consist of more than three or four maxims. . . .
> The first was to obey the laws and customs of my country, adhering constantly to the religion in which by God's grace I had been instructed since my childhood.[3]

The philosopher could not have known that the new home he was building would invite the West eventually to abandon the comfortable lodging that had housed him (and them) "by God's grace." Quite the contrary! His reason for building his new philosophy was to present rational proofs of God to unbelievers:

> I have always considered that the two questions respecting God and the Soul were the chief of those that ought to be demonstrated by philosophical rather than theological argument. For although it is quite enough for us faithful ones to accept by means of faith the fact that the human soul does not perish with the body, and that God exists, it certainly does not seem possible ever to persuade infidels of any reli-

gion, indeed, we may almost say, of any moral virtue, unless, to begin with, we prove these two facts by means of the natural reason.

. . . Few people would prefer the right to the useful, were they restrained neither by the fear of God nor the expectation of another life; and although it is absolutely true that we must believe that there is a God, because we are taught in the Holy Scriptures, and, on the other hand, that we must believe the Holy Scriptures because they come from God . . . we nevertheless could not place this argument before infidels, who might accuse us of reasoning in a circle.[4]

Descartes had an evangelist's heart linked to a philosopher's mind. These foundational ideas—the existence of God and the soul—were the first two glass panels, sterile and pristine, he installed in his new house.

But this new house of Descartes was not a comfortable Cape Cod where Jesus stands at the door and knocks, and we open the door and invite Him in, to love and to be loved. It was a glass house with no door or even airlock to God. It allowed people to view God from a safe distance—to see Him as through a pane of plexiglass. But to sense Him? Speak to Him? Hear Him? Commune with Him? Delight in Him? Never.

The Risk of the Cartesian Method

This grand experiment was a chancy one. The apostle Paul had already expressed doubts about any such approach:

My message and my preaching were not with wise and persuasive words, but with a demonstration of the Spirit's power, so that your faith might not rest on men's wisdom, but on God's power.
1 Corinthians 2:4–5

Jesus Himself had attributed a very different method to God: "You have hidden these things from the wise and learned, and revealed them to little children" (Luke 10:21).

Nevertheless, Descartes put forth many proofs of God and the soul, such as this one:

. . . How would it be possible that I should know that I doubt and desire, that is to say, that something is lacking in me, and that I am not quite perfect, unless I had within me some idea of a Being more perfect than myself, in comparison with which I should recognize the deficiencies of my nature?[5]

Out of a new epistemology came a new power. Remember that Augustine, by accepting reliable witnesses about the power of God, had learned to trust God's power to tame human savagery. Descartes refused to accept such testimony, insisting on rational deduction as the only shovel that can dig down to the bedrock of truth.

This premise contained its own conclusions: that the power of God, whenever it cannot be rationally understood, is an illusion. A mind that rejects everything it cannot understand rules out the power of God before it begins to think. The rational mind soon becomes the trusted source of power for living, replacing the power of God. Brass heaven builders believe that the rational mind saves us from our problems, that Jesus Christ is irrelevant to most human endeavors.

Descartes himself lived as a Christian and built his glass house for the "infidels." But the infidels observed his method of building and admired its possibilities. They could scarcely wait to take over his project. They were even willing to let him keep his first two glass panels in place (God and the soul) for a time as a memorial to his inventiveness and honesty. But they were after the liberated power of the mind, which they wanted to turn to the advantage of humanity—and to their own advantage, too. For whoever excelled at Descartes' method could use his or her powers to any desired end.

The risk of this Cartesian experiment was that those "infidels" who are "restrained neither by the fear of God nor the expectation of another life" might prefer "what is useful to what is right," as Descartes himself had prophesied.

Because Descartes lived in a Christian house with an Augustinian foundation, he perceived right from wrong and God's revelations from human error. But the new house he built would lead future generations to abandon the Augustinian worldview as a foundation and build an altogether new one.

Pascal, his contemporary, foresaw this eventuality when he wrote in his *Pensees*,

I cannot forgive Descartes. In all his philosophy he would have been quite willing to dispense with God. But he could not help granting him a flick of the forefinger to start the world in motion; beyond this, he has no further need of God.[6]

Pascal's foreboding would be confirmed in a remarkably short time with the anarchy and futility of the French Revolution.

Reaction Sets In

Because Descartes' alternative was a radical departure from the most basic assumptions about how we gain knowledge, it was opposed from almost every corner of Europe. It was opposed first by the Italian scientist Galileo, then by the Calvinist Voetius, then by the Jesuit Father Bourdin.

It may surprise you that Galileo was one of Descartes' chief opponents. We have the impression today that Galileo was an objective scientific observer, while the Catholics and Calvinists were closed-minded dogmatists. But this "objectivity" is a myth. Our worldview influences the most "scientific" objectivity, for our science, and not only our theology, rests on our worldview. All of us feel threatened when our worldview is challenged.

Galileo was no exception. Descartes was a philosophical revolutionary. Most people ran away from his ideas—at first. And because of Galileo's opposition, Descartes very nearly decided to publish nothing of his writings.

But after the initial shock waves had passed, a host of scientists, beginning with men like Isaac Newton, descended on Descartes' building site and offered to add a new panel here, a new wing there. On top of the epistemology of Descartes they built a completely new Western worldview. They developed the experimental methods and mathematical descriptions to validate the vision of a world as a vast machine of matter and motion, obeying clearly defined natural laws discernible to experience and to rational deduction.

The questions we must ask as we trace Descartes' ideas to their logical conclusion are these: Did his critics not see farther than he, and were they not justified in their apprehension?

The heart of the transition from Augustine's worldview to a modern Western worldview had to do (as we have seen) with epistemology—the theory of how we know. In the Middle Ages, Western leaders followed Augustine in accepting what was handed down to them by those of proven authority. Doctrines were accepted and believed because the Bible, the Pope, Thomas Aquinas, Plato or Aristotle said they were true.

Also, the older leaders of Western culture believed that knowledge was to be gained by participating in the thing to be known. To them, knowledge was not only rational but relational. God was to be known by a relationship characterized by faith and obedience, as the Reformer John Calvin wrote:

> . . . You cannot behold Him clearly unless you acknowledge Him to be the fountainhead and source of every good. From this, too, would arise the desire to cleave to Him and trust in Him, but for the fact that man's depravity seduces his mind from rightly seeking Him.[7]

In this view there is no abstract knowledge of God. We find out about God, according to the Reformers, from revelation, which is relational. Then we cleave to God and trust Him in ways He shows by His Word.

Studying the New Architecture

The Cartesian model of reality was valid in part. It ignited the scientific and technological revolution that has changed the world and brought us material prosperity. But let's stop for a moment and evaluate this revolution. The new architecture had three major flaws.

First, when the rationalistic approach to knowledge was adopted that proved so fertile in some fields, knowledge gained by credible witnesses became suspect.

But Augustine's point still holds. Even scientific knowledge must be spread about by the testimony of credible scientists who have done Cartesian experiments. None of us has the time to conduct scientific experiments on every subject for ourselves, nor even to examine scientific journals to see whether others have done their experiments properly. We cannot live without credible witnesses.

Second, the emphasis on rationality distorted the nature of scientific discovery. Most major scientific discoveries are not birthed in rational thought but in intuition and visionary experience. They arise not from conscious logical processes but out of revelations from the subconscious. Rational deductions come later as an attempt to prove the point. This was true of Descartes himself, who received his inspiration in three dreams and believed them to be revelations of the "Spirit of Truth." He wrote, "On November 10, 1619, when I was filled with enthusiasm, I discovered the foundations of the wonderful science."[8]

Arthur Koestler in his book *Act of Creation* sees this principle everywhere—that science does not develop along purely rational lines. Time after time he shows that the most significant scientific advances did not come through Descartes' methods. For example:

> Let us leave the borderlands of pathology. Nobody could have been further removed from it than the mild, sober, and saintly Einstein. Yet, we find in him the same distrust of concious conceptual thought, and the same reliance on visual imagery.[9]

Today philosophers like Karl Popper, Thomas Kuhn and Paul Feyerabend have roundly questioned the concepts of logical positivism that were so thoroughly accepted until the 1970s. The Cartesian experiment is shown to be a design poorly suited as a home for scientists.

Third, Descartes' epistemology resulted in the mechanization of the universe. The result: a world devoid of the wonderful. The wonder and mystery of the spiritual realm were seen as pollutants in the pure air of rationality.

We believe, on the other hand, that all people have a spiritual hunger. This, at least, is the testimony of the Bible and of Augustine. The result of an epistemology that constricts our knowledge to rational processes is to give us a two-dimensional universe devoid of life and freshness. As G. K. Chesterton observed:

> So these expanders of the universe had nothing to show us except more and more infinite corridors of space lit by ghastly suns and empty of what is divine. . . . The idea of the mystical condition quite

disappeared; one can neither have the firmness of keeping laws nor the fun of breaking them. The largeness of this universe had nothing of that freshness and airy outbreak which we have praised in the universe of the poet. This modern universe is literally an empire; that is, it is vast, but it is not free. One went into larger and larger windowless rooms, rooms big with Babylonian perspective; but one never found the smallest window or a whisper of outer air.[10]

Since human beings are spirit and not only mind, the geodesic house turns out to be unsuited not only for scientists but for everyone.

Brassing Over the Glass: Sigmund Freud

Tracing the history of the Western worldview in the writings of a few of its most significant thinkers, we pass over Charles Darwin for the moment (we will return to him in the next chapter) and jump to Sigmund Freud, the father of psychoanalysis. Freud represents a generation of intellectuals that clearly expounded the new worldview and encouraged people to place complete confidence in it.

Freud, following Descartes, seized the power of mind over matter as the great hope of the human race:

> We believe that it is possible for scientific work to discover something about the reality of the world through which we can increase our power and according to which we can regulate our life. . . . Science has many open, and still more secret, enemies among those who cannot forgive it for having weakened religious belief and for threatening to overthrow it. . . . [11]

Freud kicked out Descartes' low-level windows—God and the soul. Then he brassed over the glass of Descartes so that what was transparent became opaque. Freud had no interest in viewing God even from a distance. All he wanted was Descartes' powerful methods; that was all. Freud believed that God and the soul were illusions—which he defined as anything that cannot be proven by scientific method: "These which profess to be religious dogmas are not the residue of experience, or the final result of reflection. They are illusions, fulfillments of the oldest, strongest, and most insistent wishes of mankind."[12]

Because Freud had never experienced the power of God in his own life, he assumed that all Christian teachings "are not the residue of experience." That he should have entertained this notion at all shows the peculiar blindness produced by a worldview, particularly since his contemporary, William James of Harvard University, had just assembled the most convincing demonstration of Christian "residues of experience" ever assembled between the covers of a book.

In *The Varieties of Religious Experience* James wrote of the power of God:

> To suggest personal will and effort to one all sicklied o'er with the sense of irremediable impotence is to suggest the most impossible of things. What he craves is to be consoled in his very powerlessness, to feel that the spirit of the universe recognizes and secures him, all decaying and failing as he is. Well, we are all such helpless failures in the last resort. The sanest and best of us are of one clay with lunatics and prison inmates, and death finally runs the robustest of us down. And whenever we feel this, such a sense of the vanity and provisionality of our voluntary career comes over us that all our morality appears but as a plaster hiding a sore it can never cure, and all our well-doing as the hollowest substitute for that well-being that our lives ought to be grounded in, but, alas! are not.
>
> And here religion comes to our rescue and takes our fate into her hands. There is a state of mind, known to religious men, but to no others, in which the will to assert ourselves and hold our own has been displaced by a willingness to close our mouths and be as nothing in the floods and waterspouts of God. In this state of mind, what we most dreaded has become the habitation of our safety, and the hour of our moral death has turned into our spiritual birthday. The time for tension in our soul is over, and that of happy relaxation, of calm deep breathing, of an eternal present, with no discordant future to be anxious about, has arrived. Fear is not held in abeyance as it is by mere morality, it is positively expunged and washed away.
>
> . . . Religious feeling is thus an absolute addition to the Subject's range of life. It gives him a new sphere of power. When the outward battle is lost, and the outer world disowns him, it redeems and vivifies an interior world which otherwise would be an empty waste.[13]

Such power lay outside the scope of Sigmund Freud's life, of course. And because he had ruled out credible witnesses from his epistemology, there was no way he could access that power. Unwilling to examine his own assumptions about life, Freud contented himself to challenge the assumptions of Christians:

> The scientific spirit engenders a particular attitude to the problems of this world; before the problems of religion it halts for a while, then wavers, and finally here too steps over the threshold. In this process, there is no stopping. The more the fruits of knowledge become accessible to men, the more widespread is the decline of religious belief, at first only of the obsolete and objectionable expressions of the same, then of its fundamental assumptions also.[14]

Whereas Augustine had found in the rational mind no power over human savagery, Freud believed that the rational mind alone could overcome it: "Now we have no other means of controlling our instincts than our intelligence," he wrote.[15] Because the psychiatric profession prefers Freud to William James (even if Freud enjoys less favor currently), the profession has been crippled by Freud's positivistic epistemology. Categorically excluded from this field, from the early years of this century, have been the realm of the spirit, the voice of conscience and the role of faith.

William James saw the tragedy as it was happening in 1902 and tried to give fair warning:

> I state the matter thus bluntly, because the current of thought in academic circles runs against me, and I feel like a man who must set his back against an open door quickly if he does not wish to see it closed and locked. In spite of it's being so shocking to the reigning intellectual tastes, I believe that a candid consideration of piecemeal supernaturalism and a complete discussion of all its metaphysical bearings will show it to be the hypothesis by which the largest number of legitimate requirements are met.[16]

There were voices besides James' in those years to defend the biblical paradigms bequeathed by Augustine. So if the West built for itself a brass heaven, it did so by choice and not by necessity.

A Second Wing of the New House: Marx and Engels

What Freud did in the realm of human nature, Karl Marx and Friedrich Engels did in the realm of politics. Seizing the ability to know right from wrong as the prerogative of their own minds, and rejecting the authority of God, the Church, the Bible or any other previous philosophers, they laid the philosophical basis for Communism. Like Freud, they blocked out the spiritual realm and prophesied the demise of religion. In *The Communist Manifesto* they continued Freud's work of brassing over the glass panels of Descartes:

> When the ancient world was in its last throes, the ancient religions were overcome by Christianity. When Christian ideas succumbed in the 18th century to rationalist ideas, feudal society fought its death-battle with the then revolutionary bourgeoisie. The ideas of religious liberty and freedom of conscience merely gave expression to the sway of free competition within the domain of knowledge.
>
> "Undoubtedly," it will be said, "religious, moral, philosophical, and juridical ideas have been modified in the course of historical development." But religion, morality, philosophy, political science, and law constantly survived this change.
>
> There are, besides, eternal truths, such as Freedom, Justice, etc., that are common to all states of society. But Communism abolishes eternal truths, it abolishes all religion, and all morality, instead of constituting them on a new basis; it therefore acts in contradiction to all past historical experience.[17]

Marx and Engels used Descartes' freedom from authority to build a political system based on no authority except their own faith in "the state," a construct of the rational mind.

Sigmund Freud was well aware of the affinity of his own work with that of Marx and Engels. They were building two wings of the same house. In *The Future of an Illusion*, Freud imagined a traditionalist's "futile" arguments against an absolute faith in science (arguments that today sound remarkably cogent). Mouthing the traditionalist's objections, Freud wrote:

> Besides, have you learnt nothing from history? Once before such an attempt to substitute reason for religion was made, officially and in

the grand manner. Surely you remember the French Revolution and Robespierre, and also how short-lived and how deplorably ineffectual the experiment? It is being repeated in Russia at present, and we need not be curious about the result. Do you not think we may assume that man cannot do without religion?[18]

Freud answered in his own voice that the French Revolution had been an idea brought forth before its time. He was sure, now that more of the glass and brass house had been built by Westerners, that Communism would succeed.

Communism has proven, of course, to be one of the most colossal failures of all time. Communist ideas, rooted in the modern Western worldview, have enticed the West for 75 years and cost her some of her most wrenching agonies. The truths of Christ, on the other hand, and the Christian worldview provided by Augustine (which Freud, Marx and Engels claimed to abolish) live on and provide a source of new life in the very carcass of Communism.

On a more personal plane, and back in our own time, Charles Colson described the unsuitability of the brass and glass house as a place to live, by tracing the lives of its builders:

> Freud could not be comforted after his daughter's death, as if he was grieving at the finality of life without God. In his last days Marx was consumed with hatred. . . . These men were simply reaping the logical consequences of their own philosophies.[19]

The Western Church: Rudolf Bultmann

The Cartesian worldview has not only shaped the development of psychology and politics; it has also imposed its paradigms on the Church. Most Western churches have adapted their worldviews to its proclamations. A great sifting has occurred as theologians have tried to adapt the Christian Gospel to a brass heaven generation.

Rudolf Bultmann, theologian and professor of Marburg, Germany, best represents these twentieth-century sifters. Believing that the human race had now developed a secure way to separate truth from illusion, he (like many others) turned to evaluate the Scriptures under brass light fixtures. He stated his philosophical pre-suppositions in his book *Jesus Christ and Mythology:*

> The worldview of the Scripture is mythological and is therefore unacceptable to modern man whose thinking has been shaped by science and is therefore no longer mythological. Modern man always makes use of technical means which are the result of science. In case of illness, modern man has recourse to physicians, to medical science. In case of economic and political affairs, he makes use of the results of psychological, social, economic and political sciences, and so on. Nobody reckons with direct intervention by transcendent powers.
>
> Of course, there are today some survivals and revivals of primitive thinking and superstition. But the preaching of the Church would make a disastrous error if it looked to such revivals and conformed to them.
>
> . . . It makes no difference in principle whether the earth rotates round the sun or the sun rotates round the earth, but it does make a decisive difference that modern man understands the motion of the universe as a motion which obeys a cosmic law, a law of nature which human reason can discover. Therefore, modern man acknowledges as reality only such phenomena or events as are comprehensible within the framework of the rational order of the universe. He does not acknowledge miracles because they do not fit into this lawful order. When a strange or marvelous accident occurs, he does not rest until he has found a rational cause.[20]

Bultmann believed that science had so thoroughly established itself as the arbiter of truth that it was futile to resist its proclamations. To him, the Cartesian foundation was the one that gave hope to the human race, and the only foundation worth building on. The Church, he insisted, might as well start learning how to cut glass and work with brass plating. Bultmann rejected biblical power paradigms, calling them "primitive." Every verse that described spiritual power impinging on human lives had to be "demythologized"—treated as illusion, a throwback to primitive thinking.

That Bultmann was not alone in his conscious rejection of biblical paradigms we will see in chapter 13 on biblical hermeneutics, the science and methodology of interpreting the Bible.

Darwinism:
The Geodesic Framework

Doug: No one better reflects the edge on which Western culture was teetering during the 1930s than my great uncle, Elmer Ellsworth Brown. Dr. Brown organized the Department of Education at the University of California, was Commissioner of Education for the United States and chancellor of New York University. To celebrate New York University's one hundredth anniversary in 1932, Dr. Brown drew eleven hundred scholars from universities around the world to a conference on "The Obligation of Universities to the Social Order." This conference, perhaps the most extraordinary gathering of intellectuals in this century, was held at the Waldorf-Astoria Hotel November 15–17.

The conference culminated in a series of addresses on the subject "The University and Spiritual Values." In one of them, Alfred Noyes, English philosopher and poet, clearly portrayed the crisis of the West in the twentieth century. I quote him at some length here because his observations are so apt.

> During the last fifty years a change has been coming over the civilized world, a change not unlike those that heralded the downfall and destruction of former civilizations: a change that is due to one cause, and one cause only: the loss of any central and unifying belief. Not only have dogmas, creeds and traditions been impatiently thrown aside by a crowd of mediocre thinkers, . . . we have lost the spirit

that once vitalized, informed, and developed those dogmas, creeds, and traditions. We have lost it in arts and letters; and we have developed nothing of a higher order to take its place.

We are saved from chaos today, so far as we are saved, merely by what we may call the rules of the traffic, the rules of the road, by conventions that depend for their validity on the very beliefs that we have abandoned. All the pseudo-intelligentsia of modern literature are engaged in the sublime task of pointing out that even these conventions are worthless and valueless, and a vague belief has insidiously been spread by all the machines of publicity throughout the world that the pseudo-intellectuals are right. Wherever there is a straight issue between moral good and moral evil, the popular press nearly always describes the latter as "more advanced."

When those conventions, upon which our civilization depends, are put to the test . . . they are bound to collapse, for there is no reality at the present time behind them. They are like a paper currency with nothing, not even credit, in reserve. . . . No thoughtful and sincere mind looking over Europe today can fail to realize that we are separated from complete chaos by a far thinner barrier than we believed; that the whole fabric of our civilization is being tested by attacks from without and from within and from a thousand directions; and that neither Europe nor America is so secure as we once imagined from the fate of older civilizations.

Mr. Noyes was virtually prophesying the rise of Nazism six years later. He went on:

The chief characteristic of the intellectual world during the last fifty years is its gradual loss of the old simplicity and integrity which went so deep, went right down to the roots of life with men like Milton and Wordsworth in literature, or Abraham Lincoln in statesmanship. This deep integrity of spirit has been replaced everywhere by a shallow cynicism, a spirit of mockery, sometimes clever mockery, but nonetheless a shining surface with nothing behind it.

. . . In the far simpler conditions of our forefathers, the things that belonged to our peace were often found because they had the vision, though distant, of that . . . divine pattern of which our earthly best is but a poor symbol and shadow. Our forefathers believed that the soul of man was created for that vision and its ultimate realization. In its possession, though it were only a faint gleam caught from a great way off, there was happiness, because it gave a meaning and purpose to life. Bereft of it, as the greater part of art and literature testifies today, the human spirit is in torment.

The position is complicated by the fact that this inner loss is very largely due to some of the great achievements of the race.

Here Mr. Noyes mentioned the two revolutionary theories of the scientific world, the theories of Copernicus and Darwin. He continued:

But it is not the scientists or the philosophers who are responsible for the troubles from which we are suffering today; it is the pseudo-intellectuals who have followed on their trail. . . . Small, clever minds have been exalted into leaders of sects and schools of thought, chiefly on account of their quickness in seizing isolated fragments of truth—fragments that are not even true until they fall into place as parts of an organic whole. In isolation these fragments may appear to be new and sensational, and are therefore seized upon by all the machines of publicity. . . .

The result is that there was never a time so chaotic in all its judgments of art and literature, so unable to discriminate between the good and bad, and so bewildered about all the essentials that belong to our peace.

. . . Not one of the essentials that belong to our peace has been left to us in its integrity—the religious life has gone, for the majority, and the family, with the affections, is following. In literature the passions are often brutally depicted. . . . The young, though their reticence does not always betray the fact, have been robbed of their birthright in Christendom by the jaded cynicism of elderly men of letters, who have been untrue to their intellectual responsibilities. The young . . . go down from the university carrying away in their minds nothing that can compensate them for what they have lost, and in the silence and emptiness of their hearts they must often hear a distant echo of that bitterest of all human cries, "They have taken away the Lord . . . and we know not where they have laid Him."[1]

As I reread these words, I realize that Alfred Noyes could have written them this morning. Nothing has changed in the last sixty years. If anything, we are farther down the road he described than when he spoke.

Relating to Evolutionary Paradigms

It was Darwinian theory, as Alfred Noyes said, that provided the framework for the new worldview that has "taken away the Lord." Darwin provided the framework of the brass heaven, just as Descartes provided the foundation. Like Descartes, Darwin was a man of Christian faith who was convinced that God had shaped the creation. We do not have space here to trace his personal journey of faith as he developed his theory of origins. Others have done so; we recommend Michael Denton's book *Evolution: A Theory in Crisis*.

Darwinism became the geodesic frame on which many other Western paradigms were riveted. But Darwin himself, a careful scientist who followed the truth wherever it led, rejected the evolutionary conclusions that the "pseudo-intellectuals" (as Noyes called them) had forced on Western thought. "The mind revolts at the idea," wrote Darwin, "that the species have appeared as the result of blind chance."

Evolutionary teaching—the belief that the world appeared and developed by chance working through natural law—grows out of a broader paradigm: that nothing happens in this world except by natural law. Biblical paradigms reject that concept. They tell us that, quite apart from natural law, the spiritual world impinges on the material world in the creation; in the covenant with Abraham; in the incarnation, resurrection, ascension and promised Second Coming of Jesus; and in the "powers of the age to come" in the Holy Spirit. Christianity is thus incompatible with the worldview of the brass heaven, which is built exclusively on natural law.

Yet many Christians have tried to develop a worldview that combines Christian paradigms with brass heaven thinking. As we have incorporated evolutionary paradigms, the basic faith that "God created the heavens and the earth" has been eroding away, causing much of the cynicism and skepticism toward the power of God that Mr. Noyes described more than sixty years ago. Western Christians have felt that science required them to accept evolutionary paradigms, that anyone who does not do so is either a fundamentalist or a fool. They have believed that evolution is based on fact, whereas the creation paradigm is based on mere Bible stories.

Brad and I challenge this assumption. Today universities are examining more deeply the philosophy of science. As this field of study has grown, scientists have had to admit that science itself grows out of a worldview and is dependent on it.

Parallel to this development is the growing realization that evolutionary theory is not necessarily based on fact. It is a philosophical paradigm, a geodesic framework, by which some scientists organize data.

This idea was expressed by Canadian biologist W. R. Thompson in his introduction to the centennial edition of Darwin's *Origin of Species* in 1959:

> Darwin did not show in the *Origin* that species had originated by natural selection; he merely showed on the basis of certain facts and assumptions how this might have happened, and as he had convinced himself, he was able to convince others. But the facts and interpretations on which Darwin relied have now ceased to convince. Long-continued investigations on heredity and variation have undermined the Darwinian position. . . . Darwin himself considered that the idea of evolution is unsatisfactory unless its mechanism can be explained. I agree. And since no one has explained to my satisfaction how evolution could happen, I do not feel impelled to say that it has happened. I prefer to say that on this matter our information is inadequate.
>
>   . . . It appears to me that a great deal of this work has been directed into unprofitable channels or devoted to the pursuit of will-o'-the-wisps. Much time was wasted in the production of unverifiable family trees. By plausible but unconvincing arguments, zoologists have "demonstrated" the descent of vertebrates from almost every group of invertebrates. Deficiencies of the data were patched up with hypotheses, and the reader is left with the feeling that if the data do not support the theory, they really ought to. A long-enduring and regrettable effect of the success of the *Origin* was the addiction of biologists to unverifiable speculation. The success of Darwinism was accompanied by a decline in scientific integrity.[2]

In writing this introduction, Thompson was behaving as a true scientist following the methods of Descartes. Until an idea was proven, he refused to believe it, no matter how many "authoritative" voices supported it. He drew a line between fact and philosophy.

Few scientists of his day, however, paid much attention to that line. Who among us has not seen those fanciful pictures of humanity's long march from ape turning to *Homo habilis* turning to *Homo erectus* turning to *Homo sapiens*? We have seen them in *Time* and *National Geographic* magazines, in textbooks and museums. In the same precincts we have seen paintings of the evolution of the horse from *eohippus* and *mesohippus*, and so on.

Scientific Backpedaling

For a long time these fancies have been set aside not only by creationists, but by evolutionists. Many scientists no longer believe that the ape evolved into *Homo sapiens* or that *eohippus* evolved into the horse. More than a decade ago, David Raup, curator of the Field Museum of Chicago and one of the most knowledgeable paleontologists of our day, wrote:

> The record of evolution is still surprisingly jerky, and ironically we have even fewer examples of evolutionary transition than we had in Darwin's time. Species appear in sequence very suddenly, show no change, then abruptly go out of the record, and it is rarely clear that their descendants are better adapted than their ancestors. By this I mean that some of the classic cases of evolution, such as the evolution of the horse in North America, have had to be discarded or modified because of more detailed information. The more you look at the horse series, the more you find that instead of a nice progression, the horses are living at the same time, overlapping each other, with no connection, or with sudden jumps at the most. The same is true of elephants, and everything else. There is no evolutionary transition anywhere in the fossils.[3]

Stephen Jay Gould, a leading evolutionist, has admitted to a dismal lack of evidence for Darwinism in fossils.

> The absence of fossil evidence for intermediary stages between major transitions in organic design, indeed our inability, even in our imagination, to construct functional intermediates in many cases, has

been a persistent and nagging problem for gradualistic accounts of evolution.[4]

Yet despite these admissions, and dozens of others like them, we still see the same artists' conceptions in publications and museums. Because a worldview is a tenacious habit, most of us do not change its basic paradigms easily. Those who have adopted evolutionary paradigms will try to find some excuse—any excuse—to avoid rethinking their worldview.

Punctuated Equilibrium

Recent theories of origins follow the lines of "punctuated equilibrium." According to this theory, a few primitive species appeared and remained stable for millions of years. Then, by some unknown mechanism, new species appeared suddenly, ushering in a new era of equilibrium, and so on. Darwinian-style gradual evolution through minute, incremental mutations and natural selection is now an obsolete paradigm. The facts do not support it.

Yet how tenacious is the idea of evolution itself—a habit of mind that functions independently of fact. Theories of punctuated equilibrium bear no explanation for the mechanism by which "jerk-it-and-leave-it" evolution might have happened, any more than Darwin explained how gradual evolution might have occurred. And as both Darwin and W. R. Thompson pointed out, evolution is dead in the water as science unless some mechanism for it can be proven.

Microevolution vs. Macroevolution

Scientists now distinguish between microevolution and macroevolution. Microevolution—the idea that species adapt to their surroundings—is an observable fact. Cartesian science has established that species do adapt to their surroundings.

But macroevolution—the idea that species evolve into other species—has not been established as fact. It is a philosophical paradigm that works independently of fact. As Steven Stanley, paleontologist at Johns Hopkins University, wrote, "Macroevolution is decoupled from microevolution."[5] That the gypsy moth grew darker to adapt to trees polluted with coal dust in Britain is no longer considered proof that apes evolved into people or that *eohippus* evolved into the horse. To believe that species adapted themselves into other species leaps from science to philosophy.

The eminent zoologist, Pierre Grasse, summarizes:

> Naturalists must remember that the process of evolution is revealed only through fossil forms. . . . Only paleontology can provide them with the evidence of evolution and reveal its course or mechanisms . . .
>
> Today, our duty is to destroy the myth of evolution, considered as a simple, understood and explained phenomenon which keeps rapidly unfolding before us.[6]

Michael Denton, in his *Evolution: A Theory in Crisis*, draws the same line between fact and philosophy:

> It is not surprising that, in the context of such an overwhelming social consensus, many biologists are confused as to the true status of the Darwinian paradigm and are unaware of its metaphysical basis. As the following quote from Julian Huxley at a conference in 1959 makes clear: "The first point to make about Darwin's theory is that it is no longer a theory but a fact. . . . Darwinianism has come of age, so to speak. We are no longer having to bother about establishing the fact of evolution. . . ."
>
> Now, of course, such claims are simply nonsense. For Darwin's model of evolution is still very much a theory and still very much in doubt when it comes to macroevolutionary phenomena. Furthermore, being basically a theory of historical reconstruction, it is impossible to verify by experiment or direct observation as is normal in science. Recently the philosophical status of evolutionary claims has been the subject of considerable debate. Philosophers such as Sir Karl Popper have raised doubts as to whether evolutionary claims, by their very nature incapable of falsification, can properly be classed as truly scientific hypothesis. Moreover, the theory of evolution deals with a series of unique events, the origin of life, the origin of intelligence and so on. Unique events are unrepeatable and cannot be subjected to any sort of experimental investigation.[7]

We add the astonishing remarks of Colin Patterson, senior paleontologist at the British Museum of Natural History in London:

I think always before in my life when I've got up to speak on a subject, I've been confident of one thing—that I know more about it than anybody in the room, because I've worked on it. Well, this time it isn't true. I'm speaking on two subjects, evolutionism and creationism, and I believe it's true to say that I know nothing whatever about either of them.

One of the reasons I started taking this anti-evolutionary view, or let's call it a non-evolutionary view, was that last year I had a sudden realization. For over twenty years I had thought I was working on evolution in some way. One morning I woke up and something had happened in the night, and it struck me that I had been working on this stuff for more than twenty years, and there was not one thing I knew about it. It's quite a shock to learn that one can be so misled for so long. Either there was something wrong with me or there was something wrong with evolutionary theory. Naturally I know there is nothing wrong with me, so for the last few weeks I've tried putting a simple question to various people and groups.

Question is: Can you tell me anything you know about evolution? Any one thing, any one thing that is true?[8]

A Post-Cartesian, Postmodern World

How far we have backtracked since the 1950s and '60s! Thomas Kuhn and Paul Feyerabend of Berkeley have written extensively on the philosophy of science, underscoring the drift away from Cartesian thinking:

What is still probably the most generally held view of science, among both scientists and the public, is one that was shaped during the 1930's and 1940's by the school of positivist philosophers known as the Vienna Circle.

According to this view, science is a strictly logical process. Scientists propose theories on the basis of inductive logic, and confirm or refute them by experimental tests of predictions deductively derived from the theory. When old theories fail, new theories are proposed and adopted because of their greater explanatory power, and science thus progresses inexorably closer to the truth.

Logical empiricism, as this view is known, deliberately ignores the historical context of science as well as the psychological factors which many people would consider important in science, such as intuition, imagination, and receptivity to new ideas.[9]

Today many Westerners recognize the limits of the dream of Descartes—to achieve a knowledge as secure as mathematics. So today Augustine reasserts himself.

We cannot get away from personal faith, nor from the opinions of people of stature, nor from God, who made us for Himself. We are not just cold-hearted thinking machines, even if we want to be. We are a people of culture and of spirit. Since we all have world-views, and since our thoughts are ordered by unconsciously held paradigms, the best we can hope for is to retain a little honesty in the way we distinguish fact from opinion. Rather than kid ourselves about our grand objectivity, we must admit that our science is full of assumptions, intuitions and guesses. We must stop filling in the blanks for which we have no information and twisting evidence that does not fit our worldview until it does fit.

This realization, which is spreading rapidly through the West, is producing a widespread paradigm shift into post-modernity, as we will describe in chapter 19.

Is the World a Machine or an Organic Garden?

This paradigm shift is opening the ceiling to a mysterious universe. The world is not a mechanism waiting for us to understand it. Life eludes analysis. Why does healing take place? Why do white blood cells crush and cleanse away foreign bodies from our bloodstream? Do we now understand any more about instinct than in the days when Indians called it *manitou* and *sumesh*? Is it provable that we do not have an existence beyond the grave and apart from our bodies? Why do we have a sense of right and wrong independent from rational thought? Do we really know anything at all about the origin of species?

For a century Westerners have despised the idea that the cosmos is mysterious. We saw the world as a machine waiting to be understood and worked because we wanted to be the ones who worked it. While this concept has yielded abundant fruits, we must admit that the creation has resisted many of our attempts at discovery, yielding frustration and a degree of disillusionment.

Toward the end of his life, Elmer Ellsworth Brown (the chancellor who convened the conference at New York University) recognized this unexpected turn:

> Before Emerson had passed from this earthly scene in 1882, the physical sciences were advancing to the intellectual conquest of the world, and were laying down their law upon the world of human intelligence. Another decade, and in the eyes of devotees their conquest was complete, and all that remained to be done was a mopping up of particulars, "in the fourth decimal place." But . . . now some of the ablest of our scientists, some of those most loyal to the scientific tradition, find themselves driven to philosophizing, and that not only for the mastery of an avalanche of new information, but still more for the mastery of meanings, which new discoveries demand and do not themselves supply.[10]

Dr. Brown's words were prophetic. Science is backing down from its confidence, built on the foundation of a mechanical universe easily discoverable. The assertions of former generations have diminished to a whirlwind of whispered questions. Today it is the evolutionist who inherits the wind, for it is as difficult to lay hold of the secrets of our origins as it is to grasp the wind with one's hand.

Let Reason and Mystery Shake Hands

It is time to return to the sane and balanced views of Blaise Pascal, who wrote, "If we submit everything to reason, our religion will have no mysterious and supernatural element. If we offend the principles of reason, our religion will be absurd and ridiculous."[11] Cannot reason and mystery shake hands in our minds as they shook hands in the mind of Pascal?

It was Pascal, not Descartes, who developed the more balanced worldview. Pointing to the rational mind, he wrote, "It is incomprehensible that God should exist, and"—pointing now to the visible creation—"it is incomprehensible that He should not exist."[12] Again, speaking of the skeptics of his age:

> What reason have they for saying that we cannot rise from the dead? What is more difficult, to be born or to rise again; that what has never

been should be, or that what has been should be again? Is it more difficult to come into existence than to return to it? Habit makes the one appear easy to us; want of habit makes the other impossible.[13]

There is nothing primitive about seeing the world as a place of mystery, where revelations of God are everywhere and the power of the spirit world is evidenced in the visible world. The mystery of creation is unfolded by science itself, though many scientists, still clinging to a positivist worldview, cannot see this point. But a new generation is clinging to a different philosophy of science. To return to Michael Denton:

> To grasp the reality of life as it has been revealed by molecular biology, we must magnify a cell a thousand million times until it is twenty kilometres in diameter and resembles a giant airship large enough to cover a great city like London or New York. What we would then see would be an object of unparalleled complexity and adaptive design. On the surface of the cell we would see millions of openings, like the port holes of a vast space ship, opening and closing to allow a continual stream of materials to flow in and out. If we were to enter one of these openings we would find ourselves in a world of supreme technology and bewildering complexity.
>
> ... Although the argument for design has been unfashionable in biology for the past century, the feeling that chance is an insufficient means of achieving complex adaptations has continually been expressed by a dissenting minority.
>
> ... It is the sheer universality of perfection, the fact that everywhere we look, to whatever depth we look, we find an elegance and ingenuity of an absolutely transcending quality, which so mitigates against the idea of chance. Is it really credible that random processes could have constructed a reality, the smallest element of which—a functional protein or gene—is complex beyond our own creative capacities, a reality which is the very antithesis of chance, which excels in every sense anything produced by the intelligence of man?[14]

The complexity and intelligent design of the world beggars description and baffles every theory of origins. A new generation of scientists is doing what W. R. Thompson and Colin Patterson have done. It is learning to say more frequently, "I don't know." This newfound humility contains the potential for a rediscovery of our Creator, of the revelations He has vouchsafed to us and of the manifestations of His power. Once our worldview admits to the revelations of God in one place, our eyes are opened to see Him in many other areas of life—until all of life attests to His glory and power.

9

Like Waves
in a Pool

Doug: To some, the creation-evolution debate is a tennis ball to lob back and forth in a game of scientific debate. But the debate is no game because paradigms do not stand alone. One paradigm affects its neighbor, and so on, like waves in a swimming pool. The water may seem as hard as a mirror until the new paradigm is dropped into it. Suddenly waves of change spread to the farthest corner of the pool.

The most tragic and unavoidable impact of the evolution paradigm has come in the area of morals. Evolutionary paradigms affect ethical paradigms. Since Darwin provided a structure for a new worldview, cultural leaders have drawn out the implications of that worldview in every area of life. Recent Western history tells the story of this trend.

Evolutionary theory and natural selection have been peculiarly pernicious paradigms, providing the basic philosophy for the regimes of Marx, Stalin and Hitler, who drew these teachings to their logical conclusion. Perhaps this political and moral development in Europe explains why the late scientist Jacques Monod, who watched Nazism rise up next door to his native France, commented in his last radio address in 1976:

> [Natural] selection is the blindest and most cruel way of evolving new species and more and more complex and refined organisms. . . .

The struggle for life and elimination of the weakest is a horrible process, against which our whole modern ethics revolts. . . . I am surprised that a Christian would defend the idea that this is the process which God more or less set up in order to have evolution.[1]

Monod was confronting the Christian Church, part of which was (and still is) blind to the implications of certain evolutionary paradigms.

The Wings of the House Must Fit Together

Western Christians have been trying for decades to fit evolutionary theory into Christian ethics. This attempt has been a futile one, like building a geodesic dome onto a Cape Cod. *It has no integrity of design.*

Do we live in a world of righteousness and justice that has temporarily fallen into barbarity, or a world in which barbarity is the norm and righteousness is meaningless and out of place? Evolutionary theory proposes the latter; creation paradigms propose the former. Each of us must decide which to believe.

We do not imply, of course, that all evolutionists are barbarians. But they have removed the gold standard from their own ethical currency. Sooner or later a culture that has accepted such a worldview will collapse, as Germany's worldview collapsed under Hitler.

Many evolutionists understand perfectly well the connection between ethics and a theory of origins. In his book *Ends and Means*, Aldous Huxley made this candid confession:

I had motives for not wanting the world to have a meaning; consequently I assumed that it had none, and was able without any difficulty to find satisfying reasons for this assumption. . . . The philosopher who finds no meaning in the world is not concerned exclusively with a problem in pure metaphysics; he is also concerned to prove that there is no valid reason why he personally should not do as he wants to do, or why his friends should not seize political power and govern in the way that they find advantageous to themselves. . . .

For myself as, no doubt, for most of my contemporaries, the philosophy of meaninglessness was essentially an instrument of liberation. The liberation we desired was simultaneously liberation from a certain system of morality. We objected to the morality because it interfered with our sexual freedom; we objected to the political and economic system because it was unjust. The supporters of these systems claimed that in some way they embodied the meaning (a Christian meaning, they insisted) of the world. There was one admirably simple method of confuting these people and at the same time justifying ourselves in our political and erotic revolt: we could deny that the world had any meaning whatsoever.[2]

Not all evolutionists are of the same stamp as Aldous Huxley. Many cling to evolution because they honestly wish to seek the truth wherever it is found. They view the moral integrity of science as a search for truth. But we hope we have made a case in the previous chapter that evolution does not necessarily arise from the search for truth. It is merely a way of putting facts together—a philosophical paradigm.

In this chapter we wish to show that Darwinian ideas, which move beyond the foundations of science, deserve to be jettisoned by sincere Christians. These paradigms do not fit with Christian ethics, nor with the Gospel in any of its paradigms.

White-Indian Relations in the American West

The impact of Cartesian and Darwinian philosophy on Adolf Hitler and Karl Marx is well-known. So let's look at another illustration: the impact of evolutionary ideas on the relationship between whites and Native Americans.

As European civilization encroached on Western tribes, most of the first leaders who influenced Anglo-American policy toward Native Americans believed in biblical paradigms. David Thompson, explorer and cartographer of the Northern Rockies, and Jedediah Smith, explorer and cartographer of the Southern Rockies, were devout Christians. They respected the tribal peoples they met because their worldview invited them to do so. They believed that all people are created in the image of God and come from common stock: Adam. This habit of thought was cemented into their worldview.

William Clark, the first Superintendent of Indian Affairs (and an Anglican), gained great stature among the Western tribes, as did

David Thompson and Jedediah Smith. Insofar as these men were the first whites to break in upon certain Western tribes, their loving and respectful influence gave to white-Indian relations a profoundly positive beginning.

The same can be said of Dr. John McLoughlin, chief factor for the Hudson's Bay Company at Fort Vancouver. McLoughlin married a full-blooded Indian woman, Margaret, whom he loved dearly all his life. He required his employees to take off their hats in her presence and to give up demeaning sexual liaisons with Indian women. As autocratic baron of the Columbia Department, his anti-racist policies prevailed throughout the Pacific Northwest for a quarter of a century.

Because McLoughlin believed in the dignity and integrity of human beings created in God's image, he opposed the slavery practiced among the Chinooks who lived around Fort Vancouver. His anti-slavery policies reflected the influence of the Clapham Sect, a group of Christians in a suburb of London who influenced English politics through William Wilberforce in Parliament and through Benjamin Harrison, a director of the Hudson's Bay Company. These men believed that all people are created in God's image.

We do not suggest, of course, that all Christians were nonracist. Many of them—like George Simpson, for example, governor of the Hudson's Bay Company's Northern Department—clung to views that do not fit with biblical paradigms. Then, as today, Christians held it as their prerogative to pick and choose from the Bible the paradigms that suited their convenience. Nevertheless, when the biblical teaching concerning the image of God influenced Christians, racism in this country was sidestepped. This teaching, part of the larger creationist paradigm, is worth recovering today because it has usually brought integrity and morality into human affairs.

Evolutionary Ideas Enter the Arena

But as the theory of evolution began to creep into American universities, it affected the prevailing Western worldview. Evolutionary ideas, particularly where they concerned white-Indian relations, actually encouraged racism. Some universities abandoned the concept that all people are created in the image of God. This idea is not, after all, provable. On the surface the opposite seems true—that people have evolved as animals and reflect the image of the animal kingdom. *Time* magazine's March 1994 cover story on evolution, for example, begins, "No single, essential difference separates human beings from other animals—but that hasn't stopped the phrase-makers from trying to find one."[3]

Dr. Garland Hurt, who presided over the Bureau of Indian Affairs in the territory of Utah during the 1850s, had a well-publicized debate with Captain James Simpson, government explorer and head of the team that mapped and plotted the first roads and railroad through Nevada and Utah, over the nature of the human race. Dr. Hurt contributed the anthropological part of the report, describing the natives of the Great Basin who, up to that time, had eked out a hand-to-mouth existence and lived in squalid conditions.

The Expedition Report, published a year after Darwin's *Origin of Species*, reveals a growing debate throughout the U.S. even before Darwin's time. Dr. Hurt wrote:

> It appears to be the opinion of a large number of our modern phil-anthropists that all beings possessing the human form were originally endowed with an equality that ever forbids the idea of inferiority.
>
> With an eye single to this similarity in physical form, they seem to overlook the mental inequality, or attribute it to a want of culture; and hence the misguided zeal for the improvement of many of the colored races, whose mental inferiority is a fixed and demonstrable fact, which must ever and inevitably define their position in the scale of political importance, and renders the idea of their future elevation to an equality with the Caucasian race utterly preposterous, and can only exist in the misguided wanderings of a perverted imagination. They have shown from their earliest generations their incapacity for any except the most simple forms of government, such as would assimilate them to some species of the gregarious animals, whom they approximate to in this respect and imitate as much as they do the higher orders of their own species.[4]

Without burdening our readers with more of Dr. Hurt's views, we will summarize his conclusion: that governments were wasting their money in trying to spread the benefits of European learning to spare aboriginal peoples the pain of starvation and extermination.

Captain Simpson, a Christian, took issue with Dr. Hurt's theories. He prefaced Dr. Hurt's report with these remarks:

> I know it is the habit of many excellent and scientific men, as the doctor has done, to leave out in their philosophy a great truth—the greatest that has been divulged to the world—that the great I AM has spoken to man in his ignorance, and has given to him certain primary truths, which if he regard, he will assuredly live in light; but which if he disregard, he will as assuredly walk in darkness himself, and lead others into darkness. Among these great primary truths, I hold, is the unity of the race; and before any one, in my judgment, has a right to disbelieve it, he must first show that the source of knowledge of the Holy One, the Bible, which unbelievers have as yet only served to strengthen by their cavils and objections, is untrue, and therefore unworthy of being received as the grand text-book of individuals as well as of nations.[5]

It is not hard to imagine, in light of Dr. Hurt's comments, why the Bureau of Indian Affairs began to reflect dehumanizing influences during the 1850s. William Clark had provided an excellent beginning for the relationship with Native Americans. But unbiblical concepts eroded the philosophical base on which interracial respect was built. As Christians began to incorporate these concepts into their worldview, it affected their Christian witness.

Cultural Evolution

The eminent California historian H. H. Bancroft also demonstrates how evolutionary theory affected white-Indian relations. Bancroft was, like an increasing number of nineteenth-century intellectuals, a cultural evolutionist—a geodesic builder. The first volume of his *Works* conveys his evolutionary beliefs:

> Thus, to sum up the foregoing premises: in society, between two or more individuals, there is at work a mysterious energy, not unlike that of the force between molecules or life in the organism; this social energy is under intelligent governance, not fortuitous nor causeless, but reducible to fixed law, and capable of being wrought into a science. . . . This energy acts on the intellect, and through the intellect on the organism; acts independently of the will, and cannot be cre-

ated or destroyed by man; is not found in the brute creation; is not transmittable by generation through individuals; is wrought out by man as a free-will agent, though acting unconsciously; and is the product of good and evil.[6]

The world is not governed by a personal God, in other words, but by immutable, predictable evolutionary laws that permeate even social relationships. It is the task of science to study these laws and learn to control them. This idea gave birth at the turn of the century to the social sciences.

Yet the danger of this philosophy as it affects moral ideas is apparent because evolution, in Bancroft's own words, "is the product of good and evil." It is morally blind. Moral categories are meaningless in the face of the power that allegedly guides all things into the way of progress.

How, then, did H. H. Bancroft's evolutionism affect his understanding of white-Indian relations in the West? His discussion of Dr. McLoughlin's decision to marry an Indian woman is self-explanatory:

> I never could understand how such men as John McLoughlin, [or] James Douglas . . . could endure the thought of having their name and honors descend to a degenerate posterity. . . . Surely they were possessed of sufficient intelligence to know that by giving their children Indian or half-breed mothers, their own Scotch, Irish, or English blood would then be greatly debased. . . . They were doing all concerned a great wrong. Perish all the Hudson's Bay Company thrice over, I would say, sooner than bring upon my offspring such foul corruption, sooner than bring into being offspring of such a curse.[7]

Like McLoughlin, Christian explorers Peter Skene Ogden, Alexander Ross and David Thompson all cherished their full-blooded Native American wives until death did them part. Bancroft would have gagged over this matrimonial habit of Christians:

> Intermixtures of civilized with savage peoples are sure to result in the total disappearance of refinement on the one side, or in the extinction of the barbaric race on the other. . . . Left alone, the nations of America might have unfolded into as bright a civilization as that of Europe.[8]

These sentiments, which we hear even today, seem to imply respect for indigenous cultures—a sentiment we would agree with if it were true. But Bancroft's desire to leave tribal cultures alone came not from respect but from contempt. Native Americans should have been left alone, he felt, so that the mysterious forces of evolution could bring them forward to civilized forms of thought in a way appropriate to their culture.

The Effect of Creation Teaching

The creation paradigm, when accepted among Christians, brought with it the opposite ethic with regard to Native Americans. The concept that all people are created by the same God and in the image of God came attached to a moral paradigm—that we are our brother's keeper.

William Clark, on his seminal trip west in 1804, expressed his concern for the condition of tribal peoples:

> The condition of many tribes west of the Mississippi is the most pitiable that can be imagined. During several seasons in every year they are distressed by famine, in which many die for want of food, and during which the living child is often buried with the dead mother, because no one can spare it as much food as would sustain it through its helpless infancy.[9]

William Clark felt it his moral duty to share the fruits of Western civilization with tribal peoples, as well as the ideas and world-view that produced those fruits. Cultural evolutionists, still committed to "leaving people alone," would describe these hopes as imperialistic and paternalistic. Nevertheless, Clark wanted to teach both agriculture and Christianity in an attempt to address basic human need.

He was not unusual in this. His assumptions about God, the world and human nature were identical to those of the Anglicans at Red River Colony (alias Winnipeg—here lived the first Protestant missionaries in the American West) and the Franciscans of California. All believed in investing themselves in native peoples, sharing the fruits of European civilization in bringing them out of what today we would call the Stone Age. These groups invested themselves in personal relationships with native peoples, learned their languages, tried to bridge cultural chasms and love a people very different from themselves.

The Missions of California

The Franciscans, for example, took the trouble to learn Native American language and culture, as Geronimo Boscana's book *Chinigchinich* bears testimony. They dealt at close quarters with native peoples on a daily basis. The Franciscans vowed not to own one acre of land, but to develop the land—thousands of square miles of farmland, orchards and grazing land full of horses and cattle— and a lucrative hide-and-tallow industry, eventually to be turned over to the Indians they were discipling according to Roman Catholic standards.

It was not Catholicism per se that produced paternalism and violent subjugation of California natives. The Spanish identified themselves above all as the *gentes de raisón*, the people of reason. Their epistemology had given them control over the material world, which they had used to produce superior weapons and other outgrowths of material power. The Californian Franciscans were saddled with an inebriated military system that during the 1830s came increasingly under the control of the ideas of the French Revolution. These ideas boiled up into raw political power ploys that destroyed both the Catholic missions and the native tribes with one blow. H. H. Bancroft, the cultural evolutionist and historian, championed these California revolutionaries and their tactics.

Bancroft's particular champion was a Spaniard named José María Echeandía, first official governor of California. Having discovered republican government, Mexico was modeling itself after revolutionary France. Just as the French Revolution had plundered the coffers of the Catholic Church, so Echeandía moved illegally during the last years of his governorship to seize the Franciscan missions, handing over mission properties to government administrators—his personal friends one and all.

Ostensibly his motives were to liberate the natives from "slavery." The whole world, he believed, was being liberated from a

Christian worldview and freed by "the people of reason" from unenlightened thinking. But despite his liberation rhetoric, Echeandía was no more a lover of Native Americans than was Bancroft. He believed not in love but in enlightenment. A chronic hypochondriac, he avoided personal contact with all but his closest friends. He did not learn the languages of native peoples, did not study their cultures, did not befriend or love them in any personal way. He believed in leaving them alone. Perhaps that is why H. H. Bancroft found in Echeandía a kindred spirit.

As a result of his policies, Spanish landowners were permitted to pillage and plunder the industries that the padres had prepared for the natives. Nine million acres of mission lands were apportioned away immediately. The rest were taken by artifice from the natives during the 1840s and '50s.

In his *History of California*, H. H. Bancroft excuses this highway robbery. Speaking of Echeandía's right-hand man, Bancroft remarks:

> And if he also held up before the eyes of the Carrillos, Osios, Vallejos, Picos, Alvarados, Bandinis, and others, bright visions of rich estates to be administered by them or their friends, their young enthusiasm should by no means be termed hypocrisy or a desire for plunder.[10]

The Franciscans had the misfortune to see their life's work annihilated, and the people in whom they had invested their lives exterminated. Within twenty years the entire mission system lay in ruins and whole tribes of natives were wiped out by "the people of reason." This was the result of leaving the natives alone.

The Christian explorer Kit Carson wrote in his memoirs:

> When I first went over into California in 1829, the valleys were full of Indian tribes. Indians were thick everywhere, and I saw a great deal of some large and flourishing tribes. When I went there again in 1835, they had all disappeared, and when I inquired about certain tribes I had seen on the very spot where I then stood, I was told by people living there that they had never heard of them.[11]

Behind these tragedies lay an emerging worldview conceived and supported by the philosophers of eighteenth-century France—the builders of the brass heaven. The new worldview preceded Darwinian theory, of course, but Darwin gave shape to it, providing the geodesic framing and creating a fascination for it that would grip Western intellectuals for decades to come.

The Puzzle Pieces Have to Fit

The point is that the various parts of a worldview must fit together like the pieces of an interlocking puzzle. Epistemology, ethics, origins, theology, Christology, hermeneutics—all bear upon one another and must fit together. Apart from this integrity of worldview, we cannot be whole; we will be fragmented, not healed, by our culture. Those who see the world as a collage of shattered fragments will themselves be such a collage.

Many leaders of Western culture—leaders like my great uncle—sincerely believed they were advancing to new frontiers of scientific thought that would bring great reward. Now we see that those rewards are limited. Blaise Pascal and Alfred Noyes offered perceptive assessments of the spiritual and moral catastrophe brewing. Descartes and Darwin, as soon as their ideas were removed from a Christian environment, provided us with a formula for the erosion of civilization. Today we are sprinting backwards into savagery and have forgotten whence the power comes to get us moving forward again.

That the brass heaven offers no such power was demonstrated painfully in the 1930s and '40s in Germany, from which came many of its most talented builders.

We now trace the pathetic developments that led to two world wars—for it was the brass heaven paradigms dropping into Germany that created the cataclysmic waves that nearly destroyed Europe.

10

The Sting

Germany, a leader in the great Reformation and often a leader of Western culture, was once a nation infused with biblical paradigms. These paradigms—as we will explore in this chapter—show us that the spirit world on earth is filled with principalities in rebellion against God.

But God proved Himself victorious over all such powers through the death and resurrection of Jesus Christ. Jesus came to destroy the works of the evil one, and He showed His disciples how to fight those principalities. He died to disarm "strong men" (Matthew 12:29) and "elemental spirits of the universe" (Colossians 2:8, RSV). After His death and resurrection, He was enthroned with all authority and power in heaven and on earth, and He comes again to put His enemies under His feet.

In Job 1 and Zechariah 3, Satan is portrayed as a sort of heavenly prosecuting attorney. But Jesus' death cost Satan his job. An angelic battle followed, and Satan was cast out of the courts of heaven (Luke 10:18, Revelation 12:7–8). He takes vengeance for this eviction by harassing Jews and Christians (Revelation 12:17). But we can overcome him through faith in the cross of Christ, by which he was entirely disarmed (Colossians 2:15).

Paganism, the Reformation and the Demonic

We have seen that Augustine accepted biblical paradigms. He taught, following Paul's teaching of 1 Corinthians 10:20, that paganism was really demon worship. In *The City of God*, he argued so persuasively that he led the way in burying paganism in the West:

> No longer, then, follow after false and deceitful gods; abjure them rather, and despise them, bursting forth into true liberty. Gods they are not, but malignant spirits, to whom your eternal happiness will be a sore punishment. . . . The demons have not the power they are supposed to have. . . .[1]

Martin Luther, an Augustinian monk, also accepted biblical paradigms and lived by them. He knew how to fight demonic powers:

> We are surrounded by the kind of enemies who will not stop until they have knocked us down, and as individual poor men we are much too weak to withstand so many enemies. For this reason God says in the prophet Zechariah (12:10) that He will give to those who are His own "the Spirit of grace and supplication" to preserve them while they are on the field of battle and to guard and protect them against that wicked and pernicious spirit. Therefore it is the particular work of Christians, who have the Spirit of God, not to be lax and lazy but incessant and constant in their praying.[2]

Luther wrote that the evil one is perfectly content to let us endow colleges, build sanctuaries, write anthems, read, sing and multiply ceremonies beyond measure, for these things in no wise hinder him. For "when prayer is subordinated, nobody takes anything from him and nobody resists him." It is prayer that defeats "that wicked and pernicious spirit."

In Luther's writings we find three power paradigms. First, demon powers exist to harass and seek to corrupt us. Second, the power that Jesus entrusts to the Church surpasses demonic power. Third, we wield that superior power through the prayer of faith in the name of Jesus.

Luther practiced what he preached. He habitually prayed three hours a day—not the empty prayers of medieval Catholicism but prayers of faith in Jesus' name. In Luther we see the power behind the Reformation, which broke up the clouds of deception that had entered a corrupt Church. Martin Luther, apostle of faith, rediscovered the prayer of faith.

Confronting the Spirit of Magic

During the eighteenth century, however, Christians in Germany decided that these beliefs in spiritual warfare were medieval. By the nineteenth century Protestants had become skeptical about the existence of demonic powers. To many, prayer became an exercise of pious ritual.

In this milieu, Lutheran pastor Johann Christoph Blumhardt moved in 1841 to a new pastorate in the village of Mottlingen. During a pastoral visit in the home of a parishioner, Gottliebin Dittus, he was confronted by what he recognized as demonic powers. He soon learned that this woman's parents had taken her as a young girl to a practitioner of magic, hoping to cure her of a childhood illness. From that time on she had suffered from fainting spells, fits, apparitions, mysterious voices and painful physical maladies.

Blumhardt knew nothing of spiritual warfare, for the thinking of the founder of his denomination had been abandoned. But love required him to learn. Taking others with him whenever he ministered to Gottliebin, Blumhardt tried to bring healing and relief to her torment. He began by using the short prayers of the Lutheran Church and by reading Scripture to her. These provided only temporary relief. Soon he taught her to speak the name of Jesus for herself. Later he cast demons out of her by the name of Jesus, which he found effective and powerful. But even then, other demons would soon appear and trouble her more intensely than the first.

Blumhardt became distraught. Yet at the suggestion that he enlist the aid of white magic, he replied, "The Lord [has] always led me to stay with the honest weapons of prayer and the Word of God." To these he added the discipline of fasting, which seemed to add power to his prayers.

The battle for Gottliebin's release culminated after two years of prayer warfare. During one important struggle, the demons being exorcised cried out, "The alliance goes to pieces. It is all over. It is your fault—with your constant praying." The Lord showed Blumhardt that the ruling spirit he was fighting was the chief of all magic powers, and that God had appointed Blumhardt to deal a severe blow to the kingdom of darkness.

Finally, in December 1843, he was given the power to pray and fast forty hours without feeling the slightest weariness. On the 28th of that month, at 2 A.M., the prince of magic came out of Gottliebin, shrieking loudly so that the whole village heard: "Jesus is Victor! Jesus is Victor!"

Gottliebin was freed of all demonic manifestations for the rest of her life. She was also healed instantly of a twisted backbone, a short foot and stomach trouble. The pastor wrote a full report (verified by witnesses) and submitted it to his synod.[3] Blumhardt became a man of extraordinary compassion and power who spent the rest of his life ministering to the terminally ill at an asylum he founded at Boll.

During the next fifty years, there seems to have been a waning of magic arts—which most Germans attributed, no doubt, to their more enlightened culture. Germany was leading the brass heaven builders to sift the Bible of its "myths" and "illusions." But after Blumhardt's death the spirit of magic returned to Germany, in no way hindered by the power of the German intellect. The last state was worse than the first.

Demonic Power and World War I

Late in the century, a white-bearded magician named Guido von List celebrated the summer solstice by burying a number of wine bottles in the form of a swastika or hermetic cross—the sign of Aryan supremacy in the Order of the Golden Dawn.

In 1907 Adolf Lanz von Liebenfels ran up the swastika on a flag from his temple of magic. It was the sign of an emerging faith that replaced Christianity with an Aryan neo-paganism.[4]

In April 1904 an Englishman, Alistair Crowley, traveled to Egypt with his wife and prayed an invocation to the god Horus, Egyptian god of war. A being named Aiwass appeared to him and dictated

The Book of the Law, a proclamation that the world was entering into a new age, the age of Horus.

> It asserted that before the religion of the new age could take effect, the old aeon must be swept away as ruthlessly as was the pagan world of the Roman Empire, and that the planet would therefore be bathed in blood. Barbarism, lust and cruelty were prophesied, and the destruction of all Christian sentiments. The Book of the Law therefore challenged the cultural tradition of two thousand years.
>
> It asserted the reality of magic, of mysterious and irrational forces, of Unknown Supermen, one of whom was its author.[5]

The spirits of paganism were trying to undo the work of the early Church fathers and Augustine, who had brought their demise by asserting the name of Jesus against them. They managed to have their way now because the people who listened to them believed them, and because the brass heaven Church had set aside spiritual warfare as medieval. The work of Johann Christoph Blumhardt was forgotten—an anachronism in a brass heaven world.

At that time various occult practitioners gained stature with certain European heads of state. One of these was Houston Stewart Chamberlain, an Englishman who moved to Germany, divorced his wife and married Eva Wagner, daughter of the composer Richard Wagner. Chamberlain became one of the great figures in the world of occult, Gnostic, Germanic paganism, and he was a demonized man, as William Shirer described in *The Rise and Fall of the Third Reich*:

> Since he felt himself goaded on by demons, his books (on Wagner, Goethe, Kant, Christianity and race) were written in the grip of a terrible fever, a veritable trance, a state of self-induced intoxication, so that, as he says in his autobiography *Lebenswege*, he was often unable to recognise them as his own work, because they surpassed his expectations.[6]

This man became advisor to Kaiser Wilhelm II—a veritable shaman to the German head of state. Wilhelm allowed himself to be used as an instrument in the hands of Chamberlain and the spiritual forces that drove him. The Kaiser became convinced that he had a messianic mission to dominate the world on behalf of the people of Germany. Allied with Austria-Hungary, he declared war on Serbia, thus igniting World War I. In this way, the Kaiser led his nation into the worst disaster Germany had yet known.

After it was over, he fled to retirement at an estate in Doorn, Holland, where he amassed a library of occult books, trying to figure out why his faith in occult powers had so entirely failed him. H. S. Chamberlain lingered on after the war, confined to a wheelchair and bitterly disillusioned.

Hitler, the Occult Messiah

But the powers that had enticed them were not finished with Germany. They moved on and found a new mark in a bearded Bohemian dropout named Adolf Hitler. During his residence in Vienna, where he talked with occultists like Lanz von Liebenfels, Hitler became acquainted with occultism, yoga, hypnotism, astrology, Eastern religions and German paganism. Gerald Suster summarizes this formative period in Hitler's life:

> Power was his object, and power alone. From ponderous and verbose writings he extracted scraps of method, not caring whether his sources advocated good or evil. . . . And, as all do who study occultism with the slightest seriousness, he experimented with the exercises that enhance the faculties and lead to states of transcendent consciousness.[7]

In 1919 Hitler met Dieter Eckart, who was to play the same role in his life that Chamberlain had played for Kaiser Wilhelm. As high priest of the occult, Gnostic Thule Society, Eckart said of the young Hitler, "Here is the one for whom I was but the prophet and forerunner." Later, in 1923, he wrote to a friend, "Follow Hitler! He will dance, but it is I who have called the tune. We have given him the means of communication with Them. Do not mourn for me: I shall have influenced history more than any other German."[8]

Hitler came to believe, in his turn, that he was destined to dominate the world on behalf of Germany. He believed, too, that the Jewish people and the Christian Church must be destroyed, and that Jesus must be exposed as a weak, pitiful, second-rate power.

Herman Rauschning, one of Hitler's closest friends, gave intimate glimpses into Hitler's attitude toward Christianity in his book *The Voice of Destruction*. Some samples: "Whether it is the Old Testament or the New, it's all the same old Jewish swindle." "You cannot be both a German and a Christian." "We need free men who feel and know that God is in themselves. . . ." The Church has destroyed "the whole secret knowledge of nature, of the divine, the shapeless, the daimonic." "Through the peasantry we shall really be able to destroy Christianity because there is in them a true religion rooted in nature and blood."

Hitler went well beyond Kaiser Wilhelm in his exploration of the occult. He was taken over by demonic powers that ruled him. He became, as Rauschning called him, "a sort of great medicine man."[9] Rauschning added:

> One cannot help thinking of him as a medium. For most of the time mediums are ordinary, insignificant people. Suddenly they are endowed with what seem to be supernatural powers which set them apart from the rest of humanity. . . . The medium is possessed. Once the crisis is past, they fall back again into mediocrity. It was in this way, beyond any doubt, that Hitler was possessed by forces outside himself—almost demoniacal forces of which the individual named Hitler was only the temporary vehicle.[10]

Rauschning's descriptions reveal a man whose occult involvement had led to demonization:

> Hitler stood swaying in his room, looking wildly about him. "He! He! He's been here!" he gasped. His lips were blue. Sweat streamed down his face. Suddenly he began to reel off figures, and odd words and broken phrases, entirely devoid of sense. It sounded horrible.
> . . . Then suddenly he screamed, "There! There! In the corner!"[11]

Most Germans ridiculed demonic paradigms. Yet it appears that Hitler was in the grip of spirits that used mediums and occult societies to gain executive privilege with heads of state. These powers influenced all the leaders of the Third Reich, especially Heinrich Himmler, head of the SS, the Nazi elite forces, which Himmler turned into a society of black magic. These facts have been well established in the last twenty years by postmodern historians.[12]

Neo-Paganism and Christianity

Lewis Sumberg summarized well the results of this postmodern analysis of the Third Reich: "Nazism is only the most recent manifestation of a militant neo-Paganism locked in a death struggle with its arch-enemy, traditional Christianity, a struggle which will go on until the end of time."

"In this cosmology," he continued,

> the key word is Gnosis: integral, absolute, Ultimate Knowledge, transmitted to man by the gods through the ancient runic writings and exemplified in the symbolism of the pagan Aryan Grail. In the mind of the Church, nothing could be further removed from the faith and ethics of traditional Christianity than the Gnostic doctrines promulgated by the racists Zoroaster and Mani, with their emphasis on an elite's attainment of Primordial Knowledge and their belief in the two worlds, one created by the good god and the other by the bad god. . . .
>
> The ability of neo-Paganism to reaffirm itself militantly and contest with Christianity for men's minds and bodies tells us that the Nazi nightmare is the most recent but not the final act in a larger human tragedy that is still being played out. It would be foolish to see the phenomenon as a specifically "German problem"; how unbelievably shallow-rooted the Christian faith and ethic are was amply demonstrated by the unparalleled recrudescence of neo-Paganism everywhere the swastika went.[13]

This assessment of the spiritual situation was affirmed by Hitler himself, who saw clearly the weakness of the brass heaven Church:

> Do you think these liberal priests, who have no longer a belief, only an office, will refuse to preach *our* God in their churches? I can guarantee that, just as they have made Haeckel and Darwin, Goethe and Stefan George the prophets of their Christianity, so they will replace the cross with our swastika.[14]

These words proved pathetically true in many cases, but Hitler's even more daring challenge to Christ and His Church did not: "This revolution of ours is the exact counterpart of the great French Revolution. And no Jewish God will save the democracies from it."[15]

The shallowness of Christian faith in Europe can be traced to builders of the brass heaven who decided to abandon biblical power paradigms in favor of brass heaven paradigms. These leaders could not see what was happening in Germany because they were blinded by their worldview.

Dietrich Bonhoeffer, the best of Germany's theologians, writing from a Nazi prison camp, expressed brass heaven confidence with eloquence: "Man has learned to cope with all questions of importance without recourse to God as a working hypothesis. In questions concerning science, art and even ethics, this has become an understood thing which one scarcely dares to tilt at any more."[16] Yet he departed from Rudolf Bultmann in his rejection of the supposedly mythological power paradigms of the Bible, feeling that these paradigms must be retained.[17] Accordingly Bonhoeffer was able to prophesy:

> The day will come when men will be called again to utter the word of God with such power as will change and renew the world. It will be a new language, which will horrify men, and yet overwhelm them by its power. It will be the language of a new righteousness and truth, a language which proclaims the peace of God with men and the advent of his kingdom.[18]

But for the time being, the loss of biblical power paradigms was a bitter tragedy for Germany. Most Germans believed in neither satanic power nor the power of the cross of Jesus over the demonic.

If biblical paradigms are accurate, on the other hand, then the Church is the only community that can successfully oppose the evil one. We possess the keys of the Kingdom, and the gates of hell cannot prevail against the Church.

A Victory Won in Prayer

In the face of the raw evil of neo-paganism and its power to pollute faith and love, to invite war and to degrade body, soul and spirit, postmodern historians are baffled how such a "recrudescence of evil" may be opposed. Gerald Suster ends his study of Nazism by telling us to exert our willpower more forcefully. But this advice describes the problem, not the solution.

The French Catholic Jean-Michel Angebert speaks glowingly of the power of dungeon and sword so often used by Catholics to oppose neo-paganism in the past.

Both writers seem unaware of the power of God, as are most Westerners, who have grown up under the brass heaven. The tragedy is that even the Church seems unaware of the power of God.

But God's power was vindicated during World War II, despite the brass heaven that had closed God out of European culture.

During the Welsh revival of 1904, God had begun to prepare a simple man of faith to exorcise the demons from Germany—Rees Howells, son of a coalminer. His life would become a gripping testimony to the power of Jesus Christ over satanic *archons*.

The early chapters of his biography by Norman Grubb show God's gentle but firm dealings with him. Before he could be an intercessor among intercessors, he had to become a mature disciple of Jesus. He learned to rely on God for provision, gain mastery over the flesh and live the way of love, all in preparation for the prayer ministry that would consume the last years of his life, 1939–1945.

In March 1936, Howells, then director of the Bible College of Wales, began to sense that Hitler was Satan's vehicle to prevent the Gospel from being carried to the ends of the earth. "In fighting Hitler," he said, "we have always said that we were not up against man, but the devil. Mussolini is a man, but Hitler is different. He can tell the day this 'spirit' came into him."[19] Considering that most Westerners did not believe in the devil, this Welshman had remarkable insight to concur with what we know today—insight from the Holy Spirit working through biblical paradigms.

At the heart of Howells' ministry was the same bedrock of prayer that had anchored Luther and Blumhardt. He led his college in prayer every evening throughout the war from seven to midnight.

The culmination of this spiritual warfare occurred in the Battle of Britain, when Hermann Göring sent his *Luftwaffe* across the English Channel, bombing England to prepare her for Nazi invasion. During the following days, with bombs exploding everywhere around Wales and south England, Howells journalized:

> The important thing is to find out where God is in this. . . . If God is going to deliver from this hell, there will have to be some power released. . . . If you can believe that you have been delivered from hell, why can't you believe that you have been delivered from air raids? . . . This peace the Saviour gives is not an artificial one. It is so deep that even the devil can't disturb it. You can't hear things in the Spirit, while you have any turmoil or fear in you. You can't take a shade of fear into the presence of God. [20]

On September 12, 1940, the crisis came. Howells wrote in his journal:

> We prayed last night that London would be defended and that the enemy would fail to break through, and God answered prayer. Unless God can get hold of this devil and bind him, no man is safe. If we have protection for our properties, why not get protection for the country? What wonderful days these are. [21]

And two days later:

> Because we have believed, God has made known to us what is to come to pass. Every creature is to hear the Gospel; Palestine is to be regained by the Jews; and the Saviour is to return.[22]

The following day, September 15, just when Göring had victory in his grasp, the *Luftwaffe* mysteriously turned back and gave up their raids. Norman Grubb's chapter on the Battle of Britain concludes with a quote from Air Chief Marshal Lord Dowding, who commanded the battle:

> Even during the battle one realized from day to day how much external support was coming in. At the end of the battle one had the sort of feeling that there had been some special Divine intervention to alter some sequence of events which would otherwise have occurred.[23]

The faith that had prevailed against the *Luftwaffe* continued to guide Rees Howells and his intercessors through Rommel's invasion of Africa, Goebbels' invasion of Russia, the fight for Stalingrad and the culmination of the war. Howells' journals reveal a prayer battle that coincided with a military one—the victory won in prayer *before* it was won militarily. In each case God gave the intercessor the confident insight (or faith) to proclaim victory for the Allies, though it looked hopeless at the time of his assertions.

Faith, Not Knowledge

The human mind has always betrayed a weakness for clever deception. Perhaps that is why Jesus chose unlettered fishermen, not intellectuals, as His disciples.

Jean-Michel Angebert, in *The Occult and the Third Reich*, gets to the bottom of the issue when he contrasts Christian faith with the "knowledge" of the Gnostic "spirit guides" so attractive to New Agers today:

> A philosophy which finds its place within Christianity while claiming to transcend it, Gnosis offers its believers a cosmogony—that is, a conception and an explanation of the universe, material as well as spiritual—an outlook which was bound to attract large numbers of the intellectual elite unsatisfied by the apologetic commentaries on the Gospels. The Gnostics possessed an esoteric knowledge, in contrast to the common "Pistis," or belief of the masses. This true doctrine, as revealed to an elite, was not to be spread among the common people.[24]

The contrast between elite Gnosticism going back to Manes and Zoroaster, and simple Christian faith going back to Christ and the apostles, is never seen more clearly than when we place Hitler side by side with Howells. Which side will win the conflict?

Let Joseph Goebbels, who was responding to his defeat at Stalingrad, give the answer: "Do you realise what has happened? It is a whole school of thought, an entire conception of the universe that has been defeated. Spiritual forces will be crushed, the hour of judgement is at hand."[25]

And so it was—and will be.

What Have We Learned?

The Bible gives us paradigms that we cannot gain except by revelation from the One from above. These paradigms are essential to the survival of the West as we have known it. Science, in its tendency to overstep its bounds, destroyed those paradigms for Europeans during the first half of this century. By accepting brass heaven paradigms, the German Church tied its own hands and became powerless in its struggle against spiritual darkness.

If Lewis Sumberg is right, if "the Nazi nightmare is the most recent but not the final act in a larger human tragedy that is still being played out," then neo-paganism is about to reassert itself throughout the Western world. Let the Church remove her blinders, take up the weapons of her warfare and learn to fight the good fight of faith. Let Christians learn again to respect biblical paradigms. Let us open our eyes to our real enemy, and to the One from above who alone can save us.

Part **3**

Rediscovering
Biblical Paradigms

11

The Nature
of God

Doug: The convocation of scholars at New York University (mentioned in chapter 8) concluded with a story and anguished question from Philip M. Brown, professor of law at Princeton University:

One boy comes to my mind as a sort of type. His father is dying in the hospital. His mother ought to be in the hospital but keeps on for her husband's sake. The boy is compelled to leave college because there are no funds. He is facing a great moral defeat in his own life, and is asking me what is the answer. What can I give him at such a time to enable him to face things?

. . . He revealed to me first of all this deep cry: "Oh, that I knew where I might find [God]," and then told me, "I don't find Him in courses of philosophy, which are destructive and negative and not affirmative. I don't find Him in courses of religion, which are dissecting religion as though it were a dead corpse; I do not find Him in talks about social service and social problems, which tell me that I ought to do this, and that I ought to have education; I do not find Him in humanism; I do not find Him in behaviorism, which teaches me here in this college that we are in a sense irresponsible beings."

Such a student is rising right up and challenging us in our colleges and universities. What have we got to offer him in that great question of his?[1]

The universities lost the power to answer such questions when they divorced themselves from the power of God and began to build the brass heaven.

What Do We Mean by *God?*

It is a conviction of brass heaven philosophy that God is not personal but a system of impersonal laws. A recent issue of *U.S. News & World Report* focused on how Western scientists think about God. Here are comments from two of them:

> If we do discover a complete theory (of everything) . . . we shall all, philosophers, scientists and just ordinary people, be able to take part in the discussion of why it is that we and the universe exist. If we find the answer to that, it would be the ultimate triumph of human reason . . . for then we would truly know the mind of God.[2]

> My feelings about God and the universe have come about entirely through my science. I hesitate to use the word "God," but in my studies of the universe I have come to the conclusion that there is some purpose to it. The universe has organized itself in such a way as to become aware of itself. As conscious beings, we are part of that purpose.[3]

These scientists can relate to God only as a set of laws. If they believe in God, they believe He is a force, not a person. Anthropomorphism, to them, is the chief of sins. As Carl Sagan wrote:

> The idea that God is an oversized white male with a flowing beard who sits in the sky and tallies the fall of every sparrow is ludicrous. But if by "God" one means the set of physical laws that govern the universe, then clearly there is such a God. This God is emotionally unsatisfying. . . . It does not make much sense to pray to the law of gravity.[4]

Sagan may have been referring to the depiction of God on the ceiling of the Sistine Chapel. But Michelangelo painted during the Renaissance, the revival of classical art that deified not God but humanity; and his Sistine ceiling, glorious as it is, was a mock-up for the brass heaven perception of later years. That "oversized white male with a flowing beard" has nothing to do with God.

Those who have encountered the God of the Bible have shied away from pictorializing Him, believing it was sacrilegious and small-minded to do so. When we speak of a personal God, we are not trying to put a nose and two eyes on Him. We speak not of paintings but of paradigms. And the paradigm of the Bible is this: that God is personal. God is three Persons: Father, Son and Holy Spirit.

It is the Church's task not only to tell people that God can be known personally, but to lead them into a firsthand encounter with Him. It is the Church, not the universities, that can and must answer Philip Brown's question. God *can* be known in the midst of our turmoil and agony. We can hear from Him, know His promises, experience His love. "Our fellowship is with the Father and with his Son, Jesus Christ" (1 John 1:3). This was the message of the apostles to the Greeks. It can and must be ours, too.

But how can we, the Church, help people to know God? What can we say to them that the universities and the elite of the West have not said?

How Do We Know Him?

All knowledge is gained through tests of one kind or another. When I was a boy, I wanted to find out what girls were like, so I decided to test out different approaches in talking to girls. Each new girl, I discovered, had a will of her own. Each one required fresh experiments. As I gained knowledge of the sex through many experiments over the years, I finally developed an intimate relationship with one, and came to choose my wife, Carla.

Relationships grow by being put to tests that give us an ever deeper understanding of one another. But these tests are different from scientific experiments. *In relationships we are part of the test. In science we are not.* In science we try to be objective, detached. In relationships, not so.

I remember my first date with Carla. After seeing *The Russians Are Coming* at a local theater, I escorted her back to her dormitory, where she said, "Doug, I have something to say to you. I think I need to say that I'm not really interested in any serious relationships right now."

My heart sank.

I learned later the reason for her statement. Frustrated in her dealings with men, Carla had surrendered to God her concern about men and marriage. She was launching out into an experiment, which included both God and me: self-surrender. She herself was part of this experiment, and her self-surrender, the proving ground. She was becoming an "experimental" Christian.

The result of her experiment? Within two months we were engaged.

Persons are not like objects. We cannot put persons to the test without being involved along with them. If the biblical paradigm is true, that God is an omnipresent Person, then we must approach Him differently than Western scientists approach Him. What the Bible calls knowledge is one thing; what modern Westerners call knowledge is quite another. Western knowledge is *rational*; biblical knowledge (as in the Hebrew word *yada*) is *relational*.

Do we hold rational or relational paradigms? Our unconscious paradigms will already have dictated how we try to know God and what we may have found as a result of our search. But only by discovering the personal God of the Bible will people like the young man Philip Brown described ever find a satisfying answer. The Church must challenge people to put themselves "on the table" and become part of the experiment of faith. This involves an act of self-surrender, without which no one can know God.

God Puts Himself on the Table

God knows that relationships develop through mutual testing. Through the prophet Malachi he says, "Put me to the test" (Malachi 3:10, RSV). On the other hand, Ahaz refused to "put the LORD to the test" (Isaiah 7:12) when God invited him to do so. In these cases and throughout the Bible, God asked His people to put themselves into the laboratory of a relationship with Him. They themselves would be part of a grand experiment.

In certain instances, putting God to the test is inappropriate and offensive. The Hebrews in the wilderness "willfully put God to the test" (Psalm 78:18) and grumbled about many things, threatening to go back to Egypt. This angered God because their "test" was to remove themselves from His laboratory.

During the temptation in the wilderness, Jesus told Satan not to put the Lord to the test. We can see the kind of relationship that exists between Satan and God—no relationship at all. That cold-blooded lizard was fond of proposing tests that he himself was never part of. "Turn these stones into bread," he would say. Or, "Why not jump off the Empire State Building and see what happens? Maybe God will save you."

Satan does not understand relationships. Testing God this way is more the way a scientist approaches God—proposing to put Him under a microscope or heat Him up over a Bunsen burner. You or I would never submit to this approach. No more does God, our Creator, the Master of the universe, who deserves to be treated with the integrity appropriate to His grand and majestic Person.

If we are not to toy with God, neither does He toy with us. Some people believe that God was toying with Abraham the day He asked him to sacrifice Isaac on Mount Moriah. But God did not test Abraham out of idle curiosity. To the contrary, He was asking Abraham to participate with Him in a prophetic drama about God's Son, who would die on Mount Moriah two thousand years later.

Yes, God was testing Abraham. That is how Hebrews describes the event (11:17–19). But for this experiment God placed Himself on the table with Abraham. In the death of Jesus, God showed how personal He wants to be with us. In requiring Abraham to walk through this death with Him, God was inviting the patriarch to enter into His personal grief.

This is the sort of thing the Bible means by "knowing God." As C. S. Lewis described so poignantly in *The Lion, the Witch and the Wardrobe*, Jesus, like Aslan the Lion, put Himself on the table in our place by His death on the cross.

No, God does not allow Himself to be put under a microscope, nor does He look at us that way. The only test He accepts is the test of our lives joined to His by the covenant of Christ's blood.

Knowledge through Surrender

The apostle Paul wrote, "I want to know Christ . . . becoming like him in his death" (Philippians 3:10). The apostle understood that God could be known only by personal surrender—dying with Christ to personal rights and desires. "Give to . . . God what is God's" (Matthew 22:21). Not our coins only, but ourselves, for it is we who have God's image stamped on us.

Dying to our rights and trusting God in self-surrender flies in the face of Western culture. Yet it is the doorway through the brass heaven and into God.

Does the principle of self-surrender hold true in times of desperation? Will it help people who are really suffering, like the student Philip Brown described?

I can think of no grimmer laboratory than a Vietcong prison camp, the setting of a book I read recently entitled *Scars and Stripes*. Navy Captain Eugene "Red" McDaniel was captured by the Vietcong in 1968 and imprisoned for more than five years. In prison he was subjected to severe torture. He was made to hold his arms in the air for hours, was beaten until his flesh was like hamburger, was subjected to electric shock. This treatment went on for weeks. One arm was broken and left untreated.

In the midst of grueling torture, Captain McDaniel went through a crisis of faith, which led to a deep surrender of his life to God. He reflects:

> I knew that if He didn't do something, reveal something of Himself to me, I could not make it. And, in my feeble way again, I said, "Lord, . . . it's all Yours . . . whatever this means, whatever it is supposed to accomplish in me, whatever You have in mind now with all of this, it's all Yours. . . ."
>
> That was all I could say. That was all I had the mental strength to frame. I knew it wasn't much, but I meant it. It was the first time I had ever prayed so straight, so directly, so meaningfully. Whatever "commitment" I had given to Him up until then had never brought from me a prayer of surrender like that. I was totally willing now to accept whatever He had in mind, whereas all the time of my life up to this point had been spent reminding God that I was measuring up to Him and therefore He would make sure I never got beyond my depth.

It was a strange prayer for me, yet so absolutely right—even in my mind that could not fully focus on my words. But there wasn't a lot of time right then to dwell on it, because I was conscious of the guard there, waiting for the next slap. . . . And yet there was something that preoccupied me even in that prayer, something that lifted the weight of fear from me. I didn't know what that prayer was supposed to accomplish for me. Nothing at all miraculous happened, and I wasn't really expecting anything.

But, in the next minute or so, I became aware of the fact that the ropes were being taken off my arms.[5]

As a pastor, I often see the principle of self-surrender as the key to the knowledge of God. A member of my congregation recently reflected on her own experience of self-surrender:

I was always told that I had a strong will. Though I never agreed with this opinion, my red hair was often used as irrefutable evidence— usually by people who were yelling at me and using me as a punching bag. Dad drank. I was abused. At 13, because of the abuse, I was sent to live with other relatives. I swore I'd never go back home. All I wanted was love, happiness and peace.

But I was lonely. I tried, during my teen years, to fill the loneliness with men, hoping to locate one who would give me happiness and security. But the men in my life destroyed my hopes with their own violent and abusive ways. Years passed in a fruitless search for men who would make me happy. On one occasion, I heard God warn me about going too far in a relationship with one of the men in my life, but I ignored the warning. Eventually rejected by that man, who I had thought would marry me, I became depressed and suicidal.

I tried counseling with my pastor. On Wednesday, September 25, 1991, I ran out of a counseling session, sobbing uncontrollably. In my car I was trying to get control of myself when suddenly I heard the still, small voice of God a second time: "Your will or mine?" I was shocked, not only by the nearness of God, but by the implication of what He was saying.

"What, Lord?" I replied, struggling with the suggestion that I had not surrendered my will to Him. I thought I had. But there it was— the reason for my miserable relationships. In a decision of self-surrender, I gave my will to God as deeply and sincerely as I could.

Two days later I met John, a kind, gentle Christian. Within six weeks, he professed his love and asked to marry me. It was as though God had waited for my surrender to Him to begin fulfilling His promises for me.

Not that life was all peaches and cream from then on. During that time my house burned down and all my belongings went up in smoke. But John had a loving church that I felt drawn to be involved with, and one of the members offered free housing while I recovered from the loss of all my worldly belongings. As a result of moving in with them, I distanced myself from my family and was able to get a fresh start with new Christ-centered relationships. Drawn into a healing, caring church, the pain in my life began to heal. Nine months after we met, John and I had a beautiful wedding and honeymoon.

I praise God for His gracious gifts, and above all for helping me surrender my life to Him.

God is known through self-surrender, which is how we develop *any* meaningful relationship.

The Alternative to Deism

During the Enlightenment, an idea floated across the Atlantic Ocean from Descartes' France that "God," whoever or whatever that means, created natural laws and moral laws and then retired from the universe. This idea, deism, applied the method of Descartes to theology.

Treating God as a set of laws was opposed by the churches in the U.S. because it rejected what the Bible said about God. Yet it is an American fad to claim that the founders of our country were all more or less deists. This claim shows how powerfully a worldview can influence our perception of the past, causing us to see what is not there and blinding us from seeing what is. Those who believe in an impersonal God would like to revise history to match their present philosophy.

John Eidsmoe reviewed the faith of our founders in his book *Christianity and the Constitution*. Tracing the beliefs of the delegates to the Constitutional Convention, he found that "at most, Deism was the belief of 3 out of the 55."[6]

The most solidly deistic of these founding fathers, according to Eidsmoe, was Benjamin Franklin, who spent much time in France. In his *Autobiography*, Franklin described how he first got interested in deism:

> Some books against Deism fell into my hands. . . . It happened that they wrought an effect on me quite contrary to what was intended by them; for the arguments of the Deists, which were quoted to be refuted, appeared to me much stronger than the refutations; in short, I soon became a thorough Deist.[7]

But Franklin soured on deism during the course of the Revolutionary War. Although he never returned to the Presbyterian faith of his childhood, he did regain a belief in a personal God, as is reflected in his famous speech to the Constitutional Convention on June 28, 1787:

> In this situation of this assembly, groping, as it were, in the dark to find political truth, and scarce able to distinguish it when presented to us, how has it happened, Sir, that we have not hitherto once thought of humbly applying to the Father of Lights to illuminate our understandings? In the beginning of the contest with Britain, when we were sensible of danger, we had daily prayers in this room for the divine protection. Our prayers, Sir, were heard—and they were graciously answered. . . .
>
> I have lived, Sir, a long time; and the longer I live, the more convincing proofs I see of this truth, that God governs in the affairs of men. And if a sparrow cannot fall to the ground without his notice, is it probable that an empire can rise without his aid? We have been assured, Sir, in the sacred writings that "except the Lord build the house, they labor in vain that build it." I firmly believe this; and I also believe that, without his concurring aid, we shall succeed in this political building no better than the builders of Babel. . . .
>
> I therefore beg leave to move that, henceforth, prayers imploring the assistance of heaven and its blessings on our deliberations be held in this assembly every morning before we proceed to business, and that one or more of the clergy of this city be requested to officiate in that service.[8]

Ben Franklin is an archetype of the Western scientist. His spiritual journey carries weight and meaning beyond its own personal significance. How, then, did that practical, profligate, independent and scientific revolutionary come to change his mind about the nature of God?

The American Revolution had been an experiment of faith in a personal God. It led revolutionaries like George Washington to place themselves on the table with God in places like Valley Forge. By the end of the century it was as plain as day: The American Revolution, born in a Christian milieu, had succeeded. The French Revolution, born out of humanistic deism, had not.

So it was that Ben Franklin, in a request irrational for a deist, recommended prayer.

So What?

What are the implications of the paradigm that God is personal? Science runs on the fuel of predictability. Scientists cling to the hope that even God is discoverable and therefore predictable. All this gets at the purpose behind the brass heaven—bringing our world under our control. (This is also the goal, by the way, of Christian Science, which attempts to show that the spiritual world operates by laws similar to natural laws, and that we are not dealing with a God who has a will of His own.)

Jesus taught, by contrast, that we cannot get away from God's will or reduce God to a set of spiritual laws. "The Son can do nothing by himself; he can do only what he sees his Father doing, because whatever the Father does the Son also does" (John 5:19). Jesus understood that God is personal, that He *does* have a will of His own.

Jesus not only taught but demonstrated the principle of self-surrender. Because He accepted the unpredictable ways of the Father, He had to trust the Father each day, living out the experiment of faith. Of His return at the end of the age, He said, "No one knows about that day or hour, not even the angels in heaven, nor the Son, but only the Father" (Matthew 24:36).

Belief in a personal God, then, moves us in the opposite direction from science. In science we want to control. In Christian faith we relinquish control. In science we want to predict and plan. In Christian faith we surrender our predictions and plans.

During our ministry in Oregon, Carla and I sensed that God was going to move us in ten years to some new ministry. We wanted to follow His leading. In the tenth year, after one false lead, we had a call from Christ Presbyterian Church in Richmond, Virginia.

During a convocation in Dallas that year, I talked with two pastors from Richmond who advised me not to come to this church if I was happy in my present situation. They described the Richmond church as "very troubled."

Though I had been feeling a bit restless in my present church, at least it was stable and happy. So on the plane back to Oregon, I was distressed. The pastors had not told me what I wanted to hear.

What do You want, Lord? I asked.

I want you to be an Apollos, God seemed to say, *to water a church another man has planted.*

At that very moment, the woman in the seat directly behind me, a stranger, read a verse aloud out of her Bible: "I planted the seed, Apollos watered it, but God made it grow."

I was staggered! The passage confirmed my private thoughts! It was obvious that God was making His will known and requiring me to surrender my life to Him all over again. Self-surrender is not, after all, a one-time duty but a never-ending lifestyle.

So, despite the warnings from those pastors, Carla and I moved to Virginia. From the point of view of a sane, rational person seeking career advancement, I had no reason to leave my comfortable church in Oregon for a troubled congregation. But God wanted me to do it for Him and trust Him for the results. I became more deeply an experimental Christian during 1985.

After our move, we found that the warnings had been well-founded. Many of the members, tired of fighting and hurting, began to transfer their membership elsewhere. In a church of only 45 members, every loss was a catastrophe. Because the wealthier members were the first to leave, the bottom dropped out of the church budget. Carla and I asked ourselves a hundred times, "God, why did

You lead us here? Were we mistaken? Was the message about Apollos just a weird coincidence?" Through many desperate times we had to learn to trust God for our ministry and for every penny of our financial support.

In this experiment God was faithful. After a time of sifting the church, He began leading many new people into the congregation. We never wanted for anything we truly needed. In those early years I watered the church through discipleship groups to help people learn self-surrender and the experiment of faith.

Just as I have found God faithful, so have they. We have learned to be experimental Christians together. Never was pastoring so exciting or rewarding! It is easy now to see God's purposes in leading us to Virginia.

Capricious or Kingly?

If there are times God chooses to bless us, there are also times He requires us to endure deprivation and struggle. To believe in a personal God is to accept, as the apostle Paul did, both plenty and want from His hand (Philippians 4:11–12). If God sometimes performs miracles, at other times He takes them away. Then we have to learn that God is not an extension of our own wills and does not always act according to what we think best. As if this were not hard enough, He often leaves us in the dark about His reasons.

Many of God's clearest leadings for me have produced struggle and difficulty. Only later could I see His reasons. Many doors for ministry have opened up for me in Virginia (including the door for this present book) that I believe would never have opened up if we had stayed in Oregon. When closing a door to me, God has always opened a better one later on—but I would not have walked through the latter if the former had not closed!

Many people reject the paradigm of a personal God because they think such a God is capricious. They prefer to speak of Lady Luck. But if God gives us no answers for His silence or unexpected workings, it is not because He is capricious but because He is King.

12

Does God Speak?

Doug: If God is personal, and if He loves us, it is likely that from time to time He will speak to us. Love that never speaks is not love. But the concept of divine conversation has taken a terrible drubbing at the hands of brass heaven builders.

People in the Bible believed that God speaks. They believed, for instance, that "no prophecy of Scripture came about by the prophet's own interpretation. For prophecy never had its origin in the will of man, but men spoke from God as they were carried along by the Holy Spirit" (2 Peter 1:20–21). The apostle Paul wrote, "The gospel I preached is not something that man made up. I did not receive it from any man, nor was I taught it; rather, I received it by revelation from Jesus Christ" (Galatians 1:11–12).

Revelatory dreams, prophecy, visions and personal encounters with God or with messengers of God were, to biblical people, universally accepted paradigms. Behind them all lay the understanding that spiritual beings can talk with us—not only the Spirit of God, but other spirits: spirits of the dead (1 Samuel 28) and angelic and demonic spirits. Most of the books of the Bible were meticulously preserved with the understanding that the Creator had spoken through consecrated vessels—patriarchs, prophets, psalmists and apostles.

Nor did the early Church jettison the prophetic paradigm once "the last apostle died." During the apostolic and post-apostolic period, Church leaders maintained the prophetic paradigm, for they knew that God loves us enough to keep speaking to us.

The Early Church Fathers

The writings of the early Church fathers often refer to a living and active prophetic ministry. In 110 A.D., Ignatius of Antioch (himself a prophet in the Church) wrote,

> We love the prophets because they also have announced the gospel and are hoping in him and waiting for him, by faith in whom they also obtain salvation, being united with Jesus Christ.[1]

The *Didache*, written at about the same time, gave directions about prophecy to regulate its use during public worship:

> Do not test or examine any prophet who is speaking in the Spirit, for every sin shall be forgiven, but this sin shall not be forgiven. But not everyone who speaks in a spirit is a prophet except he have the behavior of the Lord. From his behavior, then, the false prophet and the true prophet shall be known.[2]

The *Didache* shows that prophecy was very much alive in the second century, and that the Church was struggling with how to keep it on the right track. Criteria had to be established to help the Church discern true prophecy from false.

In addition to the criterion of Christian character in the life of the prophet, the early Church noticed that false prophecy was sometimes violently ecstatic, while true prophecy was gentle, peaceable and upbuilding to the Body of Christ. Apollinarios of Hierapolis wrote against Montanus, leader of a cult that appeared late in the second century:

> He gave himself access to the Adversary, became obsessed and suddenly fell into frenzy and convulsions. He began to be ecstatic and to speak and to talk strangely, prophesying contrary to the custom which belongs to the tradition and succession of the church from the beginning.[3]

Apollinarios opposed the Montanists not because they prophesied, but because they prophesied *with violence,* in a manner uncharacteristic of the Holy Spirit. Violent prophecy is often satanic.

Irenaeus of Lyons rejected Montanism for another reason—exclusivity. He wrote of the Montanists,

> They set aside the gift of prophecy from the church. We must conclude that these men cannot admit the Apostle Paul. For in his epistle to the Corinthians he speaks expressly of prophetical gifts, and recognizes men and women prophesying in the church.[4]

Irenaeus opposed Montanism not because Montanists prophesied, but because they claimed that the Montanist prophets were the only true prophets; that prophecy in the rest of the Church was without value. Irenaeus also wrote:

> We do also hear many brethren in the church who possess prophetic gifts, and who through the Spirit speak all kinds of languages, and bring to light for the general benefit the hidden things of men and declare the mysteries of God. . . .[5]

Our point is simply that prophetic gifts did not cease "when the last apostle died." Church leaders sensed God wooing, encouraging, guiding, counseling and correcting them. If they spoke to Him, He also spoke to them.

God Still Speaks

Today the gift of prophecy is not so rare as many Westerners suppose. As I have moved into a walk of faith in a personal God, part of the adventure of this walk has been the unexpected ways God has spoken to me at important turning points in my life.

God Uses Other People

On June 7, 1979, I had just completed a three-day fast for my church in Hillsboro, Oregon. I had moved into my fast out of deep concern for the spiritual state of my congregation. Fasting and prayer were the only ways I could get any peace in the midst of the birth pangs of that struggling young church. I had told no one but my wife that I was fasting.

At the conclusion of the fast, on a Thursday evening, a member of my church named Raylene came to the door unexpectedly and said she had a word for me from the Lord. While I have always been cautious about such claims, Carla and I invited Raylene into our living room and she proceeded to give me a message:

"My son, I have heard your prayers. I have allowed you to go through a deep valley, so that you would know better the valley that Jesus also had to walk through. It is hard for you to see the fruits of your ministry, but even now the trees are beginning to grow buds, and the buds will soon bear flowers and fruit. I have protected the vineyard from those who would cut off the branches. Take heart, for I am leading to you undershepherds who will help you in this work; you will not have to work alone. You may leave for your vacation knowing that I have prepared this time for your renewal and refreshment. When you return, be ready to see your people through new eyes. Allow yourself to be filled with forgiveness and care for each person in your congregation. I will fill you with My love for them."

This word was clearly the answer to the three days of prayer that had preceded it. The one part that was objectively verifiable did come to pass. Within six months God led to us a retired pastor and his wife, Dick and Mary Morgan, who joined me in pastoral ministry. Also, through these words I received God's challenge to open my heart to a broader love—to pastor everyone regardless of theology, openness to the gifts of the Holy Spirit or attitudes toward me.

God Uses Parables

Several months later I experienced another instance of God speaking. I was sitting in my office when a picture came to mind. It was not a vision, just a picture I was casually thinking—a sort of parable. In it I was a gardener watering and caring for the plants in my garden. Then some people came into the garden from outside. They had not studied gardening and, though they were full of good intentions, inadvertently trampled some of the plants.

I understood this to be a parable of my ministry at that church. In particular I was concerned about several young Christians who had come into the congregation and were hurting people.

I told no one about the picture.

The next day Carla and I were in prayer, after which she said to me, "I had the strangest picture come to mind. You were a gardener in a garden. Then some people came into the garden from outside and began to trample on the plants."

That was it—the very same picture!

It was wonderful to know that God was communicating to me about my situation in the church. But why didn't He tell me what to do about these pastoral struggles? I have concluded that God does not always rescue us from our struggles because they mold our character and produce in the end a more mature ministry.

The parable, though devoid of explicit instruction, at least assured me that God was with me in the midst of my pastoring.

God Uses Any of Our Senses

Carla and I attended a General Assembly meeting of our denomination recently to help lead a prayer vigil. On the first night of the Assembly we attended the opening Communion service. But because the chairs did not fit the contour of my back, we left the service early.

On our way out of the assembly hall, we were both greeted by the foulest smell we have ever smelled—the odor of death and rotting flesh. No one else seemed to be aware of it, so it was doubtless an entirely spiritual stench, yet for us it was overpowering. We wondered what on earth could be the cause and meaning of it, and we prayed during the vigil that God would give us insight about it.

Later we shared with other intercessors this unusual experience. Among them God interpreted the stench: "Death is crouching at the door of the Presbyterian Church (U.S.A)."

The intercessors sensed, as in Matthew 24:28, that Satan is brooding over the dying body of our denomination like a vulture, hoping to pick off people from the carcass.

The story of Cain and Abel was given to further elucidate. In this passage Cain gets angry because his gift is not received. But God tells him there is a more basic issue that Cain has not faced up to: the sin that crouches at his door. So with us. Death stalks us when, in our preoccupation with our giftedness, we refuse to deal with our sin, which is of primary concern to God.

The smell of death conveyed to Carla and me the seriousness of our prayer struggle. We were in prayer after that for ten hours a day for six days, much of the vigil overlaid with compassion for the hundreds of homosexuals who had descended on the Assembly, preoccupied with their giftedness.

All this prayer—including the reassurance that Jesus, the Head of the Church, will rescue our denomination—flowed from the prophetic word triggered by the assault on our senses that God gave at the beginning of the vigil.

How Do We Know It Is God?

Brad: It is not easy to discern when we are receiving a word from the Lord and when we are just daydreaming. Discernment, especially in receiving God's guidance, is crucial. Self-deception occurs more frequently than we like to think.

My discernment process goes something like this:

1. I look for inward confirmation: Do I feel an inner peace and conviction that this message reflects God's will and intentions?
2. I check the word against the Scriptures.
3. I look for confirmation from other Christians.
4. I look for confirmation through objective circumstances.
5. Does it give glory to Jesus Christ?

Let me illustrate how this process works. When Laura and I were considering a call to missionary service in Taiwan, I stayed up late one night to pray over the decision. I told God my fears, especially my anxiety about taking Laura, who was pregnant, to a foreign land.

Opening a devotional guide I was using, Oswald Chambers' *My Utmost for His Highest*, I read these words: "Have no fear. If God calls you even to China, He will be with you."

At that I felt an infusion of peace, sensing that China was indeed God's will for us. The next day we accepted the invitation.

But I was still anxious. Being a dyslexic, I had failed in every foreign language I had ever tried to learn—Latin, Spanish, German and Hebrew. What hope had I for learning Chinese? I was tormented with doubt.

One day at a healing conference, the leader asked those who needed healing to come forward for prayer. Laura turned to me and said, "Go forward and ask for healing for your dyslexia." I did.

And as I was going forward, I was enveloped in a warm wave of God's love. I could have resisted, but it was so delicious that I just gave in to it. The next thing I knew, I was resting on the floor. From the midst of God's peace, there came deep in my heart these words: *Do not be afraid to go to Taiwan. I am healing you of your dyslexia enough so that you may learn Chinese.*

Lord, how do I know this is You and that this word is true? I asked.

A year and a half from now, you will stand in a pulpit and preach in Mandarin, came the reply.

This word spoke to my deepest fears and to the woundedness in my life caused by dyslexia. Emboldened by that word from God— a faith experiment that involved me in the testing process!—I undertook the grueling work of language study. A year and a half later, I did stand in a pulpit and preach haltingly in Mandarin!

In our decision to go to China, the Lord also spoke to Laura. (Doug and I have found that God uses our spouses to confirm His guidance and will. In fact, it is dangerous to move forward without that confirmation.) Laura was concerned that the date of her delivery was too close to our departure date.

During a time of intense personal prayer, the Lord spoke these words to her: *Do not be afraid to go to Taiwan. The baby will come early, eight weeks from today.*

This was three weeks early and would give more time to get ready for departure.

Laura asked, "Will the baby be okay?"

The Lord responded gently, *I have perfectly formed the child.*

Laura went into labor eight weeks later to the day. Our daughter Elizabeth was born a beautiful and perfect baby. We went to Taiwan full of the assurances of God.

After a number of years in Taiwan, the Lord spoke to me another specific word of guidance. Because our ministry had been successful, I assumed that God would keep us there for a long time. Yet toward the middle of our second term, there came a restlessness I could not shake. I had the sense that God wanted us to consider new options, but I did not want to hear His wishes, nor my wife's difficulty in living there long-term.

One day a Presbyterian elder offered me a large piece of land for a prayer mountain center in Taiwan. Though it was the answer to many prayers, Laura had no peace about moving to an isolated locale. When I raised the possibility with her, she replied bluntly, "It's a wonderful opportunity, and it may even be from the Lord, but you can do it with your second wife, because I'm not going."

So I went to Jesus Abbey in Korea for a week of prayer to get a "second opinion," fully expecting the Lord to change Laura's heart.

In Korea I found myself caught up in the presence of God. In image after image He showed me my life and preparation for ministry, which included marrying Laura and going to Taiwan. The images continued beyond my present time in Taiwan, showing me a broader scope to my ministry, including the rest of Asia, North America and the world.

Then the Lord said, not in audible words but as a deep knowing in my heart, *You are not to rest in Taiwan. I am calling you to an international ministry of renewal.*

I was overwhelmed. I went down the mountain and shared the word with my mentor, Archer Torrey, director of Jesus Abbey. He confirmed his belief that the word was from God.

I returned to Taiwan and told Laura, who was greatly relieved. Then we just waited to see what the Lord would do next.

Exactly two weeks later came a letter from Brick Bradford, the retiring director of Presbyterian and Reformed Renewal Ministries International, inquiring whether I would consider replacing him in his position. I found out later that my week in prayer was the very same week the board of directors of PRRMI had sought guidance about Brick's successor.

The new guidance was a complete surprise because I had practically no relationship with PRRMI. But through this invitation I am now involved internationally in a ministry of renewal, just as God said.

Scriptural Revelation—God's Ultimate Word

Some Christians do not like to give credence to "words from God." They see (and rightly so) how easily people can be led astray, either by their own thoughts or by unscrupulous "prophets" claiming to have a word from God.

The easiest way to guard against these dangers is to claim that prophecy and revelation ceased long ago, that God does not speak anymore. This idea is the logical outgrowth of deism and the brass heaven.

But the Bible tells us not to despise prophecies or hinder the prophetic gifts (1 Thessalonians 5:19–20). The Scriptures are not an exclusive outpouring of God's spoken love, but are the measuring stick by which all prophetic words must be tested.

Doug and I can affirm that our own experience of prophecy, far from detracting from the authority of the Bible, has given us a deeper respect for it by confirming the paradigm of Holy Spirit inspiration. This paradigm has dramatically changed our view of the Bible since seminary days, when we learned to scrutinize the Bible under the harsh and glaring light fixtures of the brass heaven.

13

The Bible
under the Brass Heaven

Doug: Late in the nineteenth century, Westerners brought the Bible under the brass heaven. Beginning in Germany, scholars began a grand experiment—to place the Bible (along with almost everything else under the sun) under the microscope of science. The biblical experiment was labeled "higher criticism" to distinguish it from "lower criticism," the study of biblical texts and languages.

The name itself is revealing. It shows the growing conviction that Westerners had finally attained a higher, surer way of knowing. Planting our feet on solid scientific ground, we could extract from the ancient writings a few facts available to the trained, objective scholar.

Higher criticism was another wing added to the glass-and-brass dome of the Western worldview.

Higher Criticism and Prophecy

The advent of higher criticism brought a major shift in Christian epistemology. Let's review. During the Puritan era, the Westminster divines had written, "The infallible rule of interpretation of Scripture is the Scripture itself; and therefore, when there is a question about the true and full sense of any Scripture (which is not manifold, but one), it may be searched and known by other places that speak more clearly."[1] The Bible was respected above the revelations of science and of nature.

Later, as science came into its own, a mutual regard emerged between the two ways of knowing. *All truth is God's truth* was the motto of the nineteenth century. Universities flourished, most of them founded by Christians eager to discover the truth in God's creation by the methods of Descartes. General revelation (God's revelation of Himself through the creation) and special revelation (God's revelation of Himself through Scripture) were equally appreciated.

But by the twentieth century, special revelation became a doubtful way of attaining truth. Science eclipsed divine revelation. By it we could critique from a high position the sacred writings; thus, "higher criticism."

This faith in scientific methods brought a new skepticism into Western faith. The former acceptance of all things biblical was called naïve. Did Jesus believe that Moses wrote the Torah? Now (it was said) we know better. Does the Bible speak of miracles of healing, the presence of demonic powers around us, resurrections of bodies and virgin births? Only the naïve would believe stories like that. We are children no longer. We must be honest to God.

Trust in Enlightenment philosophy led ultimately to two separate (and unsuccessful) quests for the historical Jesus—to see if any basis existed for knowing what Jesus actually did or said. All this resulted from a devout refusal to believe the testimony of credible witnesses.

The problem, of course, is that the processes of divine revelation are not available for scientific study. The higher critic, trying to escape the implications of this fact, insists that divine revelation could not happen but by natural laws. He or she has already rejected the paradigm of prophecy as the Jews accepted it. The modern scholar says, "Natural causes are what our science can study. A thinking person can believe in nothing else. If the Holy Spirit inspired these writings, He did so by natural laws working through purely human authorship."

Modern scholars do not write eloquently of the spirit of prophecy, nor of Jesus, the One from above who conveyed truth into the natural world from outside it. No, modern scholars speak of more mundane things—the vocabulary content of Ephesians as against Thessalonians, or the presence or absence of Egyptian concepts in the Pentateuch. They focus on human authorship and human cultures because these influences can be studied scientifically. Divine influences are beyond science and are not a focus of the brass heaven experiment.

But brass heaven surgical lights distort proper interpretation of the written Word of God, and that brass heaven philosophy is an inadequate basis for interpreting the Bible—for three reasons.

Higher Criticism Does Not Give Us Objective Knowledge

First, the methods of Descartes have not given us a knowledge as secure as mathematics. The ideas proposed by higher criticism have wandered all over the map, with one generation of scholars proposing one idea as fact and the next proposing its opposite.

When brass heaven hermeneutics was young, for instance, it was popular to assert that the Pentateuch (the first five books of the Bible) was a product of oral tradition. Scholars maintained that written language had not been invented until a thousand years after Abraham. Whether this idea was true or false was not the issue. The oral tradition paradigm caught on because scholars wanted to build their own wing onto the geodesic dome. German scholars like Herman Gunkel (*The Legends of Genesis*) treated the stories of Genesis as 98% non-historical. The mighty acts of God became the exaggerations of superstitious, primitive and *talkative* Hebrews.

We can now see, however, that it was Western scholars who were exaggerating—exaggerating their own rational powers. It would have been better if they had admitted that they did not know when written language was invented or how the Bible came to be written. Further research soon put the lie to the earlier theories; and the discovery of the Ebla library, dating from 2,000 years before Abraham, squashed them completely. Yet the next generation, still confident of the brass heaven experiment, proposed new theories, such as the documentary hypothesis (which says that the writings are first-millennium documents woven together by an editor).

E. B. Smick of Gordon-Conwell Theological Seminary summarizes the effect of this hermeneutic in an article on the Pentateuch:

> Modern Pentateuchal criticism is based on philosophical presuppositions that rule out the possibility of God's supernatural intervention in history. This results in an attempt to explain away not only Mosaic authorship but all supernatural events recorded in these books.

After reviewing the many brass heaven theories about how these books originated, Professor Smick concludes:

> Despite all of this divergence of opinion, the modern critical approach to the Pentateuch still clings generally to the terminology of the old documentary hypothesis, simply because the modern critic has nothing else to take its place as a humanistic explanation of how these books came into being.[2]

We could offer dozens of examples of early higher critical theories demolished by subsequent evidence, leading to new theories. The result of such backpedaling by the scholarly community has been a loss of confidence in the epistemology on which these statements are made. Descartes may have been looking for truth as secure as mathematics, but the West is losing confidence in this vision.

Biblical scholarship is not alone in this loss of confidence. It is part of a broad paradigm shift into postmodernity (see chapter 19). In the newer, postmodern worldview, science is only one of many voices to be weighed in discerning truth. This shift is bound to affect biblical hermeneutics.

Higher Criticism Distorts and Erodes Biblical Faith

A second reason to reject higher criticism as a biblical hermeneutic is this: The assumption that God does nothing except by natural law does not square with paradigms held by biblical writers, who believed in the power of God quite apart from natural law. Higher critical exegesis, therefore, is really eisegesis—distorted interpretation.

Isaiah

Take, for instance, the prophecies of Isaiah. Isaiah was forthright about the nature of his writings, purporting that they were a revelation from God given without the benefit of natural law:

> "The former things I declared of old,
>   they went forth from my mouth and
>   I made them known:
>   then suddenly I did them and they
>   came to pass.
> Because I know that you are obstinate,
>   and your neck is an iron sinew
>   and your forehead brass. . . .
> "You have heard; now see all this;
>   and will you not declare it?
> From this time forth I make you hear
>   new things,
>   hidden things which you have not
>   known.
> The are created now, not long ago;
>   before today you have never heard
>   of them,
>   lest you should say, 'Behold, I knew
>   them.'"
>   Isaiah 48:3–4, 6–7, RSV

Isaiah believed he was a vessel of revelation and that God Himself was giving him a series of messages by prophetic inspiration.

Until about a century ago, Christians accepted the prophetic paradigm. Most Christians believed that, just as Isaiah had predicted the demise of the Assyrian king Sennacherib (a death confirmed and described by the historian Herodotus) and prophesied to King Hezekiah that he had nothing to fear from Nebuzaradan, Isaiah had also prophesied the birth and death of Jesus that would take place six hundred years later.

Yet these prophecies became anathema to brass heaven scholars, who proposed an imaginary author, "Deutero-Isaiah," who must have written chapters 40–66 in post-exilic times. Otherwise, they observed, we would have to believe that (among other impossibilities) Isaiah wrote of Cyrus of Persia long before Cyrus was born. Among the higher critics, the message "I will tell you of new things, of hidden things unknown to you" falls on disbelieving ears and on foreheads of brass.

The Messiah

The Jews at the time of Jesus believed that their Scriptures prophesied the coming of a Messiah. As Alfred Edersheim wrote,

> The ancient Synagogue found references to the Messiah in many more passages of the Old Testament than those verbal predictions, to which we generally appeal. . . . Their number amounts to upwards of 456 . . . and their Messianic application is supported by more than 558 references to the most ancient Rabbinic writings.[3]

Higher criticism has been reducing those 456 Messianic prophecies to zero. It is not that these scholars disbelieve in Jesus the Messiah. Many are sincere Christians whose personal beliefs range from liberal to conservative. But they are Westerners who have adopted the Western worldview. Predictive prophecies of Christ, given four to seven centuries before Christ, are a thorn in their worldview.

Daniel

The book of Daniel provides another illustration of the distortion that higher criticism brings to the Bible. In the days of the apostolic fathers, the Church was opposed by Greek philosophers, such as the neo-Platonist Porphyry.

Platonic philosophy, even in its most Christianized form, was based on the hope that people could save their own souls through the power of thought. Porphyry believed he had attained union with God once, when he was 68. Discerning the difference between Christianity and Platonism on the power issue, Porphyry wrote fifteen books entitled "Against the Christians."

Among the efforts of Porphyry to discredit Christianity was his attempt to reinterpret the book of Daniel. The Old Testament scholar

Roland K. Harrison summarizes Porphyry's treatment of the book of Daniel (emphasis added):

> His objections to the traditional view were based on the a priori supposition that there could be no predictive element as such in prophecy. Hence the predictions in Daniel relating to post-Babylonian kings and wars were not really prophecies so much as historical accounts, and therefore of a late date. In assigning the work to the time of Antiochus IV Epiphanes, Porphyry held that the author of Daniel had lied so as to revive the hopes of contemporary Jews in the midst of their hardships. . . .
>
> This view has been reflected in one way or another ever since in rationalistic attacks upon Daniel. The shallowness of its basic philosophical pre-supposition is readily apparent from even a casual perusal of OT prophetic literature, where *the speakers not only dealt with contemporary events but also pronounced upon happenings in the future,* some of which had no particular relationship to the circumstances of their own time. The reason for this, stated simply, is that the Hebrew prophets would have had little sympathy for the modern antithesis between forthtelling and foretelling, if only because of the fact that, *for them, the future was inherent in the present in a special revelational manner.*[4]

Until recently, most Christians believed that the book of Daniel prophesied Christ at three points: Daniel 2:44–45, 7:13–27 and 9:24–27. Augustine, in *The City of God*, wrote that Daniel had predicted the exact date Christ was to commence His ministry. This date was calculated from Daniel 9:24–27, the passage beginning with "seventy weeks" (KJV), to be 483 years after the decree that allowed Ezra to return from exile in 458 B.C.—or the year A.D. 26, the year Jesus was anointed by John the Baptist.[5]

This assumption was commonly held through the nineteenth century, when Joseph A. Seiss wrote the introduction to the popular *Biblical Illustrator* commentary on Daniel. Seiss called Porphyry's theory, and that of its modern proponents, "unbelieving criticism," not "higher criticism."[6]

But already scholars like S. R. Driver and H. H. Rowley were reexamining the book of Daniel under the artificial lighting of the brass heaven. References to a coming Messiah in Daniel were found unacceptable as prophecies of Jesus. Porphyry's explanation of the book of Daniel—that it was written by a "false writer" at the time of Antiochus IV—seemed to these scholars a more understandable scenario. They could understand it by the laws of nature. Porphyry's views seemed more rational than the traditional Christian view, which seemed naïve and unscholarly. Higher critical scholars thus adopted Porphyry's idea that the "Messiah" of Daniel was Judas Maccabeus, not Jesus.

In order to make the theory stick, they had to interpret Nebuchadnezzar's dream of Daniel 2 to identify the "fourth kingdom, strong as iron" as the Seleucid empire, not the Roman Empire of Jesus' day. This was made possible by treating the Medo-Persian Empire as two empires, not one.

But the parallel prophecy of Daniel 8 does not permit such an interpretation. The "ram" of Daniel 8:3 symbolizes the Medo-Persian empire and the "goat" of Daniel 8:5 is the Greek empire of Alexander. These two empires correspond to the "silver" and "bronze" parts of the statue mentioned in Daniel 2:32. The fourth kingdom of Daniel 2:36–43 must therefore refer to the Roman Empire—during which Jesus was born, whose kingdom "will crush all those kingdoms and bring them to an end" (verse 44). In Daniel 2 God was preparing Jewish culture for King Jesus.

Yet this view has been only a minority view among modern scholars. So we find ourselves in a strange and unexpected twist of circumstances. As to prophecy, modern scholars today teach just what the enemies of the Church taught in post-apostolic times. Does this seem like a wholesome trend?

Higher Criticism Has Diseased the Church

A third reason to reject higher criticism as a biblical hermeneutic is that it does not recognize spiritual discernment; it recognizes only rational analysis—in contrast to the decisions of the apostolic fathers, for example, as to which writings among those then circulating in the Church were genuine and helpful to Christian faith.

Their decisions about the New Testament canon were based on their belief in revelation—God giving the apostles His promises and commands. The Church felt, based on this paradigm, that it had a "sure anchor to the soul." Jesus, the One from above, had spoken not as the scribes and Pharisees, but with divine authority. Because He had revealed His truth to certain credible witnesses, the Church could be "built on the foundation of the apostles and prophets" (Ephesians 2:20).

Even so, the authority of the writings was not based on simple human authorship or the authority of the eyewitness. The apostle Paul had been neither a disciple of Jesus nor an eyewitness of the resurrection. The book of Hebrews was written by an unknown author, and for that reason was put to more rigorous tests than other books. Yet Paul's writings and the book of Hebrews were accepted by virtue of the spiritual, not rational, discernment of the Church. These writings were recognized for their authority to tell us who Jesus is and what He promises and requires of us. Without this authority, there is no basis for the discipling work of the Church.

Paul tells the Ephesians, for example (or rather, the Church at large, to whom Ephesians was written):

> In reading this, then, you will be able to understand my insight into the mystery of Christ, which was not made known to men in other generations as it has now been revealed by the Spirit to God's holy apostles and prophets. . . .
> I became a servant of this gospel by the gift of God's grace given me through the working of his power. Although I am less than the least of all God's people, this grace was given me: to preach to the Gentiles the unsearchable riches of Christ. . . .
>
> Ephesians 3:4, 7–8

This claim of Paul matches his claims in other writings, like Galatians. While some challenged that claim, the early Church accepted it by virtue of spiritual discernment.

But higher critical scholarship neither recognizes nor understands spiritual discernment. Based on the power and authority of the rational mind, it boldly questions the authorship of all biblical writings. Ephesians is no exception. While few today question the Pauline origins of Ephesians, brass heaven scholars have often done so in the past, under the assumption that science bestows the right to question not only the apostles but the judgment of the apostolic fathers of the Church.

Under this hermeneutic, all the books of the Bible are to be treated as spurious if their apostolic authorship cannot be "proven." This assumption places great faith in science as capable of proving such things, and casts a pall of doubt around everything biblical.

What is the point of these higher critical debates if, in the end, God asks us to accept these writings as His Word regardless? Perhaps the answer should be obvious, but it is not.

Higher Criticism and Signs and Wonders

The spirit of prophecy is only one of the ways God has impinged on this world. He has also impacted us in signs and wonders, or what brass heaven proponents call "miracles." Signs and wonders are an offense to higher critical scholarship.

Nothing is more basic to Christian faith than the incarnation of Christ—what C. S. Lewis called the Grand Miracle. Yet the Grand Miracle, like all miracles, does not fit under the brass heaven. No matter how basic to Christian faith, every alleged work of God is jettisoned by scholars under the brass heaven, who reject the incarnation by rejecting the virgin birth—the process by which Jesus became a man. The virgin birth has been chiseled away not only by a few scholars of the radical fringe, but by the most respected of denominational scholars. Here is William Barclay, for instance, in his popular *Daily Study Bible*:

> The Virgin Birth is a doctrine which presents us with many difficulties; and it is a doctrine which our Church does not compel us to accept in the literal and the physical sense. This is one of the doctrines on which the Church says that we have full liberty to come to our own belief and our own conclusion.[7]

How is the virgin birth to be accepted, if not in the "physical" and "literal" sense? Either Jesus was born of a virgin or He was not. If we do not believe that He was conceived by the Holy Spirit in the womb of Mary, surely it is because we have built the same brass heaven over Mary that we have built over ourselves. We have taken a superior attitude toward the "miraculous" and we cannot make exceptions, not even for Jesus.

This is only one of hundreds of examples that we could look at about the offense of the power of God in the modern Western mind. Brass heaven scholarship produces unbelief by making unbelief seem higher than belief. Because of this, the legacy of higher criticism has diseased Christian faith in God's mighty acts. Higher criticism accepts the ethics of science, which encourages doubt, not faith, whereas God's Word teaches that "everything that does not come from faith is sin" (Romans 14:23).

A Hundred Years of Kitchen Analysis

The confidence we place in the paradigms of the Enlightenment has led to what J. Arthur Baird calls "the Bultmannian captivity of the Church." What is wrong with the freedom to doubt everything? Shouldn't we milk it for all it is worth? What are the dangers of applying scientific skepticism to biblical material?

The clearest impact of this scholarship on the Church was described by Baird in his book *Rediscovering the Power of the Gospel*:

> When a Christian minister stands up in the pulpit and reads from the Gospels, "And Jesus said . . .", and a small voice within replies, "Oh yes? Isn't this the word of the early church that cannot be relied upon?" then the power of the proclamation of the Holy Word goes out of his or her message. Not only are they in agony because of this intellectual-spiritual tension, but their parishioners also recognize that something is lacking.[8]

Not only is our confidence in Jesus Himself undermined, but our confidence in all biblical material. Science treats New Testament material no differently than the Pseudapigrapha or the Gnostic gospels, since higher critics, following one of Descartes' most basic principles, refuse to accept anything from previous authorities. Though the apostolic fathers long ago resolved the issue of the genuineness and helpfulness of the writings to the Church, higher critical scholars are forever questioning their judgment. Most lay people cannot understand how Christian scholars can accuse biblical writers of blatant deception, but it happens so frequently that they have grown accustomed to it. We need to gain a rational understanding of the Scriptures, but not at the expense of faith in the power of God and the straightforward statements of the Bible.

Critics have swarmed into God's kitchens to examine the way the food was prepared. They have "objectively" observed the chopping, sifting, baking and broiling of every dish from Genesis to Revelation. But in observing each slice of the knife, they fail to appreciate the transformation of the ingredients into a *pièce de résistance*. They see the tools but miss the art; see the hands but miss the heart. Western Bible scholars have, by and large, forgotten their calling—to tell us where the finest restaurant in the world can be found. We need scholars enlightened not only by science but by faith; not only by the analysis of the rational mind but by the longing of the human spirit. We need more Alfred Edersheims who have feasted on God's food and are willing to let their faith affect their scholarship.

Higher criticism will never produce such scholars. According to its most cherished assumptions, faith pollutes and dilutes fact. Science discerns no difference between faith and superstition. Science still believes in objectivity. It has placed its confidence not in God but in the power of the rational mind. This is its idolatry.

If higher critical scholarship had produced a prospering Church, we might still support it. But the experiment has cut the Church off from her root, and now the branches are dying. Look at the Church in the countries of the Great Reformation, where higher critical scholarship has taken over the seminaries. Charles Colson summarized the present state of the Church in Europe:

> Church attendance is 4 percent in . . . Germany, Scandinavia, and Austria. In France regular attendance at Mass is below 15 percent, while in Spain it has dropped to between 3 and 5 percent. And in England, site of the great nineteenth-century awakening and home of missionary movements, more people worship in mosques than in the Church of England.[9]

A hundred years of kitchen analysis have done nothing for the appetite.

"Jesus Is the Sun. The Bible Is the Moon."

Today we hear it said that "the Bible is not the Word of God; Jesus is." This cliché says less about our faith in Jesus than about our declining respect for the written Word. It masks the dishonoring of the Bible as the honoring of Christ. "If Jesus is the Sun of Righteousness," it says, "then the Bible is but a moon. It has no light of its own; it is dead. Revelationless. It has no power, nothing divine lodged within its pages. The day of the oracle has passed. In fact, there was no oracle to begin with."

Although the reaction against bibliolatry that has driven some to accept this teaching is valid, few Western Christians are in danger of bibliolatry. In decrying that cesspool, we have fallen headlong into the quicksand of unbelief. More and more our doctrine defines the Scriptures as *the words of people*. How they are the *Word of God* becomes the debatable point.

But the two revelations (Jesus and the written Word) complement each other. On the one hand, Jesus came to fulfill the Law and the prophets; all the promises of God find their *Yes* in Him. On the other, Jesus verified the writings as the expressions of Him whose thoughts are not our thoughts, whose ways are not our ways. There is a symbiotic relationship between Jesus and the Bible. Each validates the other. They are earth and tree. Without the earth, the tree does not stand. Without the tree, the earth lies barren. How then can we say that the Bible is not the Word of God?

The Demise of Brass Heaven Thinking

As our culture moves out from under a brass heaven worldview, the assumptions behind higher critical scholarship must collapse. Fewer and fewer Westerners are embarrassed about prophecy, angels, demons, miracles and spiritual power. As distasteful as this must be to an older generation, a newer generation will explore the Bible in light of postmodern paradigms that no longer outlaw the spiritual manifestations that produced the Bible.

God is moving us on from higher criticism, as the following vignette from John White (which occurred in 1985 during a John Wimber seminar in Vancouver) demonstrates:

Wimber had spoken of pastors who in the face of critical scholarship had watered down the biblical content of their preaching, thus robbing the sheep of truth. He then invited any pastors who felt convicted by God of such sin, and who wished to renounce it and preach the truth, to come forward for prayer. A large number responded. Some of these spontaneously began to weep. I stood very close to the group and estimated that about one in seven was affected in this way.[10]

The sin of the Enlightenment was this: We believed that our minds were more authoritative than the word of the One from above who sealed His testimony with His blood. We questioned the word of the prophets and apostles of the Church, who also died as martyrs for the sake of their testimony. Delighted with our liberation from authority, we questioned every credible witness God ever gave us. If their testimony came at great cost to them? No matter. They were just primitive and simple people of little importance to us moderns.

Now we must go back to basics. Do we believe in *rational* or *relational* knowledge? The knowledge paradigm we accept will determine our approach to the Bible and its fruitfulness to us. Jesus said, "My teaching is not my own. It comes from him who sent me. If anyone chooses to do God's will, he will find out whether my teaching comes from God or whether I speak on my own" (John 7:16–17). We discover a fruitful biblical hermeneutic when we put ourselves on the table with God and live by faith in Him. Luther's hermeneutic works. Bultmann's does not.

Jesus, the One from above, revealed to us the intricacies of the spirit realm and of God's will. We can deal successfully with spiritual realities because He came and showed us how. Here is the value of the Bible: It supplies the most effective and relevant paradigms available to us—Westerners and Easterners alike.

14

How Can We Become Moral Again?

Doug: During the 1930s a dramatic shift in moral philosophy occurred throughout the West. At that time Western culture departed from the Bible as an ethical guide, largely because of bitter sectarianism created by those who quoted the Bible most loudly.

Elmer Ellsworth Brown, reflecting on the course of public education, expressed his frustration:

> So long as religion is predominantly sectarian, it may not expect to regain its ascendancy over the institutions and the methods of education. Universal education gravitates toward universal knowledge and toward universally recognized forms of thought. The partial and unprevailing view of any party or sect is not at home in public schools, even though it be a view which shall eventually lead the world. Religion in its modern relations, sectarian religion, is a breeder of disturbance in those national systems of education. . . . Disturbance is often wholesome, but not disturbance of this kind; for it is full of bitterness, and often it appeals to simple prejudice.[1]

Dr. Brown, a Christian, was grieved by denominational feuding over the Bible. He, like most of his generation, looked to science to help Christians and non-Christians alike find an objective basis for truth and ethics:

Scientific education teaches men to follow truth for the sake of truth, in the full conviction that human interests and clear truth must in the end be one. In its pure devotion to truth, natural science is moral, unswervingly moral. . . .

The most vital meeting place for education and religion in this age is on the moral plane. Through its new emphasis on moral conceptions, education itself, secular education if you would call it such, may help religion to work its way through and overcome its present-day sectarianism. . . . Pure devotion to truth is found in both religion and science.[2]

Yet the hope that science would provide a clean foundation of truth from which to arrive at moral consensus has led to a frustrating and disappointing search. It was, after all, Sigmund Freud, not William James, to whom the West turned for answers, whose influence on morals in the West was truly cataclysmic.

Ethical Shipwreck

Freud chose to redefine and rename the conscience. He called it *superego* since the word *conscience* had too many spiritual and religious overtones. He wanted to remove morals from the province of an "illusory" God. Ethics, he taught, is a function of the human psyche, the result of mere cultural conditioning, and has nothing to do with God. The superego is nothing more than a psychological storage bin for parental moralizing in the brain, the "internal parent."

Many other theorists, like those of the Transactional Analysis school, followed hard on the heels of Freud to cement this notion as a Western paradigm. As universities laid hold of this teaching, the concept of conscience was discarded. Freud's analysis of human nature seemed more scientific than the idea of conscience; and *superego* replaced *conscience* as a way to describe our perception of right and wrong.

But Freud's concepts came not from research but from the brass heaven worldview. Psychologists have located no superego lobe of the brain. Nor is there a locus for morals as there is for dreams, left-handedness or logic. In his switch from conscience to superego,

Freud was constructing the base for a new ethic atop Descartes' foundation.

All American universities prior to the time of Freud offered a senior-year course on moral philosophy. This course was commonly seen as the most important part of a student's preparation for adult life. Even deists believed that we have a conscience that measures moral laws woven into the universe by God. C. S. Lewis described this older paradigm:

> We have two bits of evidence about the somebody. One is the universe He has made. . . . The other bit of evidence is that Moral Law which He has put into our minds. And this is a better bit of evidence than the other, because it is inside information. You find out more about God from the Moral Law than from the universe in general, just as you find out more about a man by listening to his conversation than by looking at a house he has built.[3]

The replacement of *conscience* with *superego* as a Western paradigm has caused enormous problems. What the apostle Paul warned of has now happened in a massive way: ". . . Some have rejected [faith and a good conscience] and so have shipwrecked their faith" (1 Timothy 1:19).

Christina Hoff Sommers, associate professor of philosophy at Clark University, shows us where this more "scientific" search for morality has led us:

> It is impossible to deny that there is a great deal of moral drift. The students' ability to arrive at reasonable moral judgments is severely, even bizarrely, affected. A Harvard University professor annually offers a large history class on the Second World War and the rise of the Nazis. Some years back, he was stunned to learn from his teaching assistant that the majority of students in the class did not believe that anyone was really to blame for the Holocaust. The graduate assistant asserted that if these Harvard students were sitting in judgment at Nuremberg they would have let everyone off. No one was to blame. In the students' minds, the Holocaust was like a natural cataclysm: it was inevitable and unavoidable. The professor refers to his students' attitude about the past as "no-fault history."[4]

Sommers goes on to quote philosopher Alasdair MacIntyre who has said that we may be raising a generation of "moral stutterers." Others refer to "moral illiteracy." Education consultant Michael Josephson says, "There is a hole in the moral ozone."

That such confusion should prevail at Harvard University is a bitter irony, since Harvard once was home to William James, who conveyed his lectures on *The Varieties of Religious Experience* to an Edinburgh audience just prior to World War I. He said:

> The lustre of the present hour is always borrowed from the background of possibilities it goes with. Let our common experiences be enveloped in an eternal moral order; let our suffering have an immortal significance; let Heaven smile upon the earth, and deities pay their visits; let faith and hope be the atmosphere which man breathes in;— and his days pass by with zest; they stir with prospects, they thrill with remoter values. Place round them on the contrary the curdling cold and gloom and absence of all permanent meaning which for pure naturalism and the popular-science evolutionism of our time are all that is visible ultimately, and the thrill stops short, or turns rather to an anxious trembling.[5]

William James prophesied only too accurately the "curdling" effect that popular science was about to have on the whole moral tone of Western culture. James believed that religious experience is a big slice of life and should be treated as a subject of scientific inquiry, rather than passed over as myth and illusion.

But the West was not interested in William James. It was too fascinated with Sigmund Freud and his brass heaven psychology.

The Scientist as Moral Guardian

Let's look at the result, in the area of ethics, of this drastic and unfortunate choice. Has science helped us find a better moral footing?

Most observers in other parts of the world comment that Western nations are consumed with male animal lust leading to violence against women. Today we lack even the cautious and prudent self-awareness of the ancient Stoic and Epicurean philosophers, who would teach us to lust moderately or not at all. We jump with our whole bodies into self-gratification as even the Greeks recoiled from doing. This all-consuming passion exploits women and devours the men and women who surrender to it. Women violated by rape and incest build prisons of bitterness and belligerence against the men who have violated them. An iron-hard feminism, different from that which once gained our sympathies, has overtaken the West.

How did this situation develop?

Prior to the turn of the last century, Christian moral values based on biblical convictions prevailed. Jesus taught what most men do not like to hear—that "anyone who looks at a woman lustfully has already committed adultery with her in his heart" (Matthew 5:28). One of Jesus' apostles warned us about the lust of the eyes as a power that can draw us away from God (1 John 2:16).

But as science established itself as the new arbiter of truth during the middle decades of this century, new ideas about sexual morality were entertained and propagated. Jimmy Carter became a laughingstock, in his widely publicized interview with *Playboy*, when he quoted Jesus' words about lust and "committing adultery in my heart."

Researchers in the 1960s claimed (based on Freudian concepts of sexual repression) that pornography harms no one and that it is a safety valve to release sexual tension. Berl Kutchinsky, criminologist at the University of Copenhagen, completed a study on pornography and sex crimes in which he claimed that when Denmark legalized pornography, sexual assault decreased. This study was acclaimed throughout the West and influenced American attitudes about pornography already loosened up by the famous Kinsey report.

Traditional Christian sexual ethics were said to be puritanical and unreasonable. Science had proven traditional values wrong. And since science is based on knowledge, Christian moral values could safely be set aside. Our culture eased its vigilance against pornography, allowing Hugh Hefner and others to build their empires.

Today the porn industry has sunk its teeth deeply into America. Americans relaxed their vigilance because researchers convinced them there was no harm in it. The decision was a triumph of the new epistemology. Today many Westerners tolerate and indulge in pornography because science has become her arbiter of morals.

Whoops! Maybe We Made a Mistake

Since the time of Kutchinsky, dozens of studies have shown that Jesus' warnings were right after all. Studies completed at Queens University and at the Massachusetts Treatment Center for Sexually Dangerous Persons have shown a consistent relationship between pornography and sex crimes. Not only does pornography not act as a safety valve; it encourages men to act out increasingly perverse fantasies. A study by the Delancey Street Foundation in San Francisco, based on interviews with sexually victimized prostitutes, found that 24 percent of these women said their attackers had specifically mentioned porn as they raped them. According to a University of New Hampshire study, states that have a high rate of porn readership also have a high rate of sex offenses.

One team of researchers, Zillman and Bryant, studied the effect of pornography on moral values. Their work is described in an article by Mark Hartwig of Focus on the Family:

> They found that people exposed to nonviolent pornography reported diminished satisfaction with their sexual partner's physical appearance, affection, curiosity and sexual performance. Those exposed to pornography also were inclined to put more importance on sex without emotional involvement.
>
> . . . People exposed to pornography are far more likely to accept premarital and extramarital sex. They also tolerate infidelity in their own relationships, view suppressing promiscuity as unhealthy, and devalue the importance of marriage. They were also far less likely to want their own children, especially daughters.[6]

Science, then, has reversed itself. We may ask what happened to Descartes' idea of a knowledge as secure as mathematics. How could scientists say one thing in the '70s and turn around and say the opposite in the '90s? The answer, once again, is that science is influenced by cultural paradigms and market forces. As Paul Kuhn wrote in his book *The Structure of Scientific Revolutions*, unconsciously held paradigms guide all scientific research. In the area of sexual ethics, science is not the objective basis for morals that we hoped it would be.

Also, it is virtually impossible for science to prove with certainty cause-and-effect relationships, such as "harm" as the basis for unethical behavior. The best science can offer is a "strong correlation"—in this case, between porn and sex crimes. Those who want to protect porn will always be able to squeak out from under the "knowledge" of scientific studies. As Mark Hartwig wrote in the article referred to above:

> As with studies of pornography consumption and rape, research on sex offenders and their victims can never prove that pornography actually causes rape and abuse, and so pornographers continue to claim that pornography is harmless. In this, they resemble the tobacco industry lobbyists, who steadfastly maintain that science has not yet proven that tobacco smoke causes cancer. Both invoke an unreasonable standard of proof to deny the obvious; that their products cause harm.[7]

Sexual violence and perversions have been increasing dramatically. Science opened Pandora's box but has not the power to put the demons of lust safely away again. Intelligence cannot tame our basic instincts. Augustine was right; Freud was wrong. And behind the decay of morals and the hardening of battle lines between the sexes lie more basic questions: Where can we find reliable knowledge to guide us through life? Wouldn't it have been better if we had kept listening to Jesus all along? Doesn't the tree of life instruct us better than the tree of the knowledge of good and evil?

Following Conscience or Libido?

Some twenty years ago I was walking by a pornography shop when a powerful inclination overcame me to go inside. My mind gave me all kinds of Freudian arguments—rational ideas I had learned during nine years of higher education about not repressing my libido. My spirit—my conscience—was giving me powerful messages in the opposite direction, conveying violent intuitions, destroying my peace, making my stomach churn. Yet I had learned over the years to set aside such warnings: "I'm an adult; I don't need to listen to this internalized parent."

Even my seminary professors had transmuted the word *conscience* into *superego*. And I had seen no end of Hollywood productions that made light of the conscience—depicting a demon on one shoulder and an angel on the other, or the two alter-egos arguing back and forth. Our culture has trivialized conscience to the point that the rational mind wins by default the right to arbitrate moral decisions. But the rational mind, according to the Bible, is under the power of sin and unable to arrive at a knowledge of the truth. Likewise is our conscience weakened until it is enlightened by the Holy Spirit and the Word of God.

Unfortunately, as I stood before that porn shop that day, I listened to my mind, ignored my spirit, pushed out of my mind what Jesus said about lust and went into the shop.

The lustful thoughts that resulted from that visit became obsessive. Pornography, I learned, has power—power to consume more and more of the imagination, power even to draw us away from God.

How easily I could have been pulled down by the consuming passions of the flesh! I learned the hard way that the eye is the lamp of the body. The New Testament analysis of the human condition was accurate. My flesh waged war against my spirit, and continues to do so. With God's help, after a long and difficult struggle, I backpedaled out of the porn industry—but not without learning that the conscience functions separately from the rational mind and that the conscience, informed by the revelations of Scripture, is the surer guide.

I have often had the experience since then of following conscience when reason whispered its opposite advice, and thus avoiding shipwreck.

God Alone Can Make Us Moral

God sends the Holy Spirit to awaken a conscience lulled to sleep by the alluring sirens of the world. He has not changed His ways from the days of Augustine; nor have the issues changed since fifth-century Rome struggled with depravity in its amphitheaters, brothels and homosexual baths.

As evidence of the correctness of the older paradigm of conscience, we offer the great awakenings of the past. Spiritual awakenings have been given short shrift in Western education because the Western worldview blinds us from seeing them. Brass heaven builders claim that these revivals were the result of mass hysteria or emotional manipulation by the clergy. But the moment we adopt biblical paradigms, we see these seasons as the fulfillment of New Testament promise. God is working to fill the earth with the power of the cross so that all people groups will have opportunity to serve Jesus, who will write His laws on their hearts.

The one ingredient in all spiritual awakenings is the sensitizing of the conscience by the Holy Spirit, who teaches us "by practice to distinguish good from evil" (Hebrews 5:14, RSV; see also John 16:8).

> And though the Lord give you the bread of adversity and the water of affliction, yet your Teacher will not hide himself any more, but your eyes shall see your Teacher. And your ears shall hear a word behind you, saying, "This is the way, walk in it," when you turn to the right or when you turn to the left.
>
> Isaiah 30:20–21, RSV

> I write this to you about those who would deceive you; but the anointing which you received from him abides in you, and you have no need that any one should teach you; as his anointing teaches you about everything, and is true, and is no lie, just as it has taught you, abide in him.
>
> 1 John 2:26–27, RSV

This teaching is not learned rationally through reading books, but through experience as we surrender our lives to God, trust Him to fulfill His promises in us and allow the Holy Spirit to strengthen our consciences.

The Reformation

This has happened repeatedly in Western history—for instance, in the Great Reformation. The Reformation we have read about in Western schools is a doctrinal controversy among Church leaders five hundred years ago. Behind doctrines, however, was a fresh out-pouring of the Holy Spirit and the awakening of conscience.

The Scottish Reformation provides us with plenty of examples of this. George Wishart (as described by John Knox) shows what was happening among the grass-and-heather roots of Scotland in those days:

> He came to a dyke in a moor edge, upon the south-west side of Mauchline, upon the which he ascended. The whole multitude stood and sat about him (God gave the day pleasing and hot). He contin-ued in preaching more than three hours. In that sermon God wrought so wonderfully with him that one of the most wicked men that was in that country, named Laurence Rankin, laird of Shiel, was con-verted. The tears ran from his eyes in such abundance that all men wondered. His conversion was without hypocrisy, for his life and conversation witnessed it in all times to come.[8]

Scottish professor and pastor David Dickson, ministering a cen-tury later, shows that Wishart's preaching was no mere anomaly:

> I must here instance a very solemn and extraordinary outletting of the Spirit, which about the year 1625, and thereafter was in the west of Scotland . . . under the ministry of famous Mr. Dickson . . . that for a considerable time, few sabbaths did pass without some evi-dently converted, and some convincing proofs of the power of God accompanying his Word; yea, that many were so choaked and taken by the heart, that through terror the Spirit in such a measure con-vincing them of sin, in hearing of the Word they have been made to fall over, and thus carried out of the church, who after proved most solid and lively Christians. . . . Truly, this great spring-tide, which I may so call of the gospel, was not of a short time, but for some years' continuance, yea, thus like a spreading moor-burn the power of god-liness did advance from one place to another, which put a marvel-lous lustre on these parts of the country, the savour whereof brought many from other parts of the land to see the truth of the same.[9]

The spiritual awakenings of the past teach us that morals come not only from parents and cultures but from God. It is better to speak of conscience than of superego, because the former better conveys God's power to write His laws on our hearts, according to the promise of Jeremiah 31:33 and Ezekiel 36:25–32.

The Great Awakening

We do not have space to catalog the many other seasons of spiritual awakening throughout history. To give a sense of the ebb and flow of these "outlettings of the Spirit," we mention the account of Jonathan Edwards during the Great Awakening (emphasis ours), in which the prevailing element was the reawakening of conscience:

> When this work of God first appeared, and was so extraordinarily carried on amongst us in the winter, others round about us seemed not to know what to make of it; and there were many that scoffed at and ridiculed it; and some compared what we called conversion to certain distempers. But it was very observable of many that occasionally came amongst us from abroad with disregardful hearts, that what they saw here cured them of such a temper of mind. Strangers were generally surprised to find things so much beyond what they had heard, and were wont to tell others that the state of the town could not be conceived of by those that had not seen it. The notice that was taken of it by the people that came to town on occasion of the court that sat here in the beginning of March, was very observable. And those that came from the neighborhood to our public lectures were for the most part remarkably affected. *Many that came to town on one occasion or other had their consciences smitten and awakened, and went home with wounded hearts, and with impressions that never wore off till they had hopefully a saving issue*; and those that before had serious thoughts, had their awakenings and convictions greatly increased.[10]

These awakenings have little to do with culture; they are more or less the same regardless of the culture where they appear. God is God whether He is dealing with Kampucheans, Canadians, Californians or Koreans.

Korea's Awakening

In his book *When Revival Swept Korea*, missionary Jonathan Goforth described the roots of the awakenings that have made Korea half-Christian in less than a century. In 1903 there came a great prayer movement among the small communities of Christians that had been established in Korea. The calling to prayer increased in intensity and frequency in the town of Ping Yang.

> They prayed about four months, and they said the result was that all forgot about being Methodists and Presbyterians; they only realized that they were all one in the Lord Jesus Christ. That was true church union; it was brought about on the knees; it would last; it would glorify the Most High. . . .
>
> It had now come to the first week of January, 1907. They all expected that God would signally bless them during the week of universal prayer. But they came to the last day, the eighth day, and yet there was no special manifestation of the power of God. That Sabbath evening about fifteen hundred people were assembled in the Central Presbyterian Church. The heavens over them seemed as brass. Was it possible that God was going to deny them the prayed-for outpouring? Then all were startled as Elder Keel, the leading man in the church, stood up and said, "I am an Achan.[11] God can't bless because of me. About a year ago a friend of mine, when dying, called me to his home and said, 'Elder, I am about to pass away; I want you to manage my affairs; my wife is unable.' I said, 'Rest your heart; I will do it.' I did manage that widow's estate, but I managed to put one hundred dollars of her money into my own pocket. I have hindered God. I am going to give that one hundred dollars back to that widow tomorrow morning."
>
> Instantly it was realized that the barriers had fallen, and that God, the Holy One, had come. Conviction of sin swept the audience. The service commenced at seven o'clock Sunday evening, and did not end until two o'clock Monday morning, yet during all that time dozens were standing weeping, awaiting their turn to confess. Day after day the people assembled now, and always it was manifest that the Refiner was in His temple. Let man say what he will, these confessions were controlled by a power not human. Either the devil or the Holy Spirit caused them. No divinely enlightened mind can for one instant believe that the devil caused that chief man in the church to confess such a sin. It hindered the almighty God while it remained covered, and it glorified Him as soon as it was uncovered; and so with rare exceptions did all the confessions in Korea that year.[12]

Goforth then described some instances of the Holy Spirit's work:

Such extraordinary happenings could not but move the multitude, and the churches became crowded. Many came to mock, but in fear began to pray. The leader of a robber band, who came out of idle curiosity, was convicted and converted, and went straight to the magistrate and gave himself up. The astonished official said, "You have no accuser; you accuse yourself; we have no law in Korea to meet your case"; and so dismissed him.

. . . A Japanese officer at the time of the revival was quartered in Ping Yang. He had imbibed the agnostic ideas of the West, therefore to him spiritual things were beneath contempt. Still, the strange transformations which were taking place, not only among great numbers of Koreans, but even among some Japanese, who could not possibly understand the language, so puzzled him that he attended the meetings to investigate. The final result was that all his unbelief was swept away and he became a follower of the Lord Jesus.[13]

Two things can be said about the Korean awakening. First, *it began in extraordinary prayer—a reliance on the power of the personal God of the Bible.* This prayer grew out of biblical paradigms, which those Presbyterians contrasted with the "agnostic" views of the West. Koreans made no attempt to adapt biblical paradigms to the Western worldview. The ability of Korean Christians since then to resist the brass heaven has been a key factor in the vitality of the Church there. We Westerners can learn much from Korean Christians.

Second, *the power of God created an awakening of conscience.* Those who were under conviction could not choose their own ideas about ethics. They were forced to go along with what God required. Judgment was beginning in the household of God and spreading to the surrounding culture. Rather than the Church adapting her ideas to those of the culture, the culture was invited to adapt its thoughts to God's.

The Koreans were following biblical paradigms in the way they approached ministry. Those paradigms were first vindicated at Pentecost. By following them, the Church prospered. Christians learned to rely not on their own learning but on God's power. Koreans came into the Church because the Church had power they could find nowhere else.

After many years of seeing such moves of the Holy Spirit in the Orient, Jonathan Goforth came home to Canada and preached to Presbyterians at a Canadian General Assembly. He was greeted coldly, his revival preaching was ridiculed and his call to repentance was resented. It was not scientific. Westerners were so fascinated with the brass heaven experiment that they had little interest in anything else.

But as Western Christians recognize the limitations of science as our moral guardian, we may yet rediscover the value of biblical paradigms. They served us well in the past and can guide us now through a time of violence, lust and moral decay—if we stick to basics and keep from fighting over decorative matters.

Our hope for the 1990s and the twenty-first century is the same as that which filled the hearts of Korean Christians at the beginning of this century: that God Himself will visit us, wipe away our misplaced trust in the rational mind, convict us of our depravity and write His laws on our hearts.

15

Spiritual Gifts

Brad: Now let's take a closer look at God's power paradigms. These center on the Person and work of the Holy Spirit—the power of God in the world.

Growing up under the brass heaven created a spiritual emptiness in me, which became intolerable during my college years. Partly to fill this void, I fell in love with a coed and had a wild, passionate romance for a year. By summer the romance crashed, leaving me with a broken heart and a guilty conscience. I felt unworthy to go into the ministry because of the immorality of the relationship.

Out of this need, I returned to my home church filled with loving people, among whom I sat Sunday after Sunday listening to sermons on God's love and forgiveness. But I needed more than the comfort of these sermons; I needed God's healing, forgiveness, deliverance and reassurance about my sense of call. Yet an invisible wall separated me from the words of the sermons. As the weight of my sin grew, my faith was crushed.

Is God real? I wondered. *Is there power to restore broken people?*

After a time I was drawn to a charismatic Presbyterian church. After the order and tradition of my home church, walking into this one was a shock. It was packed with young people. Excitement filled the air. People expected God to act. They also spoke in tongues and

174

prophesied. If someone preached on healing, healing prayer would follow to put the word into practice.

On one of the first evenings I attended there, a deep silence fell on the congregation. Consumed with my own hurt, I asked God, *Can You really touch my broken heart and forgive my guilt?*

A woman behind me, as if in answer to my question, stood up and gave a message in tongues. Her voice sparkled; it was as though an angel were speaking. It stirred in me a deep moving joy. I never even heard the interpretation given, for I was wrapped in Jesus' love. In that manifestation of the gift of tongues, God ministered to my torment. My faith was mysteriously restored.

The experience birthed a profound appreciation in me for the gifts of the Holy Spirit, which are given to bring the power of God into the hurts of the world. They move us beyond words into power.

J. Rodman Williams summarizes the purpose of the gifts: "Through the pneumatic *charismata* [spiritual gifts] the Holy Spirit shines forth and openly shows Himself. The Spirit who is invisible now manifests Himself visibly and audibly."[1]

In the tongue that was spoken in the church that night, I received a sort of knowledge that complemented academic knowledge, that was rooted in lived, personal experience and that blew a hole in my brass heaven.

Some people might say my experience was "just emotion." Christian experience does have an emotional component. But it is not merely emotional; it ministers to the whole person—body, soul and spirit; to physical hurts, emotional needs and spiritual longings. The Holy Spirit, by giving assurance and evidence of His presence in our lives, confirms our initial steps of faith so that we can enter a dynamic walk with God.

A brass heaven faith would have us give assent to doctrines with no experience to back them up. God desires us to move beyond mere doctrines into Himself, who meets our needs and heals our broken hearts.

J. Rodman Williams writes:

> The Church cannot be fully or freely the Church without the presence of and operation of the gifts of the Holy Spirit. What is depicted therefore in 1 Corinthians—and recurring in our day—is in no sense

a peripheral matter but is crucial to the life of the Church. For the recurrence of the *charismata* of the Holy Spirit signals the Church's recovery of its spiritual roots and its emergence in the twentieth century with fresh power and vitality.[2]

The Need for Power *and* Love

Doug: The manifestational gifts puncture holes in our brass heaven. Like Brad, I struggled terribly with doubts about God in the wake of the "God Is Dead" movement and the general brass heaven paradigms that saturated seminary life. The idea that God acts had been made to seem foolish.

Then one day I attended a prayer meeting in a neighboring Presbyterian church. A woman suddenly began writing down words in her notebook. I asked what she was writing. The woman—an ordinary organist in an ordinary church—had been receiving expressions of the love of God for the people in the group. We encouraged her to read them. The whole idea of prophecy had been so novel and unexpected, she hadn't known what to do.

Later that year, my mother, in answer to prayer, was healed dramatically of a back disability, an ulcer and a brain hemorrhage all in one day!

These manifestations of the Holy Spirit, showing forth the power of God, shattered my doubts about God's love and power and enabled me to begin to walk by faith. I could not have begun such a walk without some evidence that the doctrines I read in the Bible were true. This evidence was supplied through the manifestations of the Holy Spirit.

Brad: Doug and I suffered severe disappointments, however, a few years after the Holy Spirit punched holes in our brass heavens. Among the early charismatics there was often a lack of Christian maturity. In the traditional churches we could see love but little power. In the charismatic churches we could see power but little love.

Searching the Scriptures, we found that there are actually two distinct ways the Holy Spirit works in a believer's life. In the first, He is said to come *within* a person. This inner work is the character-building work that recreates us after the image of Jesus. When the Bible speaks of someone as "full of the Holy Spirit and wisdom," it is speaking of this dimension. (This biblical way of speaking, incidentally, differs from what many charismatics label a "Spirit-filled" person. They usually mean someone who practices charismatic gifts, whereas the Bible means someone manifesting the fruit of the Spirit.)

In the second type of working, the Holy Spirit is said to fall *upon* a person. This expression invariably refers to some gifting of a person for power ministry; it has no bearing on our character. Archer Torrey writes:

> The Bible consistently distinguishes between the external and the internal work of the Holy Spirit. The Holy Spirit upon us, or with us, or pushing us ("moving"), or leading us, is like the weapons and vehicles which a military unit has to have for its work, but which tells us nothing about the inner attitudes of those who use them.
>
> When the Bible speaks of the Holy Spirit in terms which make it clear the Holy Spirit is in one's inner being, then it also speaks of character, of fruit-bearing, of life, of wisdom to know God's will and the will to do it. These two different roles of the Holy Spirit are quite clear, unequivocal, and distinct in the Bible. . . . [3]

The brass heaven has made it difficult to achieve the balance between the two operations of the Holy Spirit because it does not accept "the Holy Spirit *upon*," only "the Holy Spirit *within*." The charismatic renewal tended to move the Church to the opposite extreme, creating polarization with traditionalist Christians aggravated by certain doctrines that crept into the renewal movement during the 1970s.

When the movement entered Protestant and Catholic churches, many people turned to the "experts" on the Holy Spirit who already had categories for the gifts and power of the Spirit—the Pentecostals. Many charismatics accepted Assemblies of God or Pentecostal Holiness paradigms to help them interpret their experiences.

The gift of tongues, for example. Assemblies of God teaching identifies tongues as "the initial evidence of the Holy Spirit in the life of a believer." Denominational pastors must adhere to this doctrine when they are licensed to preach.

Official Pentecostal Holiness doctrine approaches tongues a bit differently. *The Manual of the Pentecostal Holiness Church* (1981) presents this teaching (emphasis added):

> 9. We believe that Jesus Christ shed His blood for the complete cleansing of the justified believer from all indwelling sin and from its pollution, subsequent to regeneration (1 John 1:7–9).
>
> 10. We believe that *entire sanctification is an instantaneous, definite, second work of grace*, obtainable by faith on the part of the fully justified believer (John 15:2, Acts 26:18).
>
> 11. We believe that the Pentecostal baptism of the Holy Ghost and fire is obtainable by a definite act of appropriating faith on the part of the *fully cleansed* believer, *and the initial evidence of the reception of this experience is speaking with other tongues* as the Spirit gives utterance (Luke 11:13; Acts 1:5; 2:4; 8:17; 10:44–46; 19:6).

Both these teachings add baggage to the gift of tongues that is not taught explicitly in Scripture. (The biblical references listed above could be interpreted in any number of ways.) In the first teaching, the gift of tongues is taken to indicate that a Christian has received the Holy Spirit. In the second, it is taken to indicate that a Christian has attained moral perfection. Teachings of this sort create two classes of Christians—"ordinary" Christians and "Spirit-filled" or "perfected" Christians.

These doctrines about a "second blessing" have been a stumbling-block wherever the renewal movement has affected mainline churches, sowing division, pride and judgmentalism among Christians.

Caught Between the Brass Heaven Church and the Pentecostals

Trying to understand the work of the Holy Spirit, I turned to evangelical theologians. John Stott in his book *Baptism and Fullness* denied the distinct empowerment of the Holy Spirit for service and witness, teaching that the baptism with the Holy Spirit occurs automatically at conversion. Far more helpful to me were the writings of R. A. Torrey, who served as assistant to the great evangelist Dwight L. Moody. I read Torrey voraciously and became friends with his grandson, Archer Torrey.

I quote here from a recent interview with Archer in which he described his grandfather's predicament over the baptism of the Holy Spirit:

> My grandfather, R. A. Torrey, used the term *baptized with the Holy Spirit* to mean enduement with power. He made it very clear that this was a work separate from regeneration and had as its purpose not imparting life but giving power for service and witness. Christians are to ask in prayer for the baptism with the Holy Spirit and receive in faith. The baptism is a definite experience, though not necessarily an emotional experience.
>
> My grandfather went all over the English-speaking world teaching this with remarkable results. In 1903 and 1905, he made 'round-the-world preaching tours. In the evening sessions the topic was a basic call to salvation in Jesus Christ. In the daytime meetings he alternated between teaching on the power of prayer and the baptism with the Holy Spirit.
>
> At Moody Bible Institute, where he was superintendent, he insisted that before setting out in Christian service, the essential requirement for every worker was to have had a definite experience of being baptized with the Holy Spirit. This teaching was well-received and resulted in many moving in great power in ministry and witness.
>
> But this was before the Topeka Bible College Pentecost and the Azusa Street revival. The Holiness Pentecostal movement tied the baptism with the Holy Spirit to a second blessing which was entire sanctification, and limited the initial evidence of having received the baptism to speaking in tongues. My grandfather believed that this was a corruption of the biblical understanding of the baptism with the Holy Spirit. He got into tensions with the Pentecostals because, while accepting the empowering and affirming the gifts, he did not accept the second work of grace theology, nor would he accept the doctrine that tongues is "the initial evidence."
>
> To be completely honest, I think my grandfather's rejection of the Pentecostals, as well as the rest of the mainstream Church's rejection, was not entirely biblically based. It also had a great deal to do with social class. God chose a black man to lead the Azusa Street

revival. At that time many of those experiencing the baptism in the Holy Spirit and receiving the gift of tongues were people of little or no education. They had no status and no worldly power. They were precisely the kind of people from whom Jesus drew His first disciples. But they were the very people misunderstood by my Yale-educated grandfather and neglected by the upper-class mainstream denominations.

At Moody Bible Institute, as a reaction against the Pentecostals, R. A. Torrey was asked to stop teaching on the baptism with the Holy Spirit. This he refused to do, insisting that it was biblical. To avoid causing controversy, he left Moody, which he had founded.[4]

Upon leaving Moody, he went to Los Angeles to get the infant Bible Institute of Los Angeles (BIOLA) going. There he encountered the same problem as at Moody. He was asked by evangelicals to stop teaching on the baptism with the Holy Spirit. Once again he refused, because he believed the term to be biblical. He stuck to his original teaching because he knew that the evangelical position denied the enduement with power dimension and the present-day operation of the gifts of the Holy Spirit. After leaving BIOLA in 1925, for the same reason that he left Moody, he lived in Asheville, North Carolina, where he continued in active ministry until his death.

In the years since my grandfather's death, several evangelical publishers have asked my permission to expunge from his books the term *baptized with the Holy Spirit*. I have refused because I have found that when this term is rejected, there is often a rejection of the empowering, gift-giving work of the Holy Spirit as well. What most evangelicals have done—as, for example, John Stott—is to make empowerment part of justification and sanctification. The assumption is that everyone who is born again has received the power. Then there is no need to pray for and to receive the baptism in the Holy Spirit as a definite experience of empowerment to equip one for service.

We must reclaim from Pentecostal doctrine this valid biblical term for the empowering work of the Holy Spirit.[5]

I believe that R. A. Torrey steered a way between the brass heaven and the narrow doctrine of the early Pentecostals. Take away the distinctive tongues teaching of the Pentecostal denominations and you are left with the Church's need for the power of God in ministry. This is what Archer Torrey taught and what Doug and I teach in PRRMI's Dunamis Project conferences.[6] To break through the brass heaven and reach the spiritual realm, we need to wait in our own personal Jerusalems until we have been "clothed with power from on high" (Luke 24:49). But this does not mean the Western Church must accept all the theological baggage of early Pentecostalism.

Empowerment for Service

My experience of Holy Spirit empowerment did not catch hold until I overcame my earlier resentment of young charismatics from my college years. This came about in Korea at Jesus Abbey under the ministry of Archer Torrey.

One day after supper I asked Archer to pray for me for this "baptism." I wanted to be prayed for before the worship started because I was afraid the music would create emotional manipulation, and I wanted to experience God, not just an emotional jag. And—I didn't want tongues!

Archer and other members of the community gathered around me and laid their hands on me. Archer prayed a disappointingly simple prayer: "Lord, we thank You that You have used Brad in the past. Now please baptize him with Your Holy Spirit, that he may be even more useful to You in the future. And by the way, Lord, please give him the gift of tongues."

Now why did he go and mess everything up by throwing in that? I fumed inwardly.

A minute later everyone was dispersing and I was asking myself, *Is that all there is to it?*

The next moment I was overwhelmed by a powerful sense of God's presence. Jesus was right beside me, it seemed, pouring buckets of love over me. It was so wonderful that I found myself laughing for joy. Between fits of laughter, I was speaking in a language that was bursting forth. It was glorious!

I spent the rest of the night in the chapel in prayer. And the next morning, through an argument with Laura, the Lord let me know that my entire sanctification was a long way off!

I observed five other results besides the gift of tongues from my baptism with the Holy Spirit. First, I became ravenous for Bible study. Second, I had a terrifying encounter soon afterward with evil spirits. Third, I started in small ways to sense the guidance of the Holy Spirit. Fourth, the Spirit started to manifest His power through me in spiritual gifts. Fifth, I was able to bear witness freely to Jesus Christ. (It was this last effect that confirmed to me that the infilling with the Holy Spirit is for empowerment for service and witness.)

How did the Holy Spirit equip me to bear witness to Jesus? After that visit to Jesus Abbey, Laura and I headed back to Seoul by train. The Holy Spirit drew my attention to a soldier sitting a few seats from us on the train. He seemed downcast.

Go tell him about Jesus, came the nudge.

But I gave the Lord excuses: *My Korean isn't that good. I'd be embarrassed.* Then I said, *Lord, if You want me to witness to him, give me a sign.*

At that moment the man got up from his seat, walked directly over to me and asked in English, "Why are you so happy?"

With such an opening for the Gospel, I witnessed about Jesus as the Holy Spirit gave me words!

Empowerment for Evangelism

The apostle Paul proclaimed the Gospel "by the power of signs and wonders, by the power of the Holy Spirit" (Romans 15:19, RSV). The book of Acts is full of stories of how the Holy Spirit broke down cultural barriers in order to connect God's love for unbelievers with the preaching of the Gospel. This approach to ministry contrasts sharply with that of Western brass heaven churches.

I saw this Western bias illustrated dramatically one day when two American church professionals came to visit our presbytery in Taiwan. During a time for questions and answers with a group of Taiwanese pastors, at which I served as translator, one of the Americans asked the Taiwanese, "What is your program for evangelism?"

The pastors all turned to the Rev. Chen, motioning that he was the one most qualified to answer. The Rev. Chen's church, after having been touched by the charismatic renewal, had grown from 300 to 900 members in three years.

"Well," he answered, "every Sunday evening we have a healing service at the church. We pray for people who are sick or having problems. The Holy Spirit heals and blesses them. Many of those who are prayed for are so blessed that they accept Christ as Lord and Savior and later join the church. That is how we do evangelism."

"What I mean," responded the American professional condescendingly, "is, What is your *program* for doing evangelism?"

I retranslated the question.

"I've told you," he said, "we pray for the sick, Jesus heals them and they are brought into the church."

The American was not satisfied. "You don't have any program for doing evangelism?"

Rev. Chen looked a little defensive. "We pray for people and the Holy Spirit works. We tell them the Gospel. And that is the way Jesus is building our church."

The American shook his head and muttered in my hearing, "See, they really don't have any program at all."

He could not appreciate the Taiwanese because Americans tend to evaluate ministry from a brass heaven worldview, in which human effort and planning accomplish God's work. Americans seldom expect God to do anything, despite the plain word of Scripture that "unless the Lord builds the house, its builders labor in vain" (Psalm 127:1).

Divine-Human Cooperation

It is not, of course, an either-or situation. Often when people first start to experience the power of God, their worldview changes dramatically. They move from trusting human effort to an overly supernaturalistic paradigm in which everything is accomplished by God.

But even in the manifestational gifts of the Spirit, there is a human side. The inspiration and direction flow from God, while the language, activities and styles are human. On the one hand, "All these [gifts] are inspired by one and the same Spirit, who apportions to each one individually as he wills" (1 Corinthians 12:11, RSV). On the other hand, we are responsible to control and manifest these gifts at the appropriate time and manner so as to build up the Church (1 Corinthians 14:26–40). The Holy Spirit, unlike demons, does not take over our personalities, use a separate voice or destroy our integrity as persons.

Because of the element of human cooperation in spiritual gifts, therefore, we must learn how to receive (or discern) and how to express the gifts. We cannot control the Holy Spirit, but we can and must learn to control our responses to Him. In this way the fruit of the Spirit interacts with the gifts of the Spirit. We express the gifts in a loving, kind and patient way. The "Spirit upon us" flows through an earthen vessel that has itself been transformed by the "Spirit within us."

Ministering in the power of God takes a lot of learning, and there is only one way to learn—by experience and maturation through a life surrendered to God.

16

The Demonic

Brad: "Be self-controlled and alert. Your enemy the devil prowls around like a roaring lion looking for someone to devour" (1 Peter 5:8–9). "For our struggle is not against flesh and blood, but against . . . the spiritual forces of evil in the heavenly realms" (Ephesians 6:12).

With these words, the apostles represented the human condition as a war against spiritual foes that have great power to corrupt people and subvert God's plans. I incorporated this paradigm into my worldview in Korea after Archer prayed for me to receive the Holy Spirit. Laura's and my eyes were opened to spiritual realities, and we, like Jesus in the wilderness, started to experience the reality of the satanic.

In Korea our living conditions were poor. During that bitter winter of 1977, Laura and I had no running water and were cold most of the time. Occasionally we fled to the home of wealthy friends who lived in a well-furnished Western-style house in Seoul, for hot baths and other Western comforts. Though we always enjoyed these times, there was an oppressiveness about that house. We were also aware that the couple was having marital problems.

On one such visit I stayed up late talking to the wife. She told me she was thinking seriously of divorce. As we prayed, a wild thought came into my head: *The person she wants the divorce from is her father, not her husband.*

Tentatively I asked her what her relationship with her father was like.

"Oh, he's been dead fifteen years," she said, and fell silent. Then, with tears beginning to stream down her face, she poured out a sad account of how her father had rejected her. She expressed hurts apparently suppressed for years.

"Do you think you might be able to forgive him?" I asked at last.

"I think so," she said.

And as we prayed together, she did.

Manifesting a peace I had not seen in her before, she went off to her bedroom and I to mine.

Her forgiveness and our prayer, however, had apparently released demonic spirits from a foothold in her life.

In our bedroom I found Laura still awake.

"Something doesn't feel right, Brad," she said. "There's something in this house that hates us."

We prayed for protection and asked the Holy Spirit to guide us in how to deal with the mysterious hostility.

Suddenly something like an evil, invisible wave of uncleanness attacked us, creating in us nauseating panic. We both wanted to scream and run, but we held firm and faced the battle. We were assaulted by one wave of evil after another as names came to us—lust, materialism, greed and envy. We felt each of them coming like blasts of foul-smelling air, invoking feelings consistent with their depraved natures. As each assault came, we proclaimed the name of Jesus and commanded the spirits to leave. After several assaults, we were both standing on top of the bed, with the lights on praying in tongues at the top of our voices and exalting Jesus Christ.

After twenty minutes—which seemed an eternity—there was a lull. The room was so charged with power that Laura and I were afraid things would actually start flying around the room. We got off the bed and removed pictures, vases and other objects from the dressers and walls and put them on the floor.

Then came another series of attacks weaker than the first. During each lull, we prayed that any other demons would be exposed.

After an hour of this, the attacks stopped. Laura had a vision of a strong angel carrying a sword through every room of the house.

Finally, exhausted, we got into bed and fell peacefully to sleep.

The morning after this strange midnight foray into the super-natural, Laura and I noticed a subtle but definite change in the atmosphere of the home. Our friends seemed more settled. We never spoke to them of this battle and do not know if they heard or suspected anything.

As for me, for weeks I felt unclean. Then, at a conference, a Catholic priest confirmed this feeling.

"Oh, sure," he said. "Every time I cast out demons, I feel unclean, too."

So we prayed right then, and I was cleansed.

The couple did not, incidentally, get a divorce.

This experience shaped my worldview profoundly. It convinced me that biblical paradigms about the powers of darkness are accurate. More and more Westerners are recognizing these paradigms and incorporating them into their worldview.

Dr. William Long, pastor of Third Presbyterian Church of Richmond, one of the more evangelical churches in Richmond, recently reported the following experience during a mission trip to India:

> We went out to the Ynadies, a tribal group who, up until 1985, never let anybody come into their villages who ever went out again alive. But one village elder had come out in late '85, was brought to a saving relationship with Jesus Christ, and two years later went back to the Ynadies, led his family to Christ, and then a number of other villagers to Christ, and then many of his tribe to Christ. Well, that's the area where we went.
>
> What went on there? Well, for one thing, I witnessed the first exorcism of demons I had ever seen. Awesome. The man was a cobra worshipper, yelling, screaming, making serpentine motions, banging his head against trees. For the few minutes he was calm, three people laid hands on him and called upon the name of Jesus for the removal of this black night of bondage. Well, the man regurgitated a number of times without anything coming out of his mouth. Finally, finally, with neck and jaws swollen, he opened his mouth as though something were popping out. The swelling went down like a pin had pricked an air-filled cushion, and then he looked like he had just expired. Utterly limp. I didn't know if he had died. In about ten min-

utes, he blinked, looked all around, sat up, smiled, and just sat there, smiling and blinking and looking like the Gadarene demoniac— healed. Finally, people began to hold up hands and speak the name of Jesus. He looked around at these people again and again. Then finally he held up his arms and said "Jesus" any number of times, very calmly, very quietly. People came to him and hugged him, or took his hand and held it. And from every evidence I saw he certainly had a transformation. Well, we saw many such events.[1]

Such experiences can be so powerful that they may cause one to adopt an overly supernatural worldview that sees demons every- where. I had to deal with this lack of balance after my experience in the home of our friends in Korea.

C. S. Lewis defines the two extremes to be avoided in dealing with evil spirits:

> One is to disbelieve in their existence. The other is to believe and to feel an excessive and unhealthy interest in them. They themselves are equally pleased by both errors and hail a materialist or a magician with the same delight.[2]

Lest we think that demons trouble only people in faraway places like India and Korea, we remind our readers of the evidence of demonic activity in Germany during World Wars I and II. The demonic is far closer and far more influential in the West than most Westerners suppose. We quote Charles Kraft, who has ministered deliverance to hundreds of people:

> Demons seek to keep people ignorant of their presence and activi- ties. This strategy is particularly effective in Western societies. Demons like people to be ignorant of their presence and love it when people don't believe they exist. Demons have repeatedly referred to this strat- egy during ministry sessions. During a recent session observed by a psychologist learning about demonization, a demon became so angry it yelled, "I hate it that she [the psychologist] is learning about us. For years, we've been hiding and making them think we are psy- chological problems!"[3]

The brass heaven has aided and abetted this strategy of keeping Westerners, especially intellectuals, ignorant of the presence of demons.

If the Church is to recover her power over the demonic, she must, in a sane and balanced way, reincorporate spiritual paradigms in three areas of her life: pastoral care, the growth of local churches and the extension of Christ's Kingdom globally.

Deliverance in Pastoral Care

Pastoral care, the first area, is a vital aspect of the work of the Church. But science has seduced us into thinking that if we can give a problem a name, we know its causes and have solved it. John Richards comments:

> There is always a tendency to confuse the mere description of a thing with a statement of its meaning or its cause. In medicine I have suggested that the label "epileptic" and the label "demonic" need not be mutually exclusive. It may similarly be said of psychological and psychiatric labels, that they, also, are more descriptions of symptoms than of causes. . . .
>
> If such terms are used merely to describe certain syndromes or symptoms, then it would be logical to accept Victor White's contention that the terms manic-depression, schizophrenia, epilepsy, hysteria, and so on, are, similarly, mainly descriptive of symptoms not of causes. The ultimate cause, therefore, although sometimes within the sphere of medicine or psychiatry—as for example when schizophrenia is caused by a chemical imbalance—is not always so, and in the body/mind/spirit unity it would be logical to expect the causes of some suffering if not traceable to bodily or mental factors to be due to spiritual ones.[4]

Discernment of the difference between mental illness and demonization is a field that needs much study. Dr. Kurt Koch writes: "The mentally ill person is quick to talk about voices and spirits, whereas the truly demonized individual is typically not—evil spirits want to stay hidden."[5] Perhaps this distinction can help us begin the discernment process in pastoral counseling.

In the issue of the psychological versus the demonic, two things must be said side by side. First, psychological problems can resist healing if there is a demonic element and that element is not sooner or later discerned.

At an evening service at a conference, I noticed a young man acting in bizarre ways. We took him out of the service and began to pray for him. During a deliverance ministry lasting late into the night, a number of spirits left him that had entered through woundings inflicted during childhood.

This young man, we learned, had been through thirteen years of pastoral counseling and psychotherapy, had been repeatedly hospitalized, subjected to drug therapy and even to electric shock therapy, all to no avail and without even a clear diagnosis of what was wrong.

In the weeks following the deliverance, the diagnosis was made that he suffered from multiple personality disorder stemming from severe childhood abuse. Though the therapist dismissed the account of the deliverance, it was only after the deliverance that a diagnosis was made and the young man began to make progress in therapy. The deliverance did not solve all his problems, but it began the healing process.

At another conference, while being introduced by some parents to their ten-year-old daughter, I became uneasy, sensing a seductive, unclean spirit in the girl. Later I raised this tentatively with the father, suggesting the possibility that she might be demonized. He told me that eight months before, she had been sexually molested by an older man, which traumatized both the girl and her mother. After extensive counseling, while progress had been made, the mother and daughter remained unhealed.

I explained that when a person has been abused sexually by someone who is demonized, a demon will often attach itself to the victim and feed on the resulting hurt, shame and guilt. I suggested that, rather than go through a formal deliverance, which might frighten the girl, he go into her room at night while she was asleep and command the evil spirits, in the name of Jesus, to leave.

He did so.

A few days later I met the girl again. This time I had no uneasy feeling around her, but a sense of cleanness. Later I learned that the pain of the molestation was fading into the background for both daughter and mother.

The balancing statement that needs to be given, in the issue of the psychological versus the demonic, is this: Usually the demonic element of a pastoral problem is not the only, or even the primary, problem to be solved. Dr. Kraft confirms what many others are saying—that demons feed on emotional garbage, and until the garbage is removed, the problem is not solved. This garbage might include hurts and traumas resulting from the sins of others, long-term unrepented sin and occult involvement.

The pastoral task must include diagnosis of the demonic where it applies, and also the healing of deep wounds leading to forgiveness, repentance from sin and renunciation of occult involvement.

Oversimplification must be avoided in diagnosing spiritual and psychological problems—either that they are always demonic or always psychological. Life is complex, and our worldview must strive to admit as much of this complexity as possible, to open our eyes to realities that deserve to be acknowledged.

Spiritual Strategies in Church Growth

Oversimplifying the world has also had a negative effect on congregations. The second area in which the Church must reincorporate spiritual paradigms is the growth and care of local churches.

Leaders under the brass heaven have approached church growth like a business; we plan marketing strategies according to prevailing cultural trends. But often we are unaware that we are dealing with territorial spirits that oppose the construction of new churches, or that blight churches that already exist.

Brass heaven blindness to spiritual warfare has left the Church vulnerable to calculated strategies of malevolent beings that want nothing more than to destroy the Church. Today Church leaders are falling prey to sexual temptation, divorce, doctrinal heresy, fear and spiritual oppression, yet they are unaware of the spiritual causes of many of these problems and are ill-equipped to deal with them.

Blind warriors who cry, "Peace, peace," lay down their arms because they do not believe the enemy will hurt them. They do not even believe the enemy exists.

When I became executive director of PRRMI, I stepped onto a battlefield. The purpose of this organization is to produce growing churches equipped with the gifting of the Holy Spirit; yet the ministry was desperate financially. A pall of despair settled over the office in Oklahoma City as we looked at our debts and saw no money coming in to pay them. Why, I asked myself, had I left Taiwan, where money was never a problem and there was no brass heaven to obstruct the Spirit's work?

One week I was unable to make payroll for our few employees. I sent some of the office staff home. Only Carter Blaisdell (the associate director), Susan (the bookkeeper) and I remained at the office. In desperation I called them together for prayer.

Having no idea even how to pray, we bowed our heads and waited in discouraged silence.

God began speaking to us through images.

"You know," Susan said, "it's as if there is a heavy cloak over us, choking the life out of us."

We asked God to tell us what we were up against. Then we went into a time of confession. I confessed the sins of PRRMI and of the charismatic movement in general. Soon the Lord started giving us the names of evil spirits. *Suffocating control* was one such name. There were also spirits related to the history of Oklahoma with its oppression of Indians by early settlers.

Then we started to pray in the name of Jesus that these spirits would be bound and driven away. As we did, something started brooding in the upper corner of the office. It felt heavy, oppressive and dark. The more we prayed against it, the stronger it became, until suddenly I felt a constriction in my chest and found it hard to breathe. Something invisible was choking me.

"My God, help!" I cried out frantically. "Cast this thing out in the name of Jesus!"

Another part of me was analytical: *This is ridiculous. I'm just suffering from job stress.*

Suddenly Susan started choking, too, and Carter looked as though he were about to sink into a black hole. This was not job stress but some spirit manifesting.

We continued desperately in prayer, and as we commanded the spirit to leave, the room cleared. I had a vision of a tunnel of light being made through a cloud of darkness.

Three days later financial gifts started coming in, and the ministry began to move into financial health, which continues to this day. Our battle with invisible hostile forces marked a turnaround for the ministry of PRRMI.

As the Church dismantles the brass heaven—without jettisoning the insights of the rational mind—we can expect her to grow healthier. Repentance followed by prayer in Jesus' name will bring deliverance and protection from unseen forces that try to destroy us. Without them, the rational mind sits by helpless while the Church sinks to its own destruction.

Strategic-Level Warfare for Kingdom Advancement

The third area in which the Church must reincorporate spiritual paradigms, in order to recover her power over the demonic, is the extension of Christ's Kingdom globally.

One of Satan's aims, as Rees Howells discerned during World War II, is to prevent the Great Commission of the Church from being fulfilled. The evil one hinders the proclamation of the Gospel by distracting us with fruitless controversies and doctrines opposed to God's Word. He persecutes Christians and positions territorial spirits to guard the peoples of the earth from the Gospel.

John Calvin wrote,

> We have been forewarned that an enemy relentlessly threatens us, an enemy who is the very embodiment of rash boldness, of military prowess, of crafty wile, of untiring zeal and hate, of every conceivable weapon and of skill in the science of warfare. . . . Scripture makes known that there are not one, not two, nor a few foes, but great armies, which wage war against us."[6]

There is now, thankfully, a growing body of literature by respected Christian leaders on the subject of spiritual warfare. Charles Kraft, C. Peter Wagner and George Otis, Jr., have introduced the concept of territorial spirits and spiritual mapping. John Dawson, in *Taking Our Cities for God*, has laid out principles in dealing with demonic blocks to Gospel outreach.

I learned much about warfare against territorial spirits in Taiwan during my assignment to the Presbyterian Bible College at Hsinchu. The more familiar Laura and I became with the college, the more we wondered why God had called us there. The school had one foot in the grave; the buildings and grounds bore a look of decay. The student body was down to sixty and losing more. The faculty was laced with contention. The prevailing opinion was that the place should be closed, the land and buildings sold.

Coldness and hostility filled the atmosphere. Even on a beautiful day with a clear blue sky and blooming azaleas, one had to fight depression. Many people complained of this. One Taiwanese pastor told us that the one hour he taught there was the most difficult hour of the week. He always left with a feeling of deep oppression. Obviously this milieu did not lend itself to building up the student body, nor to conferences on spiritual renewal. But, except to pray, we were at a loss to know what to do.

In prayer, God reaffirmed to Laura and me that we were called to build a lay training center there that would help renew the Church of Taiwan. Yet this vision seemed impossible in view of the dark atmosphere of the place.

The breakthrough came in September 1982 when I attended a prayer retreat in Chiai, in southern Taiwan. While people were praying for me, David Clotfelter, a friend, had a vision: In our house there was peace but around the house were swirling currents of black, dirty water. This vision stimulated a period of spiritual warfare against demonic powers affecting the Bible college.

At one point a man from New Zealand, with no knowledge of the school, cried out suddenly, "Old bones, old bones!" Everyone asked what this meant, but no one knew. Perhaps there had been tombs or offerings to idols at the location. We prayed that the land would be cleansed.

Eventually two other visions were given, and we sensed a spiritual breakthrough. The first vision was of Jesus striding through the campus with a whip, driving out a host of demons. The second was of the fire of the Holy Spirit falling on our house, and from our house spreading to the rest of the campus. During this prayer, we all felt we had entered into supernatural conflict, but we had no objective evidence that anything had happened.

A few days later one of the members of the prayer team, who was very sensitive to spiritual realities, walked with me around the campus, praying over it and claiming it for the Lord. On this prayer walk he would stop suddenly and say, "Yes, here! There's something here." We prayed that each location be cleansed by Christ's blood.

Once again I was unsure what was being accomplished. Skeptical and embarrassed, I kept looking back to make sure no one was watching us.

My skepticism was soon blown away as changes became evident. First, the atmosphere changed. Others confirmed that the heaviness and coldness had lifted. Second, a little research showed that the land of the College had once been a Buddhist crematorium and cemetery. This confirmed the word about "old bones." The Chinese had known that the land was haunted by spirits; that was why they were willing to sell it to the foreign missionaries. Third, the Holy Spirit came with new power, paving the way for the lay training center, which eventually brought healing and deliverance to many.

Prayer was no quick fix. We were still surrounded by temples whose influence needed constantly to be resisted. We had to remain vigilant against spiritual attack, especially as the Lord increased our effectiveness in power ministry. Yet this initial spiritual warfare, in which high-level spirits were dealt with, marked the turnaround that made the lay training center possible.

I learned several lessons from this experience. First, any major undertaking that will advance the cause of Christ throughout the earth will be met with supernatural opposition. This opposition is to be overcome by the proclamation of God's Word, holiness of life and intensive prayer in Jesus' name. Second, spiritual warfare occurs as a result of following God's leadings in normal Christian ministry.

Spiritual warfare is not an end in itself, but a necessary means of bringing Christ's Kingdom. Third, spiritual warfare does not take place by shouting slogans at the devil or by using some special technique. It is the result of abiding in Jesus, worshiping Him and faithfully doing what He wants.

Spiritual Warfare in Oregon

Doug: My initiation into spiritual warfare began in 1983 in Oregon, where I heard a series of talks on revival prayer by Dick Simmons of Bellingham, Washington. Dick had studied the necessity of prayer in bringing fresh infusions of God's power to lift societies out of depravity. God used Dick to awaken my wife and me to a spirit of supplication and grace. At the conference Carla and I, simultaneously but separately, felt God calling us to two hours of prayer each day from 5 to 7 A.M.

On the second day after our return home, we were awakened mysteriously by our kitchen oven timer going off at 4:59 A.M.! We speculated that an angel set the thing off to confirm the inner guidance of the Holy Spirit. God wanted us to greatly increase our prayer in the quiet hours of the morning.

In addition to daily prayer, Dick gathered a group of intercessors together for more intensive prayer and fasting on the first Monday and Tuesday of each month. The main focus of our prayers was the Rajneeshpuram Community, which had been set up in eastern Oregon. This guru-led community proclaimed with impunity its doctrines of free sex and thinly veiled opposition to Christian teaching and morals. None of us felt led to confront the commune, either personally or politically. Our warfare strategy was confined to prayer and fasting. I felt, by the third or fourth month, that we were to pray that the leadership of the commune would explode apart.

For many months some of us prayed this way, all the while seeing no evidence that our prayers were having any effect whatever. If anything it seemed that the commune was becoming bolder and more arrogant. Anand Sheela, the second in command, would appear on talk shows preaching her doctrines and claiming that their teaching was just a higher version of Christianity. Rajneesh devotees clad in red would traverse the back roads of Oregon armed with shotguns.

That winter, surrounded by much news coverage about their compassion, the commune brought in poor people from around the U.S. and housed them in their community. These people were then instructed to vote for commune leaders in the local political election. Their political clout spread into local school boards and county government. After the election the people were dumped onto the streets of Portland, where Christian groups were hard-pressed to minister to them all.

We prayed on.

Finally it came time for Carla and me to move to Richmond. We were discouraged and tired of praying about the cult. Yet on the very day we drove out of the state, we heard the news on the radio: Anand Sheela had fled the commune, taking millions of dollars with her and depositing them in a Swiss bank account. The commune was in disarray, the leaders unable to agree about anything.

Once the spiritual power that pulled them together had been broken, the Immigration and Naturalization Service began to prosecute for extradition. I do not know why they had not gotten involved earlier, but I believe that a spiritual alliance had to be broken first.

The Rajneesh fled to North Carolina, where he was apprehended by authorities and tried in Charlotte. During the trial, St. Giles Presbyterian Church of Charlotte (among others) maintained a constant prayer battle, for one of its members was involved in the prosecution. (This is the church where Brad first encountered the gifts of the Holy Spirit.) The result: The guru was expelled from the country and his commune extinguished. Cultists continue to have meetings in Oregon, however; the battle is not ended.

I learned five lessons from this experience.

First, spiritual power is at the heart of much that is evil in the world.

Second, in some mysterious way, the hands of governmental authorities (police, military, government agencies, judicial systems, school authorities, etc.) are tied until the evil spiritual power is broken in the name of Jesus.

Third, Jesus is the only One who can break the power of the evil one. He disarmed Satan on the cross, and trained His Church to destroy the works of the devil in each succeeding generation.

Fourth, we fight these powers by arming ourselves with a mature Christian lifestyle, then waging a war of intensive prayer.

Fifth, it can take months or even years before God vanquishes the evil network built by conniving spirits among deceived people. Yet God's answer will come, and we must wait for it with patience, encouraging one another all the while.

17

Is the Church Human or Divine?

Doug: God's vision for the Church is astonishing. He "placed all things under [Christ's] feet and appointed him to be head over everything for the church, which is his body" (Ephesians 1:22–23). Jesus shares His rulership with us "that *through the church the manifold wisdom of God might now be made known* to the principalities and powers in the heavenly places" (Ephesians 3:10, RSV)—to the satanic powers, in other words, that keep this present world in torment.

Paul was experiencing the triumph of the name of Jesus over those powers, proclaiming the Gospel not by human wisdom, but "with a demonstration of the Spirit's power," so that the faith of the Church would rest not in human wisdom but in the power of God (1 Corinthians 2:4–5). The power of Christ given to the Church actually brings the Kingdom of God here on earth—a Kingdom not of talk but of power (1 Corinthians 4:20).

When we compare this divine vision with even the most successful Western churches (with their orderly committee meetings, professionally trained clergypersons, hour-long Sunday rituals and well-meaning efforts at political relevance), we cannot help but feel that something important has been lost. Many Christians sincerely want to be used by God yet are hindered by a worldview that has abandoned God's vision for the Church.

The form that "church" takes in our day is an outgrowth of our worldview, the brass heaven of Western philosophy. I heard a seminary president give a speech recently at a men's conference. He purported that the spiritual awakenings and revivals of the past are of no value and that the Church should flee any tendency toward such movements today. The Church should simply persist, he said, in her careful theology, rational teaching and orderly government.

After his speech I listened to the response of the men at the conference. Most were disgruntled; they had not been fed with the vision of God nor heartened in their faith. The conference organizers, too, were so uninspired by this purely rational approach to Christianity that they promised not to invite seminary professors to speak at conferences in the future!

Not all professors are so unsuccessful, of course, at inspiring God's vision in the Church. But that conference showed me how hungry people are for the vision of God to break through the brass heaven. Our seminaries are not preparing pastors to meet this need.

Christians and non-Christians alike are eager for the power of God to break into their lives. Needed today is not more ingenious ways to restructure the Church nor better teaching techniques to make Sunday school classes more interesting. The malaise of the Church goes deeper than that. We need to rediscover God's vision, introduced by Jesus and developed by the apostles of the Church.

The Organic vs. the Mechanistic Church

If we place our hope in the power of God, then local churches must become channels through which God's power can flow into the surrounding society. But the brass heaven worldview keeps missing this concept. Trusting in human ingenuity, we think of the Church as a machine to be controlled and manipulated by politics and good management, not as a tree that God causes to grow.

In our own denomination, Brad and I have seen endless (and fruitless) attempts to find renewal through denominational restructuring, as though the Church were merely an aggregate of committees (always with new names to give the impression of renewal), job descriptions, budgets, stewardship drives, building programs, four-color publications, *Robert's Rules of Order* and official church pronouncements. All mechanical. All human. All dead. We use the phrase *decently and in order*, which Paul used to guide the Church in the operation of spiritual gifts, to justify the absence of spiritual power and our trust in human mechanics.

In the face of all this, Brad and I offer a parable from Joel Arthur Barker's *The Business of Paradigms*. For centuries the Swiss perfected the art of watchmaking. In 1966 Swiss watchmakers came out with a novel idea—a battery-powered watch. This new concept required no mainspring, few cogs and wheels and none of the components of a serious timepiece. Swiss watchmakers regarded the design as a curiosity. They displayed it at the Watch Congress in Neuchatel in 1967 but did not even bother to patent it. It did not fit their paradigms for the watchmaker's art.

Two little-known companies, Texas Instruments and Seiko, saw in this curiosity the potential to revolutionize watchmaking. They developed the battery-powered paradigm, and the quartz watch was born.

The Swiss, trapped by ideas that were growing obsolete, lost the world market to Japanese and American firms that were willing to develop a watch around a battery. Today the Swiss, who once presided over eighty percent of the world's watch market, sell fewer than twenty percent of the world's watches.

Consider this as a parable of the Church. Jesus promised to give His Church power, guidance, wisdom, assurance and encouragement through the Holy Spirit—in a word, *life*. But we Western Christians fashion mainsprings and install cogs and wheels, building churches to function not from God's flow of life but from our own managerial skills and an outdated mechanistic worldview. Churches built around the power of God seem to be anomalies, despite the fact that they are often the ones that are growing fastest. (See the chart depicting *The Growth of Mainline vs. Charismatic/Pentecostal Churches* on p. 236.)

What, then, are the components of the "organic" church—the one that operates by the power of God? We would like to identify three.

1. Leaders Who Walk with God

The first component of the organic church is leaders who have surrendered their lives to the personal God of the Bible.

Jesus chose a few disciples who learned to walk in reliance on God's power in their personal lives. This concept could not be learned in a bookish environment. The disciples entered God's classroom by surrendering their lives to Him and learning how to walk with the Father as Jesus walked with Him. They developed the faculties of the spirit more than the powers of the mind.

It was the leaders at the Temple—the ones who rejected and crucified Jesus—who developed their religion as a mind game. The high-priestly Sadducees were the brass heaven builders of the first century. They did not believe in a spirit world, everlasting life, angels, demons, spiritual warfare, the existence of the soul, the resurrection of the body or the power of God "for today." They believed only in the political system they controlled and in the material world in which they indulged.

In Mark 1, by contrast, we see Peter's astonishment at the amount of time Jesus spent in prayer (by which He relied on God's guidance and power):

> Very early in the morning, while it was still dark, Jesus got up, left the house and went off to a solitary place, where he prayed. Simon and his companions went to look for him, and when they found him, they exclaimed: "Everyone is looking for you!" Jesus replied, "Let us go somewhere else. . . ."
>
> Mark 1:35–38

Peter, already baffled by the depth of Jesus' prayer life, must have found this reply incomprehensible. Jesus was responding not to human anxieties or the demands of other people, but to God's guidance. He gained His vision from the Father by walking with God. The priests of Peter's day did not behave that way; they had not learned to walk with God. Peter had to unlearn their way if he was to learn Jesus' way of trusting God daily.

We must do the same. Learning to walk with God is an essential first step if we want to renew the Church in the power of God.

2. Pastoral, Ministrative Structures

The second component of the church that operates by the power of God is the presence of pastoral rather than merely institutional structures. The power we want to drive a church will determine what kind of operative structures we build.

If we want the flow of God's life in our churches, Brad and I recommend discipleship groups (sometimes called home groups or cell groups), which are aimed at helping people walk with God. What pastors and mature believers have learned by walking with God can spread in discipleship groups to new believers as they meet together long enough for the "good infection" of faith and love to catch.

In an organic church, the aim is to build an environment where the power of God is welcomed and people encourage each other to speak of it, pray for it and praise God for signs of it.

Discipleship groups provide pastoral structures in which people can be led into mature discipleship. Here they learn how God "rewards those who earnestly seek him" (Hebrews 11:6). Without such pastoral structures, our people are not at all likely to learn the patterns of mature Christian living. Instead, their lives will be subconsciously shaped by the prevailing concepts and influences of their culture. In my church, in order to help people be transformed by the renewal of their minds and lives, we use my books *Bread: An Invitation to the Christian Life* and *Food Groups: A Balanced Diet for Christian Growth*.[1]

Discipleship groups are like the blood vessels that take the life of Jesus from the main aorta and feed it to the cells. The aorta (the Sunday morning worship service) is important, but it is inadequate to get the oxygen all the way to the cells and to cleanse the cells of their impurities. Discipleship groups are as necessary today as they were in New Testament times (Acts 2:42–47) to keep the Body of Christ in good health.

In the mechanical church, by contrast, administrative functions become the end, not the means. People serve on committees because committees ostensibly accomplish the work of the Church, even though no one may be learning patterns of Christian discipleship and the members of the committee may not be ministering biblical faith or love to each other.

In the organic church, the main structures are not administrative but ministrative, not institutional but pastoral. The main goal is to keep the life of Jesus flowing among the people. We erect pastoral structures to help our people "draw near to God with a sincere heart in full assurance of faith . . . [to] hold unswervingly to the hope we profess . . . [and] spur one another on toward love and good deeds" (Hebrews 10:22–24). We tell each other what has happened when we have trusted God for particulars. We pray for each other and love each other in real ways. We come together "that you and I may be mutually encouraged by each other's faith" (Romans 1:12).

An organic, ministrative structure, then, draws people together regularly in small groups to help them trust in the personal God of the Bible. In these groups they learn God's unique pattern for living—faith working through love—and they strengthen each other to live out that pattern in the rest of life.

The aim of this structure: to produce mature Christians. "The goal of this command is love, which comes from a pure heart and a good conscience and a sincere faith" (1 Timothy 1:5). God's life flows through the organic church. People are drawn to it because they see God's love, life and healing there.

3. Pastors as Equippers

The third component of the church that operates by the power of God is pastors who are equippers of people, catalysts for God's power flowing among believers. The pastoral role in such a church might look like this:

1. To teach, train and model for people the basic Christian life (1 Timothy 4:7, 11–12).
2. To teach, train and model for people how to lead others to live out the Christian life (2 Timothy 2:2).
3. To establish pastoral structures in the church through which people can make disciples (Acts 2:46).
4. To encourage people to rely on God in the obedience that comes from faith (Romans 1:5, 12).
5. To help people discern their spiritual gifts (1 Corinthians 12:4–6).

6. To protect the church from bad influences (Acts 20:29–31).
7. To minister to those with special problems beyond the capacity of lay people to handle, and sometimes to refer people for professional help—such as in case of addiction or marital strife.

By attempting to follow these principles in my own ministry, I have seen two small, nearly defunct churches attract young people and emerge into stable, exciting communities full of the life of Jesus. Helping people surrender their lives to God and walk with Him is a great privilege and the greatest reward that local pastoral work bestows.

An Example from the Eighteenth Century

John Wesley, who ministered during the Great Awakening, saw the difference between the mechanical and the organic. The churches of his day, despite their Reformation heritage, were not Christian environments full of God's love and power. Wesley judged the forms of the English church to be devoid of power, so he set about to establish his "Methodist societies"—a network of pastoral structures designed to receive people being touched by the Spirit of God, to enable them to respond biblically to their Christian calling.

Wesley describes his pastoral structure in the rules for his religious societies, of which we offer a representative sample:

It was agreed
1. That they will meet together once in a Week to confess their Faults one to another, and to pray for one another that they may be healed.
2. That any others, of whose Sincerity they are well assured, may, if they desire it, meet with them for that Purpose. . . .
3. That the Persons desirous to meet together for that Purpose, be divided into several Bands, or little Societies.
4. That none of these consist of fewer than five, or more than ten Persons.
5. That some Person in each Band be desired to interrogate the rest in order, who may be called the Leader. . . .

10. That every one in order speak as freely, plainly, and concisely as
he can, the real State of his Heart, with his several Temptations and
Deliverances, since the last time of meeting.[2]

Only one condition was required for membership in these societies: a desire "to flee the wrath to come, to be saved from their
sins."

By this "method" of Methodism, Wesley was establishing a structure that bypassed the top-heavy, cog-and-wheel structures of the
organized Church. His purpose was simple: to help people live out
the Christian life of faith, love and virtue. Wesley cared little about
programs, fund drives, committee structures and the rest. His structure was aimed at helping the life of Jesus flow from person to person in the Body of Christ. His method permitted the raw material
of God's power to be channeled into the making of sanctified, pro-
ductive human beings.

By this structure, and by the effective evangelistic street preaching of Wesley and Whitefield and their followers, enormous transformations were achieved throughout English society. But they were
achieved by people changed from the heart, and not only by the
external manipulation of laws and institutional policies.

A Warning:
The Abuse of Spiritual Power and Authority

Churches devoid of power can do neither good nor evil. They are
innocuous and impotent. But all power, even God's power, brings
with it potential for abuse. The perverse passion to control people
has frequently hindered churches—including charismatic churches
that want to make disciples. In the charismatic renewal we have
seen a succession of earnest leaders who have had to apologize later
for abusing power and hurting people.[3] What begins in the Spirit
can, if we are not careful, end in the flesh.

Our church in Richmond has ministered to many who have suffered from the abuse of spiritual power and authority in other
churches. This abuse has almost always flowed from the so-called
"chain-of-command" teaching—the idea that ordinary Christians
cannot possibly learn from the Holy Spirit as we have described in

the preceding chapters, but must have intermediaries to tell them how to live. The primary text to support this teaching is 1 Corinthians 11:3: "The head of every man is Christ, and the head of the woman is man, and the head of Christ is God."

This passage is interpreted as a hierarchy of command and sub-mission—and here is where the trouble starts. Jesus explicitly denied such a hierarchy when He warned His disciples not to treat people as the Pharisees did: "You are not to be called 'Rabbi,' for you have only one Master and *you are all brothers*. And do not call anyone on earth 'father,' for you have one Father, and he is in heaven" (Matthew 23:8–9, emphasis added). Jesus established *mutual, not one-way, submission* as the basis for relationships in the Body of Christ.

The apostle Paul taught the same thing: "Submit to one another out of reverence for Christ" (Ephesians 5:21). It is Satan, not Jesus, who thrives on a system of *oberführers* and *unterführers*.

What is headship? Jesus taught that we exercise authority by example, not by artificial authority structures in churches and fam-ilies. Headship brings with it the responsibility to lead other people to Christian maturity by our own mature faith and love. This is why personal maturity was so important in the selection of leaders in the New Testament Church (1 Timothy 3:1–7). Paul, in speaking of headship, was not establishing a chain-of-command authority struc-ture but showing that God uses some people to lead others by the example of their lives and by personal initiative.

So, that infamous verse in 1 Corinthians 11:3 is preceded by 1 Corinthians 11:1: "Follow my example, as I follow the example of Christ." Paul, in teaching about headship, practiced what he preached. Second Corinthians models this way of headship by exam-ple. Paul refused to lord it over the Corinthians and challenged them not to let anyone bully them into bondage. He wrote much the same thing in his letter to the Galatians, which establishes the principle of Christian freedom.

We must not give up that freedom to anyone, no matter how much we respect them or how much spiritual power they dem-onstrate. Far from controlling the lives of others, Paul had given up control even over his own life, as he described to the Corinthians many times (1 Corinthians 4:1–13; 2 Corinthians 4:7–12; 6:3–13; 10:1–6; 11:1–33). The source of Paul's headship was the authority that flows from a surrendered life—a life given to God.

While we do not have space to develop a picture of the sad and tiresome habit of some church leaders who abuse spiritual power and authority, others have done so. We recommend the book by David Johnson and Jeff VanVonderen, *The Subtle Power of Spiritual Abuse.*[4]

The power of God is a beautiful thing—until church leaders try to steal it and use it for their own ends.

The Brass Heaven
and the Unreached Peoples

The worldview into which the Church fits the Gospel has a great effect on her proclamation of the Gospel among the nations. In this chapter we examine the importance of biblical paradigms to mission enterprise as the Gospel crosses cultural lines. And we contrast two experiences of cross-cultural missions—one from the past, the other from the present.

On the surface these two enterprises seem similar. But in the first instance the Gospel became trapped in the forms of Western culture. In the latter it was freed from Western culture, while offering the benefits of the West to tribal people. A biblical worldview in that latter instance brought success to the mission enterprise because biblical paradigms were broad enough to span two very different cultures.

The Plateau Tribes

In 1782 the first "virgin soil" epidemic swept across the American continent—an epidemic of smallpox. During this mysterious sickness, *Yuree-rachen*, Circling Raven, a shaman of the *Sin-ho-man-naish* (the Middle Spokanes) attempted to minister healing to his people, who lived just west of present-day Spokane, Washington. Rather than heal them by his shamanistic practices, however, he lost his son to the disease, and great numbers of villagers also perished.

Yuree-rachen suffered a crisis of faith. Disillusioned and angry, he asked his brother, "If the righteous die while evil men live, why should we continue to follow our laws? Let us live like the animals."[1]

His brother persuaded the shaman to maintain his faith a while longer in their moral laws and in the God they called *Quilent-sat-men*, He-Made-Us. He also persuaded him to go to the top of Mount Spokane for four days of prayer and fasting.

At the conclusion of his fast, according to Spokane tradition, *Yuree-rachen* received a vision of men of white skin wearing strange clothes and bearing in their hands leaves bound together. He was told to counsel his people to prepare for these *chipixa*—white-skinned ones—and to pay attention to the teaching that came from the leaves bound together.

According to anthropologist Leslie Spier, the tribes of the region developed the "dream dance" (Dr. Spier calls it the "Prophet Dance") as a religious response to the widespread revival of such prophecy during the eighteenth century.[2]

Shining Shirt

The Middle Spokanes were not the only tribe to receive such a prophecy. Many other tribes throughout the area received similar prophecies. Nor was this type of prophecy, according to researchers, an isolated quirk, a delusion of primitive minds or a tale invented later by Christian-influenced reservation Indians.

Sometime during the eighteenth century, a Kalispel shaman and chief had delivered a similar message among the eastern Salish. The great cultural hero Shining Shirt, according to ethnologist Harry Holbert Turney-High, prophesied that white people would come from the East one day:

> According to the legend Shining Shirt was both a chief and a shaman. After he was a grown man and was in charge of his people, a Power made a great revelation. The Power said that there was a Good and an Evil One of which the Indians knew but little so far. Yet the time would come when men with fair skins dressed in long black skirts

would come who would teach them the truth. The Indians had never heard of a white man at that early date.

. . . The Black Robes would change the lives of the people in ways of which they but little dreamed. The Power then gave Shining Shirt a talisman of terrific strength. This was a piece of metal inscribed with a cross.

Shining Shirt forthwith assembled a council and preached and legislated in this wise. He said that in the past when a man married the elder sister of a family all the younger ones automatically became his wives. The Power considered this a grievous error. Therefore all men must cleave solely to the elder sister and put the other away. He made himself an example by promptly divorcing the younger of his two sister-wives.

Then he told them that there is a God. His true name was not revealed but he was temporarily called Amotkan, He-who-lives-on-high. It is the people's duty to pray to him, especially the chief who must do this every morning and particularly at the Midsummer Festival. Amotkan in some way made the world and all the people, and to him all those who live good lives must return. . . .

Shining Shirt then taught them that the Black Robes would give them a new moral law which they should obey. Again, these strange white men would teach them many things about making a living of which they were then ignorant, but which they must try to understand and perform as they were taught. Soon after their arrival all wars would cease. . . . Very soon after the appearance of the religious teachers other men with white skins would come and simply overrun the country. They would make slaves of all the people, but they should not be resisted. This would only bring needless bloodshed.

. . . Now the people trusted Shining Shirt and received his teaching. Even today they are convinced that he was given his power to accomplish an inevitable divine purpose.[3]

Christian Fur Trade Leaders

In 1809 David Thompson, the Christian explorer and cartographer mentioned in chapter 9, led his fur brigades into the Columbia Plateau and established British fur posts—two near the Kalispels and Flatheads and one among the Middle Spokanes. One thing led to another, and by 1825 interest in the *chipixas'* spiritual insights had grown to a fever pitch among all the Plateau tribes.

George Simpson, governor of the Northern Department of the Hudson's Bay Company, was accosted by a dozen chiefs on his first trip through the area in 1824–25, requesting teachers to come among them and teach their people from the book they had seen at company posts.[4] Simpson knew nothing of the prophecies that fueled these requests. While other tribes on the continent seem to have been interested mostly in the material benefits of white culture, Plateau tribes, by most accounts, were different. They wanted to know what the white people knew of the "Master of Life." Both Simpson and Alexander Ross of the Hudson's Bay Company were explicit about this unique characteristic of the Plateau tribes.

The best that Simpson and Ross could offer was to take two boys, the son of *Illim-spokanee* and the son of *Le Grand Queue* (Middle Spokane and Lower Kootenay head chiefs) to the Red River Colony (alias Winnipeg, Manitoba). There they were educated at the first Anglican mission station in the West by the Rev. David Jones and the Rev. William Cochran. Jones and Cochran taught them the ABCs—agriculture, Britishness and Christianity.

Spokan Garry and Kootenai Pelly

After four years these two native lads, known as Spokan Garry and Kootenai Pelly, returned to their people. Arriving at Fort Colville, they were immediately surrounded by vast crowds of natives from hundreds of miles around who wanted to hear what they might say of the Master of Life.

After Pelly fell from a horse, causing serious injury, Garry spent the winter of 1829–30 touring the area alone, preaching about Jesus Christ.

Evidence indicates a widespread spiritual awakening among the Plateau tribes as a result of Garry's preaching. Alvin Josephy, noted authority on the Western tribes, writes:

> By coincidence, the beginning of the close association between the Sahaptin-Salish peoples and large numbers of American trappers, which became significant about 1830, occurred simultaneously with a dramatic and remarkably influential introduction of Christian ideas among the home villages of those Indians. The Americans in the

mountains had nothing to do with it and were unaware of what was taking place. But . . . it worked abrupt and profound changes in the behavior of many of the plateau tribes beginning in the winter of 1829–30, and accounted in large measure for some of the Americans' attitudes about them that differed sharply from earlier British estimates of their conduct.[5]

The most obvious effect of this awakening was that intertribal hostilities, which until then had been the bane of the British fur trade, were greatly reduced, due to the new pattern of faith working through love that found its way into tribal cultures. This change was described by many American and British trappers, as were new patterns of prayer and Sabbath-keeping that made the white trappers seem like heathen by comparison.

Denominational Missionaries

But the first missionaries who came into the area in the 1840s were armed with two ideas that prevailed among them as the inheritance of Western culture:

1. God does not speak today. He spoke only in the Bible.
2. Christianity is for "civilized" people of Western culture. We must teach the natives our civilized ways before they will ever understand Christianity.

By virtue of these two paradigms, missionaries were not expecting God to have already spoken to native peoples. They ignored Spokan Garry, convinced that little good could come from an Indian. Besides, Garry's education had been Anglican, while most of the missionaries to Salish people were Presbyterian and Roman Catholic. The Presbyterians were still feuding with the Anglicans and Catholics—feuds exacerbated by blood spilled in the old country.

The Salish saw the infighting and sectarian rancor, were confused by it at first, then disgusted. They concluded that tribal warfare ran more rampant among whites than among the newly awakened natives, who for the first time were learning to love one another intertribally. Garry, for his part, was crushed by being ignored. And all natives sensed the lack of respect for them coming from these arrogant, narrow-minded whites—many of whom, of course, were not Christians. That, too, confused them. They could not understand how people who had had the "leaves bound together" for centuries would not all have become Christians. The Salish natives were discovering that, yes, the whites had brought the message about the Son of God, but few lived by the message they bore.

There came, in the wake of this disillusionment, a reevaluation of the Christian faith and a new openness to native shamanistic cults (like the Smohalla cult) that preached simple hate toward white people. Many natives were unable to separate the message of Christ from the messengers.

Later on Spokan Garry, who had become perhaps the most respected chief on the Columbia Plateau, was brutally evicted from his home and land, where he had been raising crops in the manner of the Rev. Cochran at the Red River Colony. The Americans said he needed to get a deed for the land. But when he applied for a deed, he was told he could not purchase the land because he was a "foreigner." He ended up disenfranchised and desperately poor, squatting on land that the white people had usurped. He lived to see the pride of Salish youth corrupted as prostitutes and drunks in the towns that white people had built—like Spokane, a city named after his father.

In his final years he cherished his Christian faith, the one thing remaining to him that kept him from complete despair. In order to do this, though, he had to come to the realization that Christian faith was not "the white man's religion" (as the whites themselves claimed) but the pleading outreach of a sovereign God to all nations, tribes and tongues.[6] The school that Spokan Garry built to teach his people agriculture and Christianity still exists in downtown Spokane, a belated attempt by white Americans to honor the memory of a man we cheated and dishonored in life.

As for the missionaries, their attempts to "convert" the natives went unrewarded. Presbyterian missions failed to establish a strong church among the Salish, though Catholics had more success among the Flatheads to the east who had received the prophecies of Shining Shirt. Presbyterians were saddled with a worldview that hindered the work they wanted to accomplish. Though they were great believers in the sovereignty of God, their views of how God would exercise that sovereignty were so narrow that they could not appreciate what He had already done among the Salish before they arrived, to prepare them for the Christian Gospel.

It was not until early in the present century that anthropologists, eager to listen to the few natives who still remembered aboriginal ways, discovered that shamanistic prophecy had prepared these tribes for the "leaves bound together" and for the teaching about Jesus, Son of the Master of Life.[7]

The Book of Acts Still Lives

What God did for *Yuree-rachen* and Shining Shirt was little different from what He did for the Parthian Magi described in Matthew 2 and for the centurion Cornelius described in Acts 10. How many Jews had anticipated that God would already have spoken to an "unclean" Roman centurion to prepare him for the arrival of Peter on his doorstep? So great was the cultural chasm between Jew and Gentile that Jews were not allowed even to enter the house of a Gentile! Yet God's love forced them to cross the chasm, expand their paradigms to deal with foreign worldviews and express the Gospel in terms of those worldviews without compromising the Gospel itself.

The American missionaries in the West had not anticipated that God might already have spoken to native shamans. Because of their worldview, they were not as discerning as Peter had been and could not relate to non-European paradigms.

Don Richardson has documented the phenomenon that occurred among the Plateau tribes—that God prepares cultures for the reception of the Gospel. His book *Eternity in Their Hearts* describes dozens of similar examples in which "God has indeed prepared the Gentile world to receive the gospel,"[8] introducing thought forms tailored as a matrix for the paradigms of Christ. His book *Peace Child* also conveys this truth, which has dawned on the missionary community as a whole only recently.

The point of believing in the Bible today is that it tells us what we may and may not expect of God. It gives us parameters, showing us how God works in advance of human effort to open doors for the

Gospel. What is the point of reading the Bible if we then say (as some Presbyterian missionaries did) that God has now changed His ways?

Christianity as a product of European culture has been a dismal failure. Christianity as the power of a sovereign God poured out for all nations has credibility—if we can keep from getting in the way of what God wants to accomplish.

The Motilones

By contrast to the experience of Native American missions in the West, Bruce Olson demonstrates what can happen when the Christian Church frees herself from narrow Western paradigms. This missionary to the Motilone Indians of Colombia shows us that the work of discipling the nations works best when Christians retain biblical paradigms.

Cross-Cultural Respect

As a student at Penn State, Bruce came increasingly under conviction that God was leading him to Colombia and Venezuela. He read voraciously about these countries and applied to be a missionary there. Applied—and was turned down. He lacked every credential imaginable. But he could not ignore the imperative to go to Colombia. Unable to get excited about any other life calling, he flew to Colombia and arranged a visit to a mission compound on the Mavaca River.

Bruce was not impressed with this mission work. He was particularly disturbed to see missionaries forcing a Western style on natives who were dressing like Americans and singing "Rock of Ages." And he came to the increasing conviction that he was being led to bring the Gospel of Jesus to the Motilones, a feared tribe who had killed outsiders whenever they strayed into their territory.

Bruce made his way into their villages, gained their trust, adopted their ways and learned their language. Clinging to the Gospel for his foundation, he took the good of the West and introduced it to Motilone culture in a manner respectful of their worldview. In this way he effectively helped the Motilones adapt to the material advancements of the West. This he attributed to two causes: First, he never asked the Motilones to give up their own culture; and second, he relied on the power and leading of the Holy Spirit.

God Prepared a People

Bruce's breakthrough in his Christian witness came about through the power of the Holy Spirit—and through the fulfillment of shamanistic prophecy, similar to that of the Salish peoples.

One day on a journey, Bruce and his friend Bobarishora came upon two warriors. One was shouting into a hole he had dug, "God, God, come out of the hole." The other was in a tree stuffing banana leaves into his mouth and trying to chew them while crying, "God, God, come from the horizon."

Bobarishora explained that the first man's brother had died far from home. They were praying that God—who, as the story went, had left long ago when the people were led astray—would come back and return him to life so that he could come home.

Wrote Bruce:

> A lively discussion started. The man who had been in the trees came down and joined us. He reminded us of the legend about the prophet [a tall man with yellow hair] who would come carrying banana stalks, and that God would come out of those stalks.
>
> I couldn't quite understand the idea behind the legend.
>
> "Why look for God to come out of a banana stalk?" I asked.
>
> There was a puzzled silence. It made sense to them, but they couldn't explain it. Bobby walked over to a banana tree which was growing nearby. He cut off a section and tossed it toward us.
>
> "This is the kind of banana stalk God can come from," he said. It was a cross section from the stalk. It rolled at our feet.
>
> One of the Motilones reached down and swatted at it with his machete, accidentally splitting it in half. One half stood up, while the other half split off. Leaves that were still inside the stalk, waiting to develop and come out, started peeling off. As they lay at the base of the stalk, they looked like pages from a book.
>
> Suddenly a word raced through my mind. "Book! Book!"
>
> I grabbed up my pack and took out my Bible. I opened it. Flipping through the pages, I held it toward the men. I pointed to the leaves from the banana stalk, then back to the Bible.
>
> "This is it!" I said. "I have it here! This is God's banana stalk."[9]

This incident—the death of a loved one provoking pleading prayers for God to come back—opened the door for the Gospel among the Motilones. The Holy Spirit had infiltrated their culture already to prepare them for the King of kings. Bruce Olson—a tall man with sandy hair—was the fulfillment of Motilone shamanistic prophecy. If he had denied such prophecy for today, he might have witnessed about Jesus Christ until he was blue in the face without results (as had happened among the Spokanes). As it was, virtually all the Motilones became Christians, for they saw God wooing them from within their own understanding of life.

Some Lessons

We have briefly glimpsed two tribes in which God used shamans to prepare them for the Gospel. In one case, the shamans spoke of leaves bound together, brought by people of white skin. In the other they spoke of a banana stalk out of which God would come, brought by a tall man with yellow hair. The similarity of these prophecies suggests that the same God engineered both. We wish to draw three lessons from these two experiments in Christian missions.

1. *The Western worldview has no categories with which to understand such happenings.* Cultural evolution is the paradigm that most scholars and historians use when evaluating the history of nations. To them, religion is merely a product of a culture and Christian missions is a form of cultural imperialism.

While there have certainly been many instances of cultural imperialism in the spread of Christianity during the colonial era, there has also been the working of a sovereign God (not to mention other spiritual powers). We Westerners must expand our worldview to include the influence of the spiritual realm in history including the workings of the sovereign God and of Jesus Christ, who reigns supreme.

2. *God has a will of His own, a way of doing the very thing we insist He cannot or will not do.* He chose to announce the birth of Jesus, for example, to astrologers, even though He abhors astrology—and He announced it to them through a star! We may object to such ways as being unlike God, yet God has a will of His own

and can do whatever He wants, as Peter pointed out to his fellow apostles in explaining about Cornelius (Acts 10:47; 11:17).

God does not encourage animistic religion. Shamanistic prophecy is more likely to be false than true. Aboriginal shamans were not always paragons of virtue, as Shining Shirt and *Yuree-rachen* apparently were. Yet although the colonial worldview could not recognize it, God was willing to use respected native shamans to reveal His Son to their people.

3. *The Church is not on her own.* We must, like Jesus, learn to see what God is doing and then align ourselves with it. But as long as the Church lives under the brass heaven, we will miss the leadings of our Lord whom we cannot see.

Jesus said to the brass heaven builders of His day, "My Father is always at his work to this very day, and I, too, am working" (John 5:17). Paul said, "God works for the good of those who love him, who have been called according to his purpose" (Romans 8:28). It is this vision of a God who works that we must rediscover as we move toward the fulfillment of the Great Commission of the Church.

Part **4**

Developing a More Whole and Wholesome Worldview

19

The Brass Heaven
Is Collapsing

In *The Structure of Scientific Revolutions,* Thomas Kuhn convinces us that science does not progress by the methods of Descartes, accumulating certainties through observation and deduction. Rather, scientists propose paradigms that they believe will resolve problems and solve puzzles better than older paradigms. During times of crisis a new paradigm emerges, articulated by a few innovators who are less invested in the older, accepted paradigms. As in political revolutions, the old order passes away. Behold, the new has come.

Because retooling new paradigms takes a lot of energy and trouble, paradigm shifts rarely happen without crisis. Kuhn writes: "As in manufacture so in science—retooling is an extravagance to be reserved for the occasion that demands it. The significance of crises is the indication they provide that an occasion for retooling has arrived."[1]

Times of crisis are marked by two characteristics. First, problems and puzzles remain unsolved because the accepted paradigms do not have the power to solve them. We have seen, for example, that brass heaven paradigms did not adequately explain the rise of Adolf Hitler. A new generation of scholars emerged that reinterpreted Nazism by the paradigms of occult power. These paradigms better explained what seemed a strange anomaly to brass heaven historians like William Shirer. (Today young Westerners are trying on these paradigms en masse.)

Times of crisis are also characterized by the accumulation of anomalies that do not fit the old paradigms. More and more versions of these paradigms must be invented to explain the anomalies, yet the paradigms still fail to satisfy. Kuhn writes: "[The] proliferation of versions of a theory is a very usual symptom of crisis."[2]

We have seen, for example, that variations of evolutionary theory are proliferating in the face of data that do not fit Darwinism. This is a sign of crisis for Darwinism and for evolutionary theory in general. Yet within the epistemology of Descartes, no other paradigms are appearing. These can appear only from outside that epistemology, by supplying a paradigm of God the Creator.

Kuhn summarizes the concept of scientific revolution:

> The transfer of allegiance [to a new paradigm] is a conversion experience that cannot be forced. . . . Conversions will occur a few at a time until, after the last holdouts have died, the whole profession will again be practicing under a single, but now different, paradigm.[3]

Such a conversion experience is approaching, not only for science, but for Western culture as a whole. We have arrived at a state of crisis.

The Paradigm Shift

The process Kuhn described in 1962 is happening culture-wide today. We evidenced in chapters 5, 9 and 10 the crisis of Western culture. As a result of this crisis, the West is undergoing a massive paradigm shift or "conversion experience." As the brass heaven of the "modern" era collapses, a new house is being designed out of bits and pieces from every worldview under the sun. The accepted label for the new worldview is *postmodern*, a term borrowed from a movement in architecture that replaced the cold, sterile functionalism of the modern era with a synthesis of many styles.

Postmodern thinking grows from the realization (outlined in chapter 3) that *there is no such thing as objective truth*. All data that comes into our consciousness is filtered by processes controlled by our subconscious mind and by our culture. This belief in paradigms has itself become a paradigm. The paradigm about paradigms has plopped into the serene pool of the West, producing ripples everywhere. *There is no objective truth!* We are surrounded by opinions. Because we cannot escape the influence of cultures, cultures themselves have become more significant to our worldview than they used to be. An eclectic worldview is now replacing the "modern" worldview of the brass heaven era.

Until recently we Westerners felt we had a corner on the truth. This attitude did not come from Christianity per se (which has not been a purely Western phenomenon) but from the Enlightenment (which has). Those Christians who wedded the Gospel with Enlightenment philosophy believed that the people of the developing world were lagging behind. But now we are dismayed by

- The current breakdown of Western institutions
- The baffling complexity of the natural world
- The inescapable reality of spiritual powers
- Our entanglement with the kaleidoscope of global cultures

Stung by our former naïveté, *we have become devotees of pluralism*. As Anthony Giddens writes, "The postmodern outlook sees a plurality of heterogeneous claims to knowledge, in which science does not have a privileged place."[4] The geodesic dome—pristine, symmetrical, homogeneous in design—now seems obsolete, '50ish and embarrassingly arrogant. Trying to be inclusive of all cultures, we are now building a worldview out of the best bits of all worldviews. No one, after all, wants to be arrogant.

The Neo-Pagan Glove for the Pluralistic Hand

To those convinced of the Christian Gospel, postmodernity contains both bad news and good. First, the bad news.

Postmodernity, in the words of David Harvey, "swims, even wallows, in the fragmentary and the chaotic currents of change as if that is all there is."[5] Though it grows out of a desire to rid ourselves of arrogance, the movement toward pluralism holds out no more hope for positive change than the rigid and arrogant philosophy of the brass heaven. It contains bits and pieces that never add up to a whole.

Also, pluralism is a movement that already went bad in ancient Rome and during Hitler's Third Reich. Hitler's own statements reflect a postmodern worldview:

> We are now at the end of the Age of Reason. The intellect has grown autocratic, and has become a disease of life. . . . What is called the crisis of science is nothing more than that the gentlemen are beginning to see of their own accord how they have gone off line with their objectivity and independence.[6]

Postmodern pluralism is setting the stage, potentially, for a widespread return to neo-paganism, as in Nazi Germany. Paganism makes a far more suitable set of clothes for pluralism than does Christianity. In paganism, everyone's god is equally acceptable, everyone's theology equally wise. The unforgivable sin is arrogance; all others are acceptable. If the Western Church wishes to legitimize this trend of Western culture (as the mainline churches legitimized the last one), it will end up in neo-paganism.

Things are already moving that way. Reader's Digest published an article on a recent assembly of the World Council of Churches that contained this tidbit (emphasis added):

> Before the opening worship service began at the last general assembly of the World Council of Churches (WCC) in Canberra, Australia, delegates passed through the smoke of burning leaves. This was a pagan cleansing rite. The congregation then listened to recorded insect noises and watched a male dancer impersonate a kangaroo. The next day, as two painted, loin-clothed Aborigines cavorted, South Korean theologian Chung Hyun Kyung invoked spirits of the dead and exhorted the audience of more than 4,000 to read the Bible "from the perspective of birds, water, air, trees" and to "think like a mountain." Quite a display, but was it Christian? *Some delegates protested against the animism, spiritism and New Age beliefs that were presented. "Pagan culture has infiltrated the WCC," says Vijay Menon, an Anglican delegate of Indian origin. "I left that behind to become a Christian."* [7]

The American Church is flirting with neo-paganism, too. This budding romance broke out into public view (among other displays) at the Reimagining 1993 Conference in Minneapolis, attended by some 2,000 mainline denominational women and a scattering of men. The conference was planned by various denominational leaders and supported with denominational money.

Speeches from the conference reflected the deep hurt and anger that fuel some of the feminist movement. Conference leaders did not turn to the Man Jesus for a healing of their hurts, tragically, but to other spiritual powers. And they are churning out other doctrines than those of Christ, as their speeches clearly reveal:

> As an incest survivor, I can no longer worship in a theological context that depicts God as an abusive parent and Jesus as the obedient, trusting child. . . .

> I don't think we need a theory of atonement at all . . . I don't think we need folks hanging on crosses and blood dripping, and weird stuff. . . .

> We cannot have one savior . . . just like the Big Mac, prepackaged and shipped all over the world. It won't do. It's imperialistic. . . .

> The church has always been blessed by gays and lesbians, witches, shamans and artists. . . .

The concluding litany offered the conferees a milk-and-honey ritual in honor of the goddess Sophia:

> Our maker, Sophia, we are women in your image. With the hot blood of our wombs we give form to new life. . . . With nectar between our thighs we invite a lover. . . . With our warm body fluids we remind the world of its pleasures and sensations. . . . With the honey of wisdom in our mouths we prophesy a full humanity to all the peoples. . . .

These teachings may seem innocuous to those who sympathize with the hurts women have sustained at the hands of men and who have little awareness of the history of heresies in the Church. But to those who are aware of ancient heresy, these teachings are an unwelcome reemergence of Gnosticism, against which many of the letters of our New Testament were written. Gnosticism was a clever repackaging of fertility-cult paganism in wrappings that might appeal to Christian leaders and intellectuals. The Gnostic Archontici taught, for example, that above the Creator dwells a more perfect deity, the "Mother of Lights."

There was a feminist side to ancient Gnosticism. One woman at the Reimagining 1993 Conference actually quoted Gnostic writings, lambasting the Christian Scriptures as hopelessly paternalistic and therefore harmful to women.

Is there no other healing for the hurts that fuel this type of feminism? The Christian answer to trauma and hurt (including that inflicted on women by men) is to seek the power of Jesus, who strengthens us with God's power in the inner nature (Ephesians 3:16–17) and enables us to forgive those who have hurt us—even rapists and fathers who commit incest. The satanic stronghold of bitterness, in the midst of forgiveness, melts into water, which flows into reconciliation between the sexes.

The answer of some feminists, however, is to seek a broader definition of God. One woman described her spiritual journey:

> I have spent the past two years in search of the femininity of my God. This is an ongoing struggle that has led me through the Bible and back to study the ancient Greek goddesses and back further still to Gaia and the ancient fertility goddesses. These pagan myths and histories have served as a paradigm to help me to re-define and re-visualize a more complete and omnifarious Christian God.[8]

Some denominational church leaders seem compelled, in a postmodern climate, to allow God to be redefined in any way a person may wish to redefine Him. Commissioners to the 1992 General Assembly of the Presbyterian Church (USA) were welcomed with a Native American smudging ceremony, which was, in the words of the General Assembly materials, "aimed to welcome friendly spirits and expel unfriendly ones."[9]

Christianity? Animism? What's the difference? Some Christian leaders seem to lack even the most basic spiritual discernment.

Postmodernity, like Manichaeism, is a house constructed of everyone's leftovers—a few bricks here, a bamboo frame there, a geodesic triangle there. It has no pattern. It is as likely to tell us to think like a mountain as to think like God. It aims merely to offend no one. How is this pastiche of diversity an improvement over the brass heaven or the comfortable home of Augustine? As in fifth-century Rome, the tendency toward pluralism will certainly lead to widespread pagan and syncretistic faiths—unless the Church acts now.

The options we are sorting through in the West today are no different than those Augustine investigated in the fifth century:

1. *The skepticism of science* (as in Academic philosophy), in which the spirit world and spiritual power are not recognized.

2. *The credulity of pagan and syncretistic religions* (such as Gnosticism), in which all spiritual reality is accepted with no sieve to strain out the evil, the illusory or the perverse. Truth and morals become relative.

3. *Faith in the revelations of our Creator* (biblical faith), in which God shows us the spirit realm and gives us dominion over the material realm. This third option alone promises Westerners a house built on rock, not on sand.

The Hope of a Paradigm Shift

Doug: Now we can perhaps see the good news. Just as Augustine, by his mother's prayers, tired of Manichaean and Academic philosophy and discovered the Christian alternative, so can we. The tide is in; the geodesic sand castle is washing away. The generation that built the brass heaven is watching it be dismantled before their eyes.

The younger generation, doubtful of the wisdom of their elders, are ready to build a fresh new worldview. They are ready for a conversion. Will they be converted to the pluralism and syncretism of New Age religion, or will they be converted to biblical faith? Today the West is just where ancient Rome was, for whom, in the words of Gibbons, all religions were to the people equally true, to the philosophers equally false and to the government equally useful.

During a paradigm shift, people are teachable as they are not when their views seem well assured. To the Church, the present paradigm shift presents an opportunity we did not have a generation ago, when Westerners were confident about scientific powers. If we can keep from fighting each other over decorative matters and concentrate on building the house of the Lord in its apostolic structures, we can make a good case for biblical paradigms, which work and represent the truth better than any other.

There are six areas of hope and opportunity flowing from the present paradigm shift.

1. "Supernatural" Phenomena

Andrew Greeley discovered in a 1974 survey that 39 percent of a random sample of Americans believed they had experienced a spiritual reality greater than they. But the last persons they would tell about their experiences were professional clergy because "they don't believe such things anymore." In the same year, *Psychology Today* reported that nearly sixty percent of Americans had had a spiritual experience of some kind, but few had found help from Christian churches or pastors in interpreting it.[10]

Because the Church was ignoring the spiritual paradigms she kept in her own Bible, searching Westerners have looked to gurus, psychics, cultists and panderers of psychedelics to interpret spiritual phenomena for them. I have seen several children of pastors get involved in occult activities and, as a result, become terribly demonized. Their parents were not equipped even to understand what was happening, let alone bring healing or deliverance. But when people discover the power and gifts of the Holy Spirit, the reality of God breaks in upon them, resulting in the assurance of His love and the satisfaction of their spiritual longings. In the present widespread cultural decline and paradigm shift, Westerners are more receptive to the power of God (and of the demonic) than ever before.

2. Helping People Walk with God

For several decades we pastors tried to be scientific, to develop a professional style to fit into cultural expectations. The idea that a pastor walks with God and helps others to do so was simply not *in*. But in a paradigm shift we have a fresh opportunity to rediscover the rewards of walking with God, and of helping others to do so.

Recently a woman came to my church hungry for God. Judy was dissatisfied with her life and wondering if God was not somehow the answer to her dissatisfaction. After the worship service she came forward to receive Christ into her life. The Holy Spirit was drawing her quietly into a relationship with Jesus and she was ready to say yes. I prayed that she would learn to walk with God.

During a subsequent pastoral visit, I told her that she could expect harassment from Satan, who was offended by people who become Christians; but she could also expect God to speak to her in His still, small voice. She should look to Him for guidance, since according to James 3:17, Isaiah 30:21 and 1 John 2:27 we feel peace from God when we are moving in His will, and unsettled and out of step when we are moving out of His will.

All this was news to her, and she was eager to try living according to these principles, guided by the Holy Spirit. She listened and learned, and entered quickly into this walk of faith in God's promises and commands.

The role of the church in Judy's life was to help her recognize that Jesus alone could satisfy her spiritual hunger, and to help her walk out her new faith. She attended one of our discipleship groups, learned to recognize God's ways and became a solid Christian in record time. In the process she learned how to

- Relate to a personal God
- Listen for His guidance
- Become sensitized to His definition of right and wrong
- Appreciate His written Word as her guide in life
- Sing and pray to Him
- Tell others what He was doing for her

The secular and professional training I received in seminary during the 1960s prepared me for none of this sort of ministry. Yet helping people walk with God is where we find most of the rewards of

Christian ministry. A paradigm shift offers a chance to rediscover this most basic dimension of Christian ministry.

3. Dealing with the Demonic

Our culture is coming into a growing realization that demons are real, whether or not they are scientifically verifiable. The paradigms of Scripture that we have ignored for so long can help us, by proper discernment, to free troubled people. Nowhere in experience do we see so clearly the power of the cross and the name of Jesus than in deliverance ministry.

A woman began to attend our church whose three-year-old daughter was terrorized by visions of a dragon-like creature stalking her bedroom. Nothing Chris could say to her little girl would calm her. As her daughter's outbursts of sheer terror became more and more frequent, Chris became exasperated. Finally one Sunday morning she brought her daughter to church for prayer.

My elders and I did not write off this complaint as the delusion of a childish imagination; we interpreted it as a spiritual problem. We rebuked the demon, bound it, required it in Jesus' name to vacate Chris' household, and placed the protection of the blood of Christ around her family.

Later the child reported to her mother that the "dragon" had left and was no more to be seen.

Western education would not have counseled us to treat Chris' problem in this way—as a spiritual problem. Western education, in fact, would have counseled us *not* to treat Chris' problem in this way. But we are discovering that spiritual problems require spiritual solutions.

Brad mentioned in chapter 15 that he and I have been involved with Dunamis Project conferences throughout the country, in which a team of Presbyterian and Reformed leaders attempt to help Christians build ministries that rely on the power of God. During these conferences we have seen evidence of the demonic, including the effects of Satanic ritual abuse. One conferee gave the following testimony, the like of which we find frequently in the New England states:

My father and paternal grandmother were devoted servants of Satan who actively participated in satanic worship. My father's family had been involved for generations. They were dedicated to passing down the knowledge, keeping the "blood line" active, and gaining more and more power by any means necessary. I was expected to follow the "ancient ways," and for a while I did. But God had other plans.

My mother never became involved in satanic worship. My father's and grandmother's involvement were carefully kept from her. She was a Christian, and I was taught and influenced by her faith as well as the faith of her Christian friends. Their prayers for me were many, and they were unknowingly engaged in spiritual warfare.

. . . Prior to my senior year of high school the Lord showed me how the wall between the two worlds, the light side and the dark side [in me], was beginning to crumble, and through the death of a close friend, the worlds intersected. Over the next two years the tensions intruded on each other more frequently. I became increasingly confused, depressed, rebellious, and suicidal. I used or did anything I could to numb the pain I felt. Following my senior year of high school, the two worlds again intersected. I believe it was at this time that the part of me living in the dark side stood and said, "No more."

It was not a victorious stand. I simply said, "No more. I would rather die." The spiritual battle waged over the next six months was indescribable. My life was literally on the line. I felt no hope and had no real understanding of what was happening. But God knew.

On January 1, 1971, I was gently and lovingly introduced to the Holy Spirit. I saw for the first time that the power of the Holy Spirit could defeat all darkness and that I could truly become a child of God. The chains of bondage were broken and my life was completely turned around. I was filled with a desire to live, to grow in the Lord, and to serve Him. I was delivered from the intense oppression as I experienced rapid growth and maturation. Many footholds were severed as I gave God control of my life.[11]

Satanism, witchcraft and other forms of "spirituality" have resurfaced today just as they did in pre-Nazi Germany. The Church must confront this reality, not cover it up behind the brass heaven.

Robson Gomes, a Brazilian theological student interning in my church, reports that in Brazil there is a massive popular movement of spiritism. People involved in spiritism frequently become demonized and need deliverance. Deliverance of people from demonization in his home church, Robson says, is an almost weekly occurrence. He also makes an interesting comment about America: "The demons are here, too, but they are in hiding."

His comment has been borne out in our Dunamis Project conferences, for at these conferences we have been confronted by demonized people—mostly sincere Christians who have suffered many years from spiritual problems never discerned by their churches. These have afflicted clergy and laity alike. A young pastor was delivered from a spirit of fear that had long hindered his ministry. One woman testified that after her deliverance at the conference, she slept soundly for the first time in years.

In recent years much sound teaching has been published about deliverance and spiritual warfare. Brad and I recommend Tom White's *A Believer's Guide to Spiritual Warfare* and *Breaking Strongholds*, Charles Kraft's *Defeating Dark Angels* and C. Peter Wagner's *Wrestling with Dark Angels*.

4. Junking Rusty Theories—Evolution

The coherent theory explaining creation as a product of blind chance has (as we described in chapter 8) proven less durable than some had hoped—a casualty of our shift to postmodernity. Our epistemology is changing, and with it the verities that were built on top of it.

In 1991 a Gallup poll inquired into American beliefs about creation and evolution. Only nine percent held to a strict evolutionist line. (Among college graduates, 16.5% did.) The most popular belief was a strict biblical creationist view, supported by 47% of Americans (25% of college grads). The second-most-popular belief was of the forty percent who believed that "man developed over millions of years from less advanced forms of life, but God guided this process, including man's creation." Apparently the last group was somewhere between "I don't know" and "All of the above."

If the Church greets this news about creation faith by fighting over the precise meaning of each verse of the book of Genesis, we will have missed the boat. Debate over the Bible will only remind us why Westerners abandoned biblical paradigms at the beginning of this century (see p. 130).

If, on the other hand, the Church recognizes the most basic question in every culture—*Where is the power for living?*—we can once again offer the creation as Exhibit 1 for the power of God. In light of the present paradigm shift, the Church can again preach that the earth proclaims God's handiwork, that His power can make us new creations in Christ, and that His power will recreate all things at the end of the age.

5. Power Churches

If the real issue is *Where is the power for living?* the Church has an opportunity to replace the power of the rational mind with a credible presentation of the power of God. The churches that are doing so are, if numbers of members offer any clue, among the most successful churches. A recent report listed the fastest growing congregations in America:

> According to John Vaughn, Director of the International Megachurch Research Center in Bolivar, Missouri, 31 of the fastest-growing congregations in the U.S. in 1991 were "independent charismatic" churches. Six were from such classical Pentecostal denominations as the Assemblies of God, The Church of the Foursquare Gospel, the Church of God, and the United Pentecostal Church. Other churches on the list included 23 Southern Baptist churches, seven "independent evangelical churches," five Church of Christ congregations, and five from Chuck Smith's Calvary Chapel network. Few churches from the mainline Protestant churches made the list.[12]

Those American churches that have opted to proclaim the power of God, either through preaching the Gospel with power or through an emphasis on signs and wonders, have grown. Those denominations that have opted to adapt the Gospel to the Western worldview to make it more respectable intellectually have not grown, as is evident in the graphs on the following page.

This news may baffle mainline denominational leaders who have carefully built churches on sound German theology and good management technique. But the younger generation is interested in spiritual reality, not secularism, political control, higher criticism of the

The Growth of Mainline vs. Charismatic/Pentecostal Churches

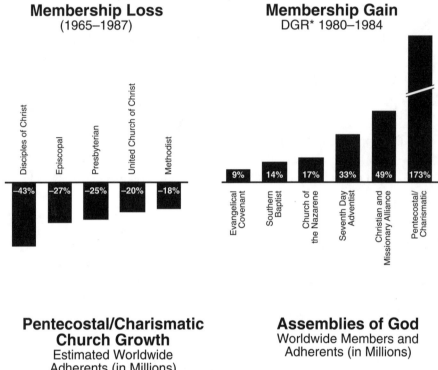

Membership Loss
(1965–1987)

Disciples of Christ: −43%
Episcopal: −27%
Presbyterian: −25%
United Church of Christ: −20%
Methodist: −18%

Membership Gain
DGR* 1980–1984

Evangelical Covenant: 9%
Southern Baptist: 14%
Church of the Nazarene: 17%
Seventh Day Adventist: 33%
Christian and Missionary Alliance: 49%
Pentecostal/Charismatic: 173%

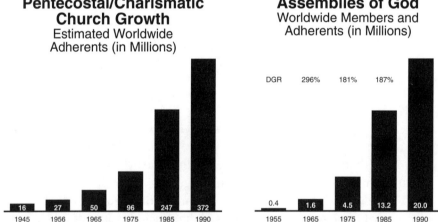

Pentecostal/Charismatic Church Growth
Estimated Worldwide Adherents (in Millions)

1945	1956	1965	1975	1985	1990
16	27	50	96	247	372

Assemblies of God
Worldwide Members and Adherents (in Millions)

	DGR	296%	181%	187%	
0.4		1.6	4.5	13.2	20.0
1955		1965	1975	1985	1990

*DGR = Decade Growth Rate. Information provided by Vinson Synan, C. Peter Wagner, and David Barrett. Graphics provided by Vinson Synan. Used by permission.

Bible, an obese church bureaucracy or clever management theory—faiths that still run strong in the mainline Protestant churches.

When the Church offers only a belated imitation of what the world already has, is it any wonder that people are not beating a path to her door? The young want to know whether God is real, whether the Gospel is true and whether Jesus still brings the Kingdom of Heaven that Paul described as "power," not "talk." The kind of church that ministered to the generations of Freud and Bultmann is no longer relevant in a postmodern world.

Paul Hiebert described the old ways that are rapidly growing defunct:

> Order, organization, planning, control, managing by objective, and production are common values in many North American churches and mission agencies. Prayer, waiting on God, and seeking his leading are used to introduce our planning meetings, or relegated to the aged or the marginalized.[13]

The geodesic assumption that God will not do anything for people has made deep inroads into the Church. All of this must now be unlearned if the Church will minister effectively to postmoderns. And it *can* be unlearned during a paradigm shift when a culture is willing to retool.

6. The Kingdom of God in the Developing World

Global communication has shrunk the world—a fact that cuts two ways. On the one hand, it brings us closer to pagan, animistic, atheistic and Islamic thinking. On the other hand, it makes us more aware of the power of God flowing freely in the developing world.

Reports from Argentina, for instance, reveal that spiritual awakening is happening there. In the days of Jonathan Goforth, the Western Church could simply ignore such reports as the wild exaggeration of primitive peoples. Today we do not have that luxury. We have been brought near these people and must acknowledge what God is doing among them. Hector Jimenez is a converted Argentinean drug dealer who now pastors a church of over 200,000. Of these new converts, many are former homosexuals. Edgardo Silvoso, a fellow revivalist in La Plata, reports that these homosexuals were healed not through counseling but through prayer and a visitation of God.

In America, by contrast, the Church tends to pay the most attention to the proclamations of science. But despite reports on the national news, scientific research is a long way from reaching many definitive conclusions about homosexuality, its causes or cures. The news that intensive prayer by the Church has created a climate of deliverance for homosexuals in Argentina must be greeted with surprise by Western Christians (if they hear it at all).

As we are trying to point out, however, the paradigms of Scripture, unshackled from higher criticism, have the power to reveal the thoughts of God and the power of God. As the Western Church is freed from the limitations of science during a postmodern age, she can rediscover her true calling—to bring the Kingdom of God on earth as it is in heaven.

Our friend Tom White describes the kind of Bible-induced processes that have brought such astonishing results in Argentina:

> Three days ago I returned from Buenos Aires, where I participated in the second annual Harvest Evangelism Institute. It seems clear to me the nation is in the midst of "vival," an expansive move of the Spirit of God to bring explosive growth to the church. For years now I have heard and read about Carlos Annacondia (former businessman turned crusade evangelist), Omar Cabrera (pastors a church of 50,000+), Eduardo Lorenzo (a Baptist pastor who learned to apply spiritual warfare to church growth), and Hector Jimenez (former drug dealer and prison inmate who now pastors a church that meets over 70 times a week and is still expanding at 200,000+). I met these men, listened to them, visited in their churches.
>
> . . . Their strength is their heart unity in Christ, and their common vision to reach their city. Their methodology is prevailing prayer for the lost—not inward, self-oriented prayer, but compassionate petition for the unsaved. And the new experimental dimension is spiritual warfare, a strategic targeting of satanic strongholds, first within the church itself (e.g., disunity, pride, apathy, ignorance of enemy schemes), then within the city (e.g., Freemasonry, New Age movement, drug trade, pornography industry, intellectualism, etc.) When these elements are working together, at the right time the Gospel is

presented to the entire city, through both door-to-door contact, radio, television and crusade meetings.[14]

In a paradigm shift, we Westerners can receive such news from other countries without the hindrance of brass heaven self-confidence and blindness. We may once again put our confidence in God's power, won by Jesus on the cross, proven by His resurrection, poured out in the Holy Spirit, and testified to by the apostles and prophets of the Church.

Helping People Expand Their Worldview

Brad: As the stranglehold of Cartesian thinking gives way to a multidimensional, relativistic, expanding universe, the Church is faced with new challenges and opportunities. These will vary depending on how any given group of Christians has accommodated itself to brass heaven thinking.

Evangelicals

Many evangelicals, though they have chosen to remain faithful to the biblical witness to Jesus, have through dispensationalism shut out the present work of the Holy Spirit. In guarding the truth that God has spoken and acted in Scripture, many evangelicals have lost the truth that God speaks and acts now. Charles Kraft summarizes:

> Instead of attempting to return to at least the more reasonable aspects of the supernaturalism that the Enlightenment overturned, Evangelicals have often argued against the liberal positions from the *same* rationalistic basis. We, like they, have often seen little of God's hand in the present and conducted our defense purely on the basis of what God used to do. We have maintained stoutly that God once did miraculous things—the things recorded in Scripture—and will again do such things at the close of the age.

In the present day, however, Evangelicals tend to believe that God has stopped talking and doing the incredible things we read about in Scripture. Now we see God limiting himself to working through the Bible (the inspired record of what he used to do), plus an occasional contemporary "interference" in the natural course of events. . . .

We pray for guidance and then mostly reason it out. We train people to do God's work by sending them to schools where they learn to reason and think philosophically. But we seldom teach them to relate that philosophical thinking either to God or to the human beings they are supposedly learning to minister to. . . . We teach church leaders how to think *about* God and to a lesser extent, human relationships. But we do not usually teach them how to *relate* to God and to other humans.[1]

We evangelicals must expand our worldview to include biblical power paradigms and the "excluded middle" Paul Hiebert wrote of (see chapter 5). Charles Kraft, John White, Paul Hiebert and C. Peter Wagner are currently championing these changes.

Liberals

For the liberal segment of the Church, the challenge requires a more radical change. Liberalism has sought God's truth not in the transcendent revelations of the Bible, but in culture. Following our culture, liberalism has celebrated the triumph of the rational mind over the power of God. But that triumph is now turning to rot. Harry Emerson Fosdick, one of the foremost leaders of liberalism during the '40s, predicted this end:

All truth, we said, is God's truth, and Christian theology can take it in, rejoice in it, and incorporate it into the understanding of the gospel.

A peril, however, was inherent in our endeavor, which liberalism as a whole was neither wise enough to foresee nor Christian enough to forestall. We were adjusting Christian thought to a secular culture. Unaware of the consequence, we made the secular culture paramount and standard. Was this or that factor in Christian thinking in harmony with the new science?—that was the test. The center of gravity was not in the gospel but in the prevalent intellectual con-

cepts of our time. We surrendered our independent standing ground
and became a movement of adaptation and accommodation.
     Some of us saw the debacle coming and were deeply concerned.[2]

Doug and I come out of liberal backgrounds. We celebrate what
is good in the liberal movement—its passion for justice and its concern for the poor and for minorities. But pulling up the anchor from
biblical revelation has cast the movement adrift on an endless sea
with no direction except the prevailing currents. The natural tendency, reacting against fundamentalism, was to accept the epistemology of science. This shift, as Fosdick wrote, caused liberalism to
become a movement of adaptation and accommodation, which to
liberals have become deeply ingrained habits. These habits now
expose them to New Age currents and the philosophy of pluralism.
     The challenge that faces liberals is to see beyond its reaction against
fundamentalism and to gain a new respect for biblical paradigms.

Fundamentalists

There are those today who claim to follow the Bible and nothing but the Bible in everything they do. Their commitment to scrip-
tural standards is laudable, but they are unaware of how our worldviews are influenced by our culture.
     One parishioner complained about her parents, who had for-
bidden her and her siblings dancing, card-playing and reading any
Bible save the King James Version. Despite the parents' fundamental orthodoxy, in which they undoubtedly took a measure of pride,
they subjected their children to verbal abuse that left many emotional scars eventually requiring inner healing. They were unaware
that their attitudes toward dancing and card-playing were largely
cultural, not biblical, and that in neglecting the weightier matters
of love and faith, they had strained out gnats while swallowing
camels. They fell prey to legalism, which poisoned their children's
attitudes about God.
     It is not easy to build biblical paradigms into our worldview. It
requires more from us than to sincerely defend the inerrancy of the
Bible. The process requires a careful walk of obedience to the commands of Christ. These commands may or may not concur with the

familiar childhood ways of a fundamentalist upbringing. It is remarkable how distinct our doctrines of inerrancy are from the process of incorporating biblical paradigms. We are reminded of Lesslie Newbigin's assessment of the liberal-fundamentalist debate:

> For Protestants at least, in the present situation, the crucial question is the authority of Scripture as it is acknowledged and exercised in the life of the Christian community. I have suggested that this question cannot be dealt with except by means of a radical critique of the reigning epistemology, the way in which we regard any claim to know the truth. On the one side there are those who claim for the Bible a kind of authority which it cannot have, an authority which would obliterate the subjective factors which are involved in human knowing of anything. On the other side are those for whom the Bible has no real authority at all because it is simply one strand of the many-stranded fabric of human religious experience. Both parties are led astray by Descartes's dream, by the false ideal of an indubitable knowledge.[3]

The challenge to fundamentalists is to recognize truthfully the limits of our knowledge of the Bible and to try humbly to live out biblical paradigms. In this process, our doctrines of inerrancy become less important than the power of God's Word to create change. In addition, the fundamentalist has settled too often for a head knowledge of what the Bible says, as opposed to a personal relationship with God, to "know the love of Christ which surpasses knowledge" (Ephesians 3:19, RSV).

What Is Involved in Expanding Our Worldview?

With these preliminary remarks behind us, we now move to examine the ways we can help people genuinely to live by biblical paradigms. What are the ingredients that invite people to enjoy the refreshing changes of Christ's Kingdom in both their thinking and their living? There are at least seven.

The Will

Jesus said, "If any one chooses to do God's will, he will find out whether my teaching comes from God or whether I speak on my own" (John 7:17). At the heart of our worldview lies a decision to believe or not to believe what God has said. This decision is connected with our readiness to submit to God and with what is occurring in the rest of our lives.

In the story of the rich man and Lazarus, Jesus warned that many people would be unwilling to believe God: "If they do not listen to Moses and the Prophets, they will not be convinced even if someone rises from the dead" (Luke 16:31). It would be no lack of evidence or credible witnesses that would cause the rich man's brothers to refuse God's warnings. It would be because they *chose not to believe* the ample evidence already given.

A well-known California preacher was preaching at a Chinese church. His sermon, which denounced the gift of tongues, was being translated into Mandarin by an elder of the church.

Suddenly the interpreter turned to the preacher and said, "Hold on a moment! What do you mean those gifts have ceased? I myself have spoken in tongues for years. In fact, I'm praying in tongues even now as I prepare to translate each new sentence."

The preacher responded, "Well, I just don't see it that way."

He chose not to see the evidence of tongues that was before his eyes, despite the claim of the interpreter of the sermon that it was actually helping the interpretation!

One summer my sister came to Taiwan to visit us before she was a committed Christian. We had conversed deeply about Jesus and the Holy Spirit; she was searching for God. One day she accompanied me on a teaching mission in a church in Taipei. The Holy Spirit came with power during the service. As people were being prayed for, some fell on the floor under the Spirit's power, others spoke in tongues, others were filled with joy. One person started to manifest an evil spirit. As I was ministering to the demonized person, I noticed my sister observing these phenomena intently, her face stamped with wonder and fear. Afterward I asked her what she had thought about the evening.

"I know Jesus is real," she replied, "and I know the Holy Spirit was at work. I saw it with my own eyes, so even though I don't understand it, I know it's true. But I refuse to believe in it for myself, because if I do, my whole world will have to change, and right now I just can't handle that."

Unreadiness, fear of the unknown, pride, traditionalism, hurt and many other factors may affect our openness to change. But the basic question behind them all is this: Are we willing to see reality more and more as God sees it? Are we willing to put away our old paradigms and accept new ones as God reveals them?

The Role of Experience

If the will to believe affects what we experience, the opposite is also true: Our experience limits our worldview. Many people cannot accept what they have not experienced.

Suppose one has never experienced a clearly answered prayer, or basic conversion, or a clear instance of God's provision, or any manifestation of the Holy Spirit. Such a person must be willing to be placed in a context where he or she will be directly confronted with the power of God. This is the second ingredient that helps to expand people's worldview.

I grew in my experience of the Holy Spirit by placing myself under the tutelage of Archer Torrey. He shaped my worldview profoundly, not so much by his formal teaching as by exercising a ministry in God's power.

Recognized for his academic excellence and leadership, Archer was assigned to rebuild the Anglican seminary in Seoul that had been closed during the Korean War. After seven years the seminary was on solid footing, but Archer was not satisfied. The seminary was doing a good job in academics, he said, but "it is not the context in which to learn theology." He believed theology needed to be learned in a live-in laboratory, not in a lecture hall. The Church, he believed, should rely on the power of God; but he could not get the students or faculty to take prayer or the power of God seriously. To them these were academic topics.

In 1965, led by the Holy Spirit, the Torreys broke with all tradition, left their comfortable place at the seminary and headed into the mountains of eastern Korea. Supported by God alone, they established Jesus Abbey as an environment in which to learn theology. The community, with a rigorous regimen of farming, community life, prayer and Bible study, provides the context in which theology becomes lived experience. Here, prayer covers everything. Miracles of provision, healings and deliverances are frequent. The Abbey has become a center of theological reflection like L'Abri in Switzerland, but also of spiritual renewal and effective social witness.

The result of the Torreys' obedience to the Holy Spirit has been costly and profound. I am one of the fruits of their obedience. I learned more practical theology at Jesus Abbey than I did in all my prior theological courses.

The Role of Obedience

The founding of Jesus Abbey illustrates the third ingredient that helps people to expand their worldview: obedience. The promises of God are intimately connected to His commands. Those who obey Him and walk by faith find His promises sooner or later, for God is a rewarder of those who seek Him. Provision, answered prayer, the gifts of the Spirit, lasting deliverance from demonic power and inner healing—all these are usually contingent on obedience.

I believed that Jesus could forgive my sins, for example, but I did not experience the joy of His forgiveness until I risked going to a brother and confessing specific sin according to James 5:16. Through obedience, the paradigm of the cleansing blood of Jesus promised to those who confess their sins (1 John 1:7–9) proved for me a valid filter for understanding reality.

I also believed God would provide for those who seek first His Kingdom and His righteousness, but I did not experience this provision until I stopped charging fees for the ministry of PRRMI. Again and again, obedience in response to the leading of the Holy Spirit has resulted for me in a *lived* experience of God's promises, confirming biblical paradigms.

Psychological Makeup and Type

People differ. The way we discern and respond to God differs, too. We must take this fourth ingredient into account as we help people expand their paradigms to include the power of God.

I am different from both Doug and Archer in that I am intuitive while both of them are more logical. Accordingly, we experience the presence and power of God in different ways.

In 1984 Archer came to Taiwan to teach 125 Taiwanese pastors on the Person and work of the Holy Spirit. During the first five days there was little worship or prayer, only dry lectures (which I helped translate) that laid intellectual and biblical foundations. As Archer exegeted the Greek and Hebrew text, the pastors listened intently. I could sense a thin stream of the Holy Spirit moving within our midst.

At the end of the lectures, Archer said matter-of-factly, "If anyone feels led to pray for the baptism of the Holy Spirit, please come forward, and we'll be happy to pray for you."

Most of the pastors came forward. As they did, there was an outpouring of the Holy Spirit the like of which I have never seen before or since. The little stream I had felt earlier became a rushing torrent. As Archer prayed and I translated, the most amazing things happened. People keeled over and rested in the Spirit; demons cried out; people tearfully confessed sins; others spoke in tongues; others had visions. Many recommitted themselves to Jesus Christ.

At one point I could sense the Holy Spirit like a torrent rushing through the room and through me. I turned to Archer and blurted, "Do you *feel* that!"

Archer whirled around and snapped sternly, "Feel what? I don't feel a thing! Learn this, and learn it well: Moving in the Holy Spirit is not a matter of feelings but of obedience! Obedience. Obedience. Not feelings."

His corrective shook me up.

"Yes, sir," I said, and turned to continue praying for the pastors.

That event, in which Archer felt nothing but acted out of obedience, was the beginning of a move of the Holy Spirit that continues in the Taiwan Presbyterian Church to this day. My experience with Archer taught me not to box God in but to let His power touch other people differently than it touches me.

Overcoming Hurts

Some people have been hurt by those who defined God's power too narrowly—and this is the fifth factor we must take into account in helping people live by biblical paradigms. Some nurse anti-charismatic or anti-fundamentalist biases because they have been hurt by charismatics or fundamentalists.

While in college, I would at times come across conservative Christians on campus who rejected me because of my long hair, beard and generally wild appearance, which did not measure up to their standards of Christian dress. Their rejection hurt me and made me less receptive to biblical ideas. Added to this were the hurts I later experienced among charismatics who rejected me for not speaking in tongues.

Only in Korea did I get beyond these hurts. The missionaries I met there saw more broadly—and loved more broadly, too. They did not believe that tongues is the "initial evidence" of the Holy Spirit in a person's life. In the midst of their love I could forgive those who had hurt me and expand my worldview to include the paradigm of tongues.

I see this same principle working in the lives of others. Once, as I was ministering in a church, I received a word of knowledge about several couples close to the front, who were experiencing tensions in their marriage.

"I believe the Lord is saying that Jesus loves you," I said, "and He wants to melt the ice that has formed between you."

Immediately several couples started to hold one another and cry softly. At the end of the service I rejoiced to find that the Lord had done a wonderful work of reconciliation. Many couples gave thanks to Jesus publicly for His love they had experienced vividly. And most who witnessed this gentle manifestation of the Holy Spirit were not only blessed but encouraged to keep growing in faith.

But not everyone rejoiced. A prominent elder reacted violently. Calling a special meeting of the session (the ruling body), he denounced me as a false prophet. The manifestations of the Holy Spirit of 1 Corinthians 12, he insisted, had ceased long ago.

"This is of the devil," he fumed.

I knew it was futile to argue with him. I was up against his brass heaven and there was no breaking through.

But just then the Lord gave me another word of knowledge, one that broke my own heart. Inserting a word into his arguments against spiritual gifts, I said, "Excuse me, sir, but I think the Lord may have given me another word. I would like to submit it to you all for your discernment."

Then I asked whether anyone who had spoken in tongues had ever hurt him.

"Perhaps the real reason for your anger," I added, "has nothing to do with theology, but with unhealed hurt."

At these words he looked stunned.

"Absolutely not!" he shouted, and rushed from the room.

The elders looked stunned, too, but with joy and astonishment. One older man offered words of praise for what God had just done. Then he prayed that this embittered brother, who had been a thorn in many people's side, would finally be healed.

Years ago, they told me, his wife had gotten involved in a charismatic group, received the gift of tongues, then run off with the group leader, leaving this elder to raise several small children by himself.

Knowing this about him, I found it easy to understand why he was so hostile toward spiritual gifts. Nothing hinders openness to new paradigms more than hurts that we associate with those paradigms.

Doug: I have led dozens of discipleship groups over the last twenty-five years in which people learn (as we saw in the last chapter) to trust God and experience His power and provision.

In every group, it seems, there is at least one person who has reservations about the Holy Spirit, and especially about the gift of tongues. These reservations often stem not from a heart hardened by unbelief, but from hurts inflicted by charismatics.

In the context of the love relationships that have grown up in the group, I am able to say that tongues has been a blessing to my own prayer life, but that I do not accept the notion of tongues as a badge of spiritual superiority. I encourage groups to accept whatever they can and allow the healing of past hurts to take place in its time.

With social pressure minimized and hurts soothed, it is remarkable how many people eventually become friends with the gift of tongues.

A Context of Love and Trust

In that same illustration we see the sixth factor that opens people to new paradigms: the trust that grows up in the context of small groups. Jesus was sent to expand the worldview of the entire human race, but He began with twelve disciples who were in a tight fellowship with Him and with one another. The same is true with us. A small group full of love and trust is usually the most powerful context to facilitate change.

In the West, church gatherings follow Enlightenment procedures aimed to help us grasp concepts with our rational minds. In our Sunday school classes we discuss biblical concepts but rarely share our personal experiences of God. Pastors preach to passive pew-sitters and feel we have succeeded when they tell us we gave them something new to think about.

Jesus' approach to ministry was different. He put no confidence in the rational mind but in the power of God. Consequently, His ministry hinged not on intellectual debate but on a relationship of personal trust with a few whom He called disciples. Based on that trust, His disciples learned to trust their Creator in a new way. As they stepped out in faith, believing God for provision, healing or deliverance, they discovered *reality*—the power of God. In this way, Jesus helped them to walk with God.

I have found these principles dynamic and effective in our discipleship groups at Christ Presbyterian Church of Richmond. The groups help people to experience God and change their paradigms about Him. Because the promises of God do not become real apart from obedience to His commands, the Church must provide the environment in which people feel comfortable trying out God's ways before they can know God's promises. This happens best in small groups where people learn to trust each other and God.

Credible Witnesses

The data that support any worldview come from either our own experience or the experience of others. Few of us have seen atoms or molecules. We believe in their existence because credible scientists attest to them.

The same is true in the realm of the Spirit. None of us was present at Jesus' empty tomb, nor were we in the room where He ate a piece of fish to prove He was not a ghost. Yet we may accept Jesus' resurrection on the basis of witnesses whom the Church has found credible.

One of the main hindrances to the expanding of worldview in mainline churches is that many people have not met credible witnesses to the power of the Holy Spirit. If our only exposure to this dimension is a television evangelist who claims to perform miracles, then begs for money the next moment and a year later has fallen into financial or sexual scandal, we are not likely to be interested in the power of the Holy Spirit.

We receive disturbing truth best from those who are most like us and who hold the same values we hold. A sincere but uneducated Pentecostal from the coal mines of West Virginia is not likely to be received as a credible witness among educated Presbyterians or Episcopalians in a big city. For the social activist, a credible witness is one who works for justice and also testifies to the power of God. In academic circles, the credible witness is a person with the "right" degrees. If worldview is to be expanded, credible witnesses are needed who can witness to and embody biblical paradigms.

In the present paradigm shift, many of us are becoming dissatisfied with our understanding of how life works. But changing our worldview can be a profoundly unsettling experience, requiring years of reevaluation of cherished beliefs. We need Christian people who are familiar with the above principles and are willing to be "fathers and mothers in Christ Jesus" to those who are rebuilding their worldview. The need for loving, mature Christians is all the more urgent in that Westerners are now exposed to a bewildering variety of worldview options from around the globe.

It is essential, therefore, that Christians gain a global, and not merely a Western, vision.

Epilogue:
Redrawing the Map of Reality

God is lifting our sights. He is showing us how to think more and more as citizens of heaven and not only as citizens of the West. By the paradigms of Christ, we have a high vantage point from which to evaluate Western culture—and Eastern as well.

Doug: I have in my church a young woman of Indian/Hindu background who was converted to Christ some ten years ago. She has been praying for her family, who remain Hindu, though they have lived in the U.S. for many years. She writes of her recent experience of the power of God helping her bridge her own personal chasm between West and East:

> Yesterday I was invited to attend a worship service at a church where the pastor was gifted in healing and deliverance. With curiosity and skepticism, I went to the service, knowing deep inside that I was bound by something I could not comprehend—something about my Hindu background and culture that crippled my ability to follow Jesus and share His love with others. As the worship began, I had a picture of myself wanting to run to God, but unable to do so because I was trying to pull the Hindu temple behind me.
>
> The pastor spoke about the renewing of our minds in Christ (Romans 12:1–2). He said that Jesus came to set captives free. He

compared us with Lazarus, who needed people to help him remove his graveclothes after Jesus raised him from the dead. He spoke of 2 Timothy 1:7 ("God has not given us a spirit of fear . . ."), a passage God had brought to my heart many times before.

When he gave an altar call, I knew that God wanted me to go forward. I had spent the whole weekend struggling with the validity of my conversion years before. My decision to follow Christ at age 14 was motivated more by a deep need for belonging and friendship than by an understanding of Christ and the cross. How I wished I could give a clearer, more powerful testimony, but I had gone to Jesus innocently as a child, not thinking through the implications of turning my back on generations of Hindu belief. Now I wanted to get beyond this mental battle with my cultural background that left me feeling inadequate, weak-minded and guilty.

At the front of the sanctuary, I pleaded and wept before God. As the pastor began praying for others, I ached with the fear of being passed over in my own time of need. But he looked at me and told me that I no longer needed to be bound to the roots of false religion and philosophy. Then he said, "You no longer serve a guru; you serve Jesus Christ!" People laid hands on me and loosed the chains of Hinduism. I could not stop crying and pleading for freedom.

During this time, I saw in my mind's eye a small Indian man with bushy hair, a painted face and many arms. Distressed, he was gyrating in front of me. I did not know what to think of him until I remembered a picture that God had given me over a year ago. (Journal entry 4/6/92: "I am in the clutches of a strong octopus—tentacles that will not allow me to move ahead.") The octopus and this wild man merged into one. I cried out and commanded him to leave. I am not sure what the little wild man or demon represented, but I know that God met me in a way that was orchestrated purely by His providence.

Later, as we continued in worship, I again saw the picture of myself, God and the temple. This time I was facing the temple, and the people inside were running out to meet God. I left the service filled with a deep assurance that I was free to serve Christ more completely.

I have spent the last ten years of my life trying to integrate my culture with my relationship with Christ. As I have encountered conflict after conflict, I have gradually understood that God is more interested in my willingness to love and serve only Him than in how much I embody my Indian/Hindu culture. In fact, as I have surrendered more of my will to Him, He has led me further away from any intellectual embracing of my heritage. On the other hand, He has given me a deepened love for Indian people, not for the sake of culture and identity, but for the sake of God's love and grace.

"You no longer serve a guru; you serve Jesus Christ. You will have life in the Spirit . . . and you are mine."

This young lady has become a global Christian, a citizen of the Kingdom of heaven. Though postmodernity accentuates cultural distinctives, God diminishes them so that we can move more freely across cultural borders. If the Western Church is to be effective in reaching people for Christ, we must get beyond thinking merely like Westerners and become citizens of God's Kingdom.

Colonial, Anti-Colonial and Global Eras

Paul Hiebert sees the Church doing just that. He traces three historical periods in the West's awareness of cultural pluralism,[1] the first two of which we have reviewed already.

The first is the *colonial period*, in which positivism was assumed to be superior to all other epistemologies. Science was said to provide an accurate photograph of reality. Colonial Westerners took a "higher critical" attitude toward the Hebrews and all non-Western cultures. Having no stance from which to evaluate Western epistemology, humility vanished (the kind of humility the apostle Paul showed toward non-Jewish people). Christians often failed to discern between Western paradigms and the paradigms of Christ.

The recent paradigm shift to postmodernity has brought us into the *anti-colonial period*, with its emphasis on pluralism and subjectivity. The paradigms of many cultures have been reexamined, appreciated and accepted even in areas unproven by science and unapproved by God's Word. Biblical, scientific and historical truth are subjected to countless interpretations as shaped by culture. Postmodernity denies that objective reality can be known; it leads to moral relativism and a sense that all interpretations of the Bible are equally valid.

By this view, objective, accurate photographs of reality do not exist. Life is a dream shaped by our subconscious mind. We are trapped in our subjective worlds, unsure how to communicate the Gospel or anything else beyond the barriers of culture and our private worlds. As hope in an agreed-upon basis for truth slips from our grasp, postmodernity has led to confusion, despair and moral catastrophe.

But this does not end the story of the maturation of the Western worldview. We are moving into a third period, according to Dr. Hiebert, the *global era*, marked by "critical realism," a synthesis of the two previous extremes. In the global era, we see that there is an objective basis for truth, but it is limited. We become "critically realistic" about our own mental powers. If we really want to be honest to God, we must recognize the shortcomings of our own minds.

We do not need (and cannot have) photographs of reality. Yet we can do more than just dream about life. God has equipped us with the means to make mental maps of reality. Thus, we have progressed from the photograph, to the dream, to the map.[2]

Elements in Global Mapmaking

Christians in the global era attempting to redraw their map of reality recognize six elements of biblical mapmaking.

God has given us, through *the paradigms of the Bible,* the key to the map we must each make for ourselves.

Science provides us with recognizable landmarks in the material world.

The power of God provides benchmarks in assessing how the spiritual world breaks into the material.

The credible witness of other mature Christians will suggest topography that we ourselves have not suspected.

Humility is a help in the process, too. Those who humbly recognize the limitations of their own mental maps are those who will likely end up with the best map in the end. (Also, as Paul wrote in Philippians 2, an important spinoff of humility is unity in the Body of Christ.) We are not, on the other hand, to be gullible about other peoples' paradigms, especially those who do not acknowledge the basic paradigms of Christ in the Apostles' Creed. "Test all things," the apostle Paul wrote. Testing what is apostolic, we sift out what is not and alter our maps accordingly, as Augustine did years ago.

Christian freedom is a final element in our mapmaking. Each of us must be left free to make our maps. It is counterproductive to destroy one another's paradigms with ridicule—a frequent manipulative tactic among brass heaven builders and some Christian dogmatists. Science and the paradigms of Christ give us a limited but valid way of discovering truth; ridicule can only jeopardize that discovery.

The apostle Paul demonstrated a global, Kingdom-of-heaven lifestyle. Though a Hebrew, he proclaimed God's paradigms in such a way that they transcended Hebrew culture and were accepted by Gentiles. The paradigms of Christ became a key that people of diverse cultures could use in their mapmaking. God revealed to him what He has done, what He will do and what He requires of us now. These teachings supply the key of the Kingdom—a unique, interlocking set of paradigms that guides people of all cultures in making maps of reality.

These key paradigms are not optional but vital and necessary. Many of the world's peoples are aware of the spirit realm and are trying to relate to it. But in some cases the evil one has inserted spiritual paradigms that conflict with God's revealed Word—the doctrines of neo-pagan Gnosticism, for example, revealed so terribly under Hitler's Third Reich and at other times in history. These paradigms may seem good at first but they prove to be deceptive and destructive. Those who accept them are walking the way that leads to death.

The Church alone has the paradigms of the New Covenant to oppose these doctrines, and we must regain our confidence in proclaiming them. Without them the world is left with the choice between brass heaven despair and New Age deception.

The Power of God

For almost a century, Westerners have treated the power of God as an illusion. But without it there is no gold standard behind the currency of Western values. Today we must return to the gold standard, for our moral and spiritual currency suffers from inflation that is spiraling out of control and bankrupting its value.

Also, as C. Peter Wagner has written, God's power is essential to the proclamation of the Gospel across cultural borderlands. Without God's signs and wonders, our preachings seem to be cultural imperialism. The power of God saves us from imperialism by giving cross-cultural validity to the preached Gospel.

The Gospel is global, not provincial or merely Western. The power of God is displayed among us to cement the paradigms of the Creator into the worldviews of diverse cultures, both Eastern and Western.

The works of God are not mere miracles.[3] The Bible speaks of them more often as "signs." They point beyond themselves to the paradigms of Christ. They remind us that God loves us, that He has a purpose for each of us, that His Son died for our atonement, rose from the dead, took power and is coming again to judge all people and to reward His servants. These paradigms are meant, in turn, to lead us beyond thought into obedience. The mental maps we make are designed to guide our steps obediently in the way of Jesus.

As we break through the brass heaven, we can rediscover the power that leads to obedience to Jesus, and so fulfill at this late hour the prophecy of Bonhoeffer: "The day will come when men will be called again to utter the word of God with such power as will change and renew the world."[4]

Notes

Chapter 1

1. John Calvin, *Institutes of the Christian Religion* III.xx.2.

Chapter 3

1. C. S. Lewis, *Miracles: A Preliminary Study* (New York: Macmillan, 1947), p. 8.

2. Charles Kraft, *Christianity in Culture: A Study in Dynamic Biblical Theologizing in Cross-Cultural Perspective* (Maryknoll, N.Y.: Orbis, 1979), p. 53.

3. Arthur Koestler, *The Act of Creation* (New York: Dell, 1964), p. 50.

4. Koestler, p. 43.

5. Charles Kraft, "Worldview and Spiritual Power," Chinese Leadership Conference on Church Renewal, Spring 1987, (School of World Mission, Fuller Theological Seminary, Pasadena, Calif.), p. 6.

6. Koestler, p. 96.

7. This account is based on a phone conversation with Delores Winder and on her book *Jesus Set Me Free* (Shreveport, La.: Fellowship Foundation, 1986).

Chapter 4

1. Charles Kraft, "Worldview and Spiritual Power," pp. 9–10.

2. *The Rebirth of America* (Arthur S. DeMoss Foundation, 1986), p. 37.

3. Richard Neuhaus, "Moral Leadership in Post-Sectarian America," *Imprimis*, Vol. 2, #7, July 1982, p. 3.

4. David C. Reardon, *Aborted Women: Silent No More* (Chicago: Loyola University Press, 1987), p. 351.

5. Those who become acquainted with the power of God must also come to grips with satanic counterfeits that enter the picture to confuse us. During seasons of spiritual awakening, both types of power can be seen. John White's book *When the Spirit Comes with Power* provides an excellent treatment of this confusing problem, in which spiritual power is used for self-aggrandizement and not for the cross of Christ. Of people who do this Jesus says, "I never knew you. Away from me, you evildoers!" (Matthew 7:23). John White speaks of satanic power as "stolen power."

Chapter 5

1. Charles Kraft, "Worldview and Spiritual Power," p. 10.

2. William J. Bennett, "Quantifying America's Decline," *Movieguide*, Vol. VIII, No. 10, May 1993, pp. 4–5.

3. Kraft, p. 10.

4. C. Peter Wagner, *Christian Life*, December 1984, p. 45 (summarizing Paul Hiebert's thesis).

5. Paul Hiebert, "The Flaw of the Excluded Middle," p. 4, reprinted by permission of Paul Hiebert, Trinity Evangelical Divinity School, Deerfield, Ill.

Chapter 6

1. Augustine, *Confessions*, translated by John Ryan (New York: Doubleday, 1960), p. 139. Ryan's translation has been used throughout.

2. *Confessions*, p. 144.

3. *Confessions*, p. 180.

4. *Confessions*, p. 202.

Chapter 7

1. René Descartes, "Rules for the Direction of the Mind," *Great Books of the Western World*, Vol. 31 (Chicago: *Encyclopaedia Brittanica*, 1952), p. 3.

2. Descartes, p. 5.

3. René Descartes, "Discourse on the Method of Rightly Conducting the Reason and Seeking for Truth in the Sciences," *Great Books of the Western World*, Vol. 31 (Chicago: *Encyclopaedia Brittanica*, 1952), p. 48.

4. René Descartes, "Meditations on the First Philosophy in Which the Existence of God and the Distinction Between Mind and Body Are Demonstrated," *Great Books of the Western World*, Vol. 31 (Chicago: *Encyclopaedia Brittanica*, 1952), p. 69.

5. Descartes, "Meditations," p. 86.

6. Blaise Pascal, *Pensees*, II, 77.

7. John Calvin, *Institutes of the Christian Religion*, I.ii.2.

8. René Descartes, *Great Books of the Western World*, Vol. 31 (Chicago: Encyclopaedia Britannica, 1952), p. ix.

9. Arthur Koestler, *Act of Creation* (New York: Dell, 1964), p. 171.

10. G. K. Chesterton, "The Ethics of Elfland," *A G. K. Chesterton Anthology*, (San Francisco: Ignatius Press, 1985), pp. 266–67.

11. Sigmund Freud, *The Future of an Illusion* (New York: Liveright Publishers, 1928), pp. 95–96.

12. Freud, p. 54.

13. William James, *The Varieties of Religious Experience* (New York: Collier, 1961), pp. 54–55.

14. Freud, p. 68.

15. Freud, p. 83.

16. James, p. 405.

17. Karl Marx and Friedrich Engels, *The Communist Manifesto* (New York: International Free Press, 1948), p. 29.

18. Freud, p. 80.

19. Charles Colson, *Kingdoms in Conflict* (New York: William Morrow/Zondervan, 1987), p. 67.

20. Rudolf Karl Bultmann, *Jesus Christ and Mythology* (New York: Charles Scribner's Sons, 1958), pp. 36–38.

Chapter 8

1. Alfred Noyes quoted in *The Obligation of Universities to the Social Order: Addresses and Discussion at a Conference of Universities under the Auspices of New York University at the Waldorf-Astoria in New York, November 15–17, 1932* (New York: New York University Press, 1933), pp. 357–63.

2. Charles Darwin, *Origin of Species*. For this and the following quotes from Raup, Gould, Grasse, Patterson and Monod, we are indebted to Dr. Henry Morris of the Institute for Creation Research in San Diego.

3. David Raup, "Conflicts Between Darwin and Paleontology," *Bulletin of the Field Museum of Chicago*, January 1979, p. 25.

4. Stephen Jay Gould, "Is a New and General Theory of Evolution Emerging?" *Paleobiology*, January 1980, p. 125.

5. Steven M. Stanley, *Macroevolution: Pattern and Process* (New York: W. H. Freeman Co., 1979), p. 69.

6. Pierre P. Grasse, *Evolution of Living Organisms* (New York: Academic Press, 1977), pp. 4, 8.

7. Michael Denton, *Evolution: A Theory in Crisis* (Bethesda, Md.: Adler and Adler, 1985), p. 75.

8. Colin Patterson, "Evolution and Creationism." Speech given at American Museum of Natural History, November 5, 1981, pp. 1–2. Also quoted by Tom

Bethell in "Agnostic Evolutionists: The Taxonomic Case Against Darwin," *Harper's*, February 1982, p. 50.

9. Nicholas Wade, "Thomas S. Kuhn: Revolutionary Theorist of Science," *Science,* July 8, 1977, p. 143. Taken from Donald E. Chittick, *The Controversy: Roots of the Creation-Evolution Conflict* (Portland: Multnomah, 1984), p. 45.

10. Elmer Ellsworth Brown, *"Guide of Life," A Few Remarks* (New York: New York University Press, 1933), pp. 227–28.

11. Blaise Pascal, *Pensees, Great Books of the Western World*, Vol. 33 (Chicago: *Encyclopaedia Britannica*: 1952), p. 222 (Pensee #273).

12. Pascal, p. 213 (Pensee #230).

13. Pascal, p. 212 (Pensee #222).

14. Denton, pp. 328, 341–42.

Chapter 9

1. Jacques Monod, "The Secret of Life," Australian Broadcasting Co., June 10, 1976.

2. Aldous Huxley, *Ends and Means* (New York: Harper & Brothers, 1937), pp. 312, 315, 316. Quoted from Donald Chittick, *The Controversy: Roots of the Creation-Evolution Conflict* (Portland: Multnomah, 1984), p. 172.

3. Michael D. Lemonick, "How Man Began," *Time,* March 14, 1994, p. 81.

4. Garland Hurt quoted in James H. Simpson, *Report of Explorations Across the Great Basin in 1859* (Reno: University of Nevada Press, 1983), p. 463.

5. Simpson, p. 459.

6. H. H. Bancroft, *Works*, Vol. I (San Francisco: The History Co., 1886), p. 24.

7. Bancroft, pp. 33–34.

8. Alberta Brooks Fogdall, *Royal Family of the Columbia* (Fairfield, Wash.: Ye Galleon Press, 1978), p. 76, quoted in H. H. Bancroft's *History of the Northwest Coast*, Vol. II, pp. 650–53.

9. William Clark to the Secretary of War, March 1, 1826. *American State Papers; Indian Affairs II*, pp. 653–54.

10. H. H. Bancroft, *History of California*, Vol. III (San Francisco: The History Co., 1886), p. 184.

11. Edwin L. Sabin, *Kit Carson Days* (New York: Press of the Pioneers, 1935), p. 56.

Chapter 10

1. Augustine, *The City of God*, II.29, *Great Books of the Western World*, Vol. 18 (Chicago: *Encyclopaedia Britannica*, 1952), p. 168.

2. Martin Luther, *Works*, Vol. 21 (St. Louis: Concordia, 1956), p. 138.

3. Johann Christoph Blumhardt, *Blumhardt's Battle: A Conflict with Satan*, Frank S. Boshold, tr. (New York: T. E. Lowe, 1970).

4. Gerald Suster, *Hitler: The Occult Messiah* (New York: St. Martin's Press, 1981), p. 25.

5. Suster, p. 29.

6. William Shirer, *The Rise and Fall of the Third Reich* (New York: Simon & Schuster, 1960), p. 105. Shirer himself, as is typical of historians of the modern era, regarded Chamberlain as a mere anomaly.

7. Suster, p. 51.

8. Suster, pp. 95, 99.

9. Hermann Rauschning, *The Voice of Destruction* (New York: Putnam, 1940), p. 259.

10. Rauschning, p. 256.

11. Rauschning, p. 256.

12. Louis Pauwels and Jacques Bergier, *The Dawn of Magic* (London: Panther Books, 1964); J. H. Brennan, *Occult Reich* (London: Futura Press, 1974); Francis King, *Satan and Swastika* (London: Mayflower Books, 1976); and Jean-Michel Angebert and Gerald Suster's works as quoted herein.

13. Lewis Sumberg quoted in Jean-Michel Angebert, *The Occult and the Third Reich: The Mystical Origins of Nazism and the Search for the Holy Grail* (New York: McGraw-Hill, 1974), translator's preface, pp. x–xiii.

14. Rauschning, pp. 50–51.

15. Rauschning, p. 233.

16. Dietrich Bonhoeffer, *Letters and Papers from Prison* (New York: Macmillan, 1953), p. 195.

17. Bonhoeffer, p. 167.

18. Bonhoeffer, p. 188.

19. Norman Grubb, *Rees Howells, Intercessor* (Fort Washington, Pa.: Christian Literature Crusade, 1973), p. 246.

20. Grubb, p. 259.

21. Grubb, p. 261.

22. Grubb, p. 261.

23. Grubb, p. 262.

24. Angebert, p. 6.

25. Suster, p. 194.

Chapter 11

1. Philip M. Brown quoted in Elmer Ellsworth Brown, pp. 423–24.

2. Stephen Hawking, *A Brief History of Time*, quoted in "The Creation," *U.S. News & World Report*, December 23, 1991, p. 58.

3. Paul Davies, *The Mind of God*, quoted in "The Creation," p. 60.

4. "The Creation," p. 61.

5. Eugene B. McDaniel with James Johnson, *Scars and Stripes* (Philadelphia: Holman, 1975), pp. 120–21.

6. John Eidsmoe, *Christianity and the Constitution* (Grand Rapids: Baker, 1987), p. 43.

7. Eidsmoe, p. 194.
8. Eidsmoe, p. 208.

Chapter 12

1. Ignatius of Antioch, "Epistle to the Philadelphians," 5.
2. *Didache*, 11.7.8.
3. Eusebius, *Ecclesiastical History,* 5.18.
4. Irenaeus of Lyons, "Against Heresies," 3.11.
5. Irenaeus, 5.6.

Chapter 13

1. The Westminster Confession of Faith, I.9.
2. *The Zondervan Pictorial Encyclopedia of the Bible*, Vol. IV (Grand Rapids: Zondervan, 1976), pp. 675, 682.
3. Alfred Edersheim, *The Life and Times of Jesus the Messiah* (Grand Rapids: Eerdmans, 1971), reprint of the 1886 original, p. 163.
4. *The Zondervan Pictorial Encyclopedia of the Bible*, Vol. II, p. 13.
5. Augustine, *The City of God*, XVIII.34.
6. *The Biblical Illustrator: Daniel* (New York: Fleming H. Revell, no date), p. ix.
7. William Barclay, *The Gospel of Matthew*, Vol. 1 (Philadelphia: Westminster, 1956, 1958), p. 10.
8. J. Arthur Baird, *Rediscovering the Power of the Gospel* (Wooster, Ohio: Iona Press, 1982), p. 14.
9. Charles Colson, *Kingdoms in Conflict* (New York: William Morrow/Zondervan, 1987), p. 219.
10. John White, *When the Spirit Comes with Power: Signs & Wonders Among God's People* (Downer's Grove, Ill.: InterVarsity, 1988), p. 89.

Chapter 14

1. Elmer Ellsworth Brown, *Government by Influence and Other Addresses* (New York: Longmans, Green & Co., 1910), pp. 64–65.
2. Brown, p. 71.
3. C. S. Lewis, *Mere Christianity* (New York: Macmillan, 1943, 1952), p. 37.
4. Christina Hoff Sommers, "Teaching the Virtues," *Imprimis*, November 1991, Vol. 20, #11, p. 2.
5. William James, *The Varieties of Religious Experience* (New York: Collier, 1961), p. 124.
6. Mark Hartwig, "Pornography Warps Men's Attitudes," *Focus on the Family Citizen*, Vol. 6, #6, June 15, 1992, pp. 10–13. All the material about pornography in this chapter was taken from this article.

7. Hartwig, p. 11.

8. Iain H. Murray, *The Puritan Hope* (Edinburgh: Banner of Truth Trust, 1971), p. 5. The quote is from John Knox's *History of the Reformation in Scotland*.

9. Murray, pp. 27–28. Taken from Robert Fleming's *The Fulfilling of the Scripture*.

10. Jonathan Edwards, *A Faithful Narrative of the Surprising Work of God* (Grand Rapids: Baker, 1975), pp. 18–19.

11. Refers to the Achan of Joshua 7 who secretly stole plunder after the victory at Jericho.

12. Jonathan Goforth, *When the Spirit's Fire Swept Korea* (Grand Rapids: Zondervan, 1943), p. 9.

13. Goforth, p. 11.

Chapter 15

1. J. Rodman Williams, *Renewal Theology*, Vol. 2 (Grand Rapids: Academie Books, 1988, 1992), p. 330.

2. Williams, p. 327.

3. Archer Torrey, "The Holy Spirit and You: On or In," *Christian Life*, April 1983, p. 33.

4. R. A. Torrey founded the Chicago Bible Institute at the request of D. L. Moody. It became Moody Bible Institute after Moody's death.

5. Archer Torrey, interviewed at The Dunamis Project, Lake George, N.Y., 1991.

6. Dunamis Project conferences take place throughout the country under the auspices of Presbyterian & Reformed Renewal Ministries International. They offer a series of six four-day conferences aimed at helping Protestant church leaders to minister in the Spirit's power.

Chapter 16

1. William R. Long, "Report on Trip to India, October 27–November 11, 1990," p. 2.

2. C. S. Lewis, *The Screwtape Letters* (New York: Macmillan, 1961), p. 3.

3. Charles Kraft, *Defeating Dark Angels* (Ann Arbor: Servant, 1992), p. 104.

4. John Richards, *But Deliver Us From Evil: An Introduction to the Demonic Dimension in Pastoral Care* (New York: Seabury, 1974), p. 106.

5. Tom White, *The Believer's Guide to Spiritual Warfare* (Ann Arbor: Servant, 1990), pp. 152–53. Quoting Dr. Kurt Koch, *Occult Bondage and Deliverance*.

6. John Calvin, *Institutes of the Christian Religion*, I.14.13.

Chapter 17

1. At the present time these books are available from the author: Douglas

McMurry, 2508 Dickens Rd., Richmond, VA 23230.

2. John S. Simon, *John Wesley and the Religious Societies* (London: Epworth Press, 1921), pp. 196–97.

3. We refer our readers to two published articles: an interview with Bob Mumford, *Christianity Today* (March 19, 1990), p. 39, apologizing for the abuses of the shepherding movement; and Ralph Martin's article in *Charisma* (July 1992), pp. 30–32, apologizing for spiritual abuse at the Word of God Community in Ann Arbor.

4. David Johnson and Jeff VanVonderen, *The Subtle Power of Spiritual Abuse* (Minneapolis: Bethany, 1991).

Chapter 18

1. This is the question posed by Albert Camus, one of the great philosophers of the brass heaven, in his book *The Plague*.

2. Leslie Spier, *The Prophet Dance of the Northwest and Its Derivatives: The Source of the Ghost Dance* (Menasha, Wis.: American Anthropological Association, 1935). The original "dream dance" or "prophet dance" was associated with moral righteousness, public confession of sin and prophecies about white people and the spiritual insights they would bring.

3. Harry Holbert Turney-High, *The Flathead Indians of Montana*, Memoirs of the American Anthropological Association, #38 (Menasha, Wis.: American Anthropological Association, 1937), pp. 41–43.

4. Frederick Merk, *Fur Trade and Empire: George Simpson's Journal 1824–25* (Cambridge, Mass.: Harvard University Press, 1931), pp. 132–36.

5. Alvin Josephy, *The Nez Perce Indians* (New Haven: Yale University Press, 1965), pp. 73–74.

6. The standard biography of Spokan Garry is by Thomas Jessett: *Spokan Garry* (Minneapolis: T. S. Dennison, 1960).

7. Other books used in this study of Plateau tribal culture and history include:

Drury, Clifford M. "Oregon Indians in the Red River School," *The Pacific Historical Review*, Vol. VII, #1, March 1938.

Johnson, Olga W. *Flathead & Kootenay* (Glendale, Calif.: A. H. Clark Co., 1969).

Lewis, William S. "The Case of Spokane Garry," *Bulletin of the Spokane Historical Society*, Vol. I, #1, January 1917.

Miller, Christopher. *Prophetic Worlds: Indians & Whites on the Columbia Plateau* (New Brunswick, N.J.: Rutgers University Press, 1985).

Ruby, Robert H., and Brown, John A. *The Spokane Indians: Children of the Sun* (Norman, Okla.: University of Oklahoma Press, 1970).

Tucker, Sarah. *The Rainbow in the North: A Short Account of the First Establishment of Christianity in Rupert's Land by the Church Missionary Society* (London: James Nisbet & Co., 1853).

Wynecoop, David C. *Children of the Sun* (Wellpinit, Wash., 1969).

8. Don Richardson, *Eternity in Their Hearts* (Ventura, Calif.: Regal, 1981), p. 28.

9. Bruce E. Olson, *Bruchko* (Altamonte Springs, Fla.: Creation House, 1973, 1978), pp. 140–41.

Chapter 19

1. Thomas S. Kuhn, *The Structure of Scientific Revolutions* (Chicago: University of Chicago Press, 1962, 1970), p. 76.

2. Kuhn, p. 71.

3. Kuhn, pp. 151–52.

4. Anthony Giddens, *The Consequences of Modernity* (Stanford: Stanford University Press, 1990), p. 2.

5. David Harvey, *The Condition of Post-Modernity: An Introduction to Theories of the Contemporary* (Oxford: Blackwell, 1984), p. 44.

6. Hermann Rauschning, *The Voice of Destruction* (New York: Putnam, 1940), pp. 222–23.

7. Joseph A. Hariss, "The Gospel According to Marx," *Reader's Digest*, February 1993, p. 68.

8. "College Women's Packet Promotes Goddess Worship," *The Presbyterian Layman*, May/June 1993, p. 19. Quoting an issue paper on inclusive language by Rebecca Todd Peters.

9. Zeb Bradford Long and Douglas McMurry, "Steps toward Renewal & Vision for the Presbyterian Church (USA)" (Black Mountain, N.C.: Presbyterian & Reformed Renewal Ministries, Inc., 1993), p. 4.

10. Morton Kelsey, *Discernment: A Study in Ecstasy and Evil* (New York: Paulist Press, 1978), p. 3.

11. Victoria Anne Orr, "God's Grace and Deliverance," *Renewal News*, Summer 1993, p. 11.

12. *North American Renewal Service Committee Timelines*, Vol. 2, #1, Winter 1992, p. 3.

13. Paul Hiebert, "The Gospel in Our Culture," unpublished paper, p. 6.

14. Tom White, *Lines of the Times*, December 1992, p. 1.

Chapter 20

1. Charles Kraft, *Christianity with Power* (Ann Arbor: Vine Books, 1989), p. 41.

2. Harry Emerson Fosdick, *The Living of These Days: An Autobiography* (New York: Harper & Row, 1956), p. 245.

3. Lesslie Newbigin, *Truth to Tell* (Grand Rapids: Eerdmans, 1991), p. 50.

Epilogue

1. Paul G. Hiebert, "Beyond Anti-Colonialism to Globalism," *Missiology: An International Review*, #19, pp. 263–81.

2. I have borrowed many of these ideas from Steve Sandage's unpublished paper, "Multi-Cultural Resources of Christian Counselors." Steve, a former student of Dr. Hiebert, is now a doctoral student at Virginia Commonwealth University.

3. See William F. Albright and C. S. Mann's *The Anchor Bible Commentary on Matthew* (New York: Doubleday, 1971), pp. cxxiv–cxxxi, for a good discussion of the New Testament basis for understanding the mighty acts of God.

4. Dietrich Bonhoeffer, *Letters and Papers from Prison* (New York: Macmillan, 1953), p. 188.